The International Struggle for
New Human Rights

PENNSYLVANIA STUDIES IN HUMAN RIGHTS
Bert B. Lockwood Jr., Series Editor

A complete list of books in the series is available from the publisher.

The International Struggle for New Human Rights

EDITED BY CLIFFORD BOB

PENN

University of Pennsylvania Press

Philadelphia

Published by
University of Pennsylvania Press
Philadelphia, Pennsylvania 19104-4112

Printed in the United States of America on acid-free paper

10 9 8 7 6 5 4 3 2 1

Library of Congress Cataloging-in-Publication Data
The international struggle for new human rights / edited by Clifford Bob.
        p. cm. — (Pennsylvania studies in human rights)
    Includes bibliographical references and index.
    ISBN 978-0-8122-4131-0 (alk. paper : acid-free paper)
    1. Human rights—Case Studies.   I. Bob, Clifford, 1958–
JC571.I6362 2009
323—dc22   2008025520

Contents

vi   Contents

Chapter 1

Introduction: Fighting for New Rights

CLIFFORD BOB

Why does the international human rights movement recognize certain issues, but not others, as rights violations? How do some aggrieved groups transform their troubles into internationally acknowledged human rights concerns, whereas other groups fail when they attempt to do so? Asking these questions has practical implications for victims of abuse, raises thorny policy questions for the rights movement, and opens new avenues of theoretical inquiry for scholars. In today's world, "human rights" are a pervasive political ideal and a compelling call to action. Nongovernmental organizations (NGOs) monitor violations around the globe. International organizations hold countless meetings on rights issues. Democratic governments proclaim human rights to be at the center of their foreign policies. And the media frequently highlight rights abuses.

For beleaguered citizens in neglectful or despotic states, these developments represent opportunities for overseas support. If aggrieved groups can portray their causes as human rights issues, they may be able to tap organizations, personnel, funding, and other strategic resources now available at the international level. If a transnational network then grows, it may succeed in pressuring national governments to change policies and ease repression. Of course, foreign assistance does not guarantee resolution of difficult national problems. Indeed, internationalizing a domestic conflict may backfire, hurting a group's chances of achieving its goals at home. Nonetheless, in recent years, many who claim they are repressed, abused, neglected, or excluded have described their situations as human rights issues. Some have succeeded in rousing the rights movement while others have failed. In other cases, where those affected may not have the capacity to depict their plight as a violation of international norms, outside champions have taken up the cause. Children are one example, with their rights developed primarily by adults. Yet here too the success with which champions have transformed underlying problems into major rights issues varies. Can aggrieved groups take steps to improve their chances?

For the rights movement, it is important to explain why significant problems have had difficulty gaining its attention. South Asia's Dalits (Untouchables), whose plight was long slighted by the rights movement, comprise 160 million Indians and another 90 million people worldwide. Physically and mentally disabled people, another huge population suffering abuse and neglect in many countries, have only recently attracted serious responses from transnational NGOs and international organizations. Even among rights that have won formal endorsement in international conventions, activism varies greatly—despite the movement's affirmation of all rights as "universal, indivisible[,] . . . interdependent, and interrelated."[1] What explains this variation? Does selection follow a rational pattern?

These issues go beyond existing theory in comparative politics and international relations. Most research has analyzed how activists use well-established human rights norms to change state policy. Risse, Ropp, and Sikkink, for instance, provide case studies in which populations suffering torture, extrajudicial executions, and other gross abuses tap transnational networks.[2] In these instances, the persecuted face difficult but well-defined tasks: alerting the world to violations of recognized norms; and convincing NGOs, international organizations, and states to act. Successful cases have common features. The perpetrators (and targets of activism) are brutal governments. The violations are civil and political, often involving widespread killings or legally sanctioned discrimination. And the evidence linking abuser to victim is relatively clear.[3]

In contrast to existing scholarship, this volume highlights more fundamental and logically prior issues. How do groups enduring problems alien to the rights movement establish new norms or energize existing but moribund ones? Why do some activists succeed and others fail? What explains the timing of success?

Definitions and Caveat

This book proposes a framework explaining the human rights movement's adoption of new rights. By "movement," we refer to the NGOs, international organizations, state bureaucracies, foundations, journalists, individuals, and others who work, sometimes together in networks, sometimes in competition with one another, to promote ideals and values denominated in international law as "human rights." Given this definition, the movement extends back centuries. We focus, however, on the post-World War II era when governments, often under pressure from citizens, ratified many international human rights declarations, conventions, and laws. Some of these entailed the foundation of international organizations or bureaucracies devoted to rights issues. More important, in the 1960s, activists organized NGOs to act as watchdogs over state implementation and violation of human rights standards.

The new rights of interest in this book are ones long omitted from international human rights law or codified but allotted few resources by the rights movement. For much of its history, the movement devoted its efforts primarily to some of the civil and political rights in the Universal Declaration of Human Rights (UDHR) and the International Covenant on Civil and Political Rights (ICCPR).[4] Even the economic, social, and cultural issues explicitly delineated in the UDHR and the International Covenant on Economic, Social, and Cultural Rights (ICESCR) spawned little activism.[5] Indeed, leaders of the movement often denigrated such rights as less fundamental than civil and political rights. Issues not explicitly noted in these and other instruments drew even less attention. From early on, therefore, certain aggrieved groups accused the movement of disregarding their concerns. As the movement's power and importance have grown since the 1970s, these groups have more loudly demanded inclusion of their issues. Meanwhile, other groups have organized for the first time to demand rights specifically tailored to their needs.

Adoption of a new right occurs when leading members of the movement accept a grievance they had previously ignored, devoting significant resources to it and in some cases promulgating international legal codes to cover it. Adoption does not happen easily. Rather the aggrieved must persuade the rights movement of the claim's import and its validity as a distinct right. In many cases, even seemingly sympathetic NGOs are resistant. However, if gatekeeper NGOs can be convinced to embrace and promote a claim, this makes wide recognition of the new right more likely. While states may also adopt new claims early, most act later, in the context of campaigns involving the wider rights movement. Given these definitions, adoption clearly has degrees, with the rights movement bolstering certain issues more fully than others.

Skeptics might argue, however, that international conventions and declarations omit few if any rights. True, the UDHR, ICCPR, ICESCR, and other declarations and conventions include lofty and expansive language. But many rights detailed in these instruments have attracted little notice—or express disavowal—from NGOs, international organizations, and states. Of course, a right's codification nonetheless helps those seeking its practical revival: barring an argument that the right has fallen into legal desuetude, claimants may cite and potentially resuscitate it. Even in these cases, however, the mainstream rights movement does not expand its agenda readily. In addition, numerous wrongs go unspecified in international law, and many groups consider the broad term "human rights" insufficient for their needs. This is particularly the case for newly formed or politicized groups anxious to stamp international approval on their identities. In these cases, activists face the daunting task of constructing a new right without explicit statutory foundation.

The Argument

We argue that the rise of new rights involves four distinct if overlapping activities. First, politicized groups frame long-felt grievances as normative claims. Second, they place these rights on the international agenda by convincing gatekeepers in major rights organizations to accept them. This is crucial because a handful of NGOs and international organizations hold much sway in certifying new rights.[6] Third, states and international bodies, often under pressure from gatekeepers and aggrieved groups, accept the new norms. Finally, national institutions implement the norms.

This book focuses on the first three parts of this struggle. While national implementation is crucial to vindicating a new right, this is primarily a question of domestic politics, albeit influenced by international developments.[7] However, this book, like most of the human rights literature, focuses on the international level. The primary rationale for this limitation is our interest in explaining both the development of new international rights and the strategic interactions between aggrieved groups and the human rights movement.

In this book, we seek to demonstrate the argument's plausibility with a series of case studies. This introduction elaborates the theoretical and conceptual backbone. The empirical chapters probe it in three contexts covering much of the ferment in current rights practice. The first three chapters discuss stigmatized minorities, including children of wartime rape, Dalits, and sexual minorities (lesbian, gay, bisexual, and transgendered [LGBT] people). The next three chapters turn to disability and health rights, describing claims made by mentally and physically disabled people, as well as those surrounding HIV/AIDs and female genital mutilation (FGM). The book concludes with two chapters analyzing economic and social rights. Although the movement long neglected these rights, since the late 1990s major NGOs have launched unprecedented activities concerning them. Here we discuss both the broad rights enshrined in the ICESCR and water rights, which have won significant recognition in recent years. In each of these three areas, the authors compare the degree to which key members of the rights movement have responded to novel claims in different periods. Such comparisons generate insights into the factors encouraging politicized groups to level rights claims, inducing gatekeepers to promote them, and persuading states to implement new norms.

Admittedly, this volume's categorization of claims is rough; some could probably be placed in different or multiple slots. Other classification systems are also possible. For instance, one might sort the cases according to the strength with which individuals identify themselves as members of the aggrieved group. This is difficult to measure, however, and is subject to change—not least based on the mobilizations for national and international rights described in this volume. One might also sort the cases by the extent to which the rights movement has adopted the claims. As a specific focus of activism, children of wartime rape remain off the agenda, with international organizations and NGOs having decided to avoid the issue. Until recently, the rights movement similarly ignored or rejected the other claims examined here. This was the case for claims without an explicit statutory basis, such as Dalit rights, LGBT rights, and water rights. It was also the case for economic and social rights, which key members of the rights movement long renounced despite the ICESCR, supposedly coequal to the ICCPR.[8] However, most of the issues examined in this book have today won support from NGOs and international organizations, albeit to varying degrees. For disabled people, the process has gone furthest, with many governments quickly signing the 2006 Convention on the Rights of Persons with Disabilities—although implementation of the convention's precepts remains uncertain.

Key Actors

Four sets of actors play the largest roles in these processes: claimants who seek new rights; major rights NGOs and international organizations, which act as gatekeepers; states, which may ratify such claims as international law and implement them as domestic law; and opponents who combat new rights.

CLAIMANTS

Most accounts have treated the first two sets of actors as components of cohesive transnational advocacy networks. But to clarify the quest for rights, this book stresses differences between claimants and gatekeepers.[9] By "claimants," we mean groups holding grievances within their home states. This includes those demanding both individual rights and group rights, such as Dalits seeking "compensatory discrimination" for centuries of subjugation.

While many claimants act autonomously, some also attract champions, individuals or organizations not part of the aggrieved group who expend extraordinary effort to advance its cause at the early stages. These outsiders, who may have little clout within the rights movement, nonetheless have resources, skills, or positions that aid the aggrieved group in projecting its cause internationally. For example, in the struggle to make HIV/AIDS a rights issue, rather than just a medical one, Jonathan Mann, director of the World Health Organization's Global Program on AIDS, acted as a champion. Champions sometimes initiate campaigns themselves or act independently of the aggrieved. This is most likely when a group is unable to speak for itself, perhaps due to legal incompetence as in the case of children. (In such cases, accountability problems are also acute, with the weak having few ways of influencing their self-appointed sponsors.)

GATEKEEPERS

We define "gatekeepers" as entities at the core of the human rights movement, whose support for a claim can boost it substantially. Typically these are organizations with the largest budgets, best staffs, and greatest credibility in the rights movement. Among them we include major NGOs such as Amnesty International and Human Rights Watch; international organizations such as the UN's Office of the High Commissioner for Human Rights and other prominent international bodies; and human rights intellectuals. When gatekeepers endorse new issues as rights violations—something they do not do readily—they can persuade other segments of the rights movement to join in. This may occur directly, through gatekeeper campaigns on behalf of a new right and its claimants. It may also occur indirectly: because gatekeepers have reputations for integrity and reliability, their choices can subtly influence less powerful "followers." The choices of gatekeepers, communicated widely because of their easy access to other NGOs, journalists, and government officials, signal the worthiness of certain causes and, by implication, the dubiousness of others. As follower organizations compete for scarce members and funding, such signals can spark bandwagons that move certain issues from obscurity to celebrity.[10]

Gatekeeper certification can be a major boon. This is especially so for claimants with limited ability to conduct campaigns themselves, although it is less so for groups capable of strong lobbying on their own. Generalizing from this point, aggrieved groups vary in their power, and these variations affect both the role of gatekeepers and the larger course of advocacy. For instance, in this book compare activism for disability rights and AIDS-related rights to that for Dalit rights. Gatekeepers appear to have played a bigger role in the latter case, probably due to Dalits' relative lack of resources to promote their cause internationally.

Human rights intellectuals are leading scholars, journalists, and others who specialize in rights issues. Through their commentary, intellectuals shape the conceptual basis for rights practice. Of course, their ideas are at best influential. They hold no formal authority over the movement, although some also head gatekeeper organizations. Yet their reputations and experience, as well as their ability to place the hurly-burly of rights work in perspective, is valuable to many in the movement. Some of today's most prominent rights intellectuals are Aryeh Neier, Kenneth Roth, Michael Ignatieff, and Samantha Power, while in the past people such as Eleanor Roosevelt, Isaiah Berlin, and Raphael Lemkin, coiner of the term "genocide," occupied similar roles.

STATES

States act as authoritative decision makers with the power to elevate novel claims into international law—or to reject them. In addition to making such momentous choices, certain governments may also shepherd nascent norms through a welter of international bureaucracies and procedures. The state role in developing the 1999 Mine Ban Treaty and the 2002 Rome Statute of the International Criminal Court was extensive and by no means confined to final ratification. This suggests a larger point: the actors identified thus far may have overlapping roles, with states, for instance, sometimes acting as champions of new norms.

OPPONENTS

Movements for new rights often trigger opposition, although most accounts ignore this or focus only on government foes. The latter are, of course, crucial to norm acceptance and implementation. But new claims face other foes. For one thing, aggrieved local groups will seldom favor internationalization unanimously, and some members may work against it. For their part, gatekeepers may oppose enlarged missions or find unfamiliar claims trivial, irrelevant, or unenforceable. This book's chapter on the rights movement's long dismissal of economic and social rights exemplifies this possibility. Most important, countermovements may arise in civil society to oppose new claims.[11] In recent years, global campaigns for the International Criminal Court, greenhouse gas controls, family planning, and other issues have galvanized opposing coalitions. Rights movements also confront well-funded countermobilizations invoking their own norms. For instance, women's groups supporting abortion rights face opposition from religious organizations promoting the right to life. Free market organizations tout property rights as a foil to those who uphold environmental rights.

The Struggle for New Rights

Rights emerge in much the same way as other policy. While this view runs counter to recent idealization of rights, it jibes with a realistic appraisal of rights claims and rights law as politics.[12] In this view, there are numerous human needs, grievances, and problems, the majority of which go unnoticed most of the time. Reframing these issues as rights violations is a strategic choice aimed at exerting greater pressure to solve them. By itself, however, such reformulation has little effect. The claim needs to draw backing from powerful audiences who believe that the right deserves acceptance. Optimally, domestic audiences embrace the claim, because national institutions offer the most direct way of achieving political goals within a state. But often national channels respond slowly or not at all. In these cases, activists may project their claims internationally. When gatekeepers adopt the claim as a rights issue, the right becomes a recognizable issue on the international scene. It enters the international issue agenda.[13] In some cases, norms also rise to the decision agenda, where states either accept or reject them as international law. Finally, even if ensconced as international law, states must implement new norms.

Of course, this model does not explain how every claim gains international acceptance. The actual process is more complex than portrayed here. Gatekeepers, rather than aggrieved populations, may inaugurate claims and then search for local "victims" to exemplify violations. In recent years, a number of global campaigns have followed this top-down pattern. For instance, efforts to control the international small-arms trade were launched in the early 1990s not by those hurt by gun violence in conflict-torn societies but by NGOs based in countries at peace.[14] The water rights case described in this volume appears to follow this pattern, with international activists starting campaigns based on opposition to World Bank privatization policies—and independently of local claimants. In all cases, there are frequent interactions between national and international levels and among the various actors. With these cautions in mind, however, we argue that the model outlined here helps clarify a complicated reality.

From Grievance to Rights Claim

The struggle typically begins with members of an aggrieved group framing their needs as rights. Despite the pervasiveness of rights language in the world today, we assume that this is a political choice and that there is nothing automatic about it.[15] Group members must perceive their grievances as injustices within evolving international practice. In today's world, leaders of many weak groups will be aware of rights rhetoric, although this may not be the case for highly deprived, isolated, or repressed populations.

Assuming that a persecuted group is aware of the human rights environment, one might expect it to portray its claims as rights. But this will happen only if group leaders see advantages to doing so. Often these are concrete and material. Presenting a claim as an internationally cognizable right may bring support to a group and pressure on its opponents. This is because, for international audiences, invoking a right can suggest a cause's worthiness—even if the underlying grievance is complicated, ambiguous, or contested.[16] In short, such framing may help a group achieve its political goals.

But not all wronged groups raise rights claims. As noted earlier, governments may accommodate the group. Even if they do not, certain groups will avoid the international sphere. Nationalists may find it unpalatable; pragmatists may forge alliances with civil organizations in their home states. International activism may also be unwise in societies that stigmatize foreign intervention. And even in domestic contexts where external aid is unproblematic, attracting it may appear too costly. In addition, framing a situation or grievance as a violation may disproportionately benefit certain segments of a group, usually those having greater familiarity with rights mechanisms and institutions. As a result, a group's decision to make such claims is often fraught, as several of this volume's studies document.

Nonetheless, leaders of many groups promote new rights to international audiences. But why do they not depict the grievances as abuses of well-accepted rights? For one thing, desired solutions may be different from those provided by existing rights. Many injured groups seek affirmative actions by a state, society, or corporation to help them improve their situation. They demand not simply that the targets of their activism end repressive, discriminatory, or offensive behavior, as required by "negative" liberties, but also that they take additional, positive steps. The latter may include economic redistributions, reparation payments, job reservations, or other policies affirmatively favoring the aggrieved group.[17] In addition, the agendas of certain groups, particularly ethnically based ones, may include territorial autonomy or national independence. If international audiences recognize their situations as discrete rights issues, group members may gain a psychological lift, and group identity may deepen. This facilitates mobilization and increases power in domestic politics. Even for groups with less ambitious agendas, recognition of rights can increase assistance earmarked for the group. Foundations, NGOs, and other transnational actors, aware for the first time of an issue, will be more likely to support it. In sum, recognition of new rights can serve as a tool for fortifying or even fashioning groups. Contrary to the assertion that rights are beyond politics, they are fundamentally political.

Reformulating grievances as violations has little consequence in itself, however. While rights may act as trumps in national contexts with well-developed legal systems, the analogy fails in a global context without enforcement mechanisms.[18] For rights to change realities, powerful actors, not just the aggrieved themselves, must recognize them.

THE INTERNATIONAL ISSUE AGENDA

When the aggrieved convince gatekeepers to promote their claims, the new right reaches the international issue agenda. Given gatekeepers' prior commitments and limited resources, their adoption of any such claim is uncertain. Yet without a gatekeeper's taking on the issue, a proposed right may not attract broader backing, including state support.

There is nothing automatic about gatekeepers' embracing problems, even those affecting millions. Despite reputations as moral actors, even well-funded NGOs and international organizations cannot accept every claim made by every group. Instead, the gatekeepers screen and frequently reject them. On what factors do gatekeepers choose? Sometimes it is a question of their having too few resources and too many issues. Choices also hinge on the match between a new claim and a gatekeeper's preexisting mandate, expertise, or method. If a proposed right does not fit, it may be rejected.[19] To avoid this, aggrieved groups may trim the claims they originally asserted as rights, thereby meeting the gatekeepers' preexisting worldview or demands.

Decisions about adopting or rejecting a new right generate controversy within gatekeeper organizations. NGOs and international organizations are not monolithic. Even if small and hierarchical, they will invariably include individuals with conflicting roles and interests. Moreover, gatekeeper missions are often vague. As a result, claimants may win individual devotees but fail to persuade the organization. Debate over FGM and economic rights roiled Amnesty International and Human Rights Watch for decades, as this volume describes.

Another issue is at stake too. Human rights intellectuals have long flagged the purported perils of rights "inflation." In 1984, Alston voiced "serious concern" about rights being "conjured up . . . 'as if by magic.'"[20] More recently, commentators have criticized the tendency to "define anything desirable as a right."[21] Among the charges, "proliferation" cheapens the human rights tradition, erodes consensus on rights, dilutes the moral power of rights, and weakens enforcers' will. Most worryingly in this view, rights come to serve as little more than rallying cries for mobilized political interests. To stem the threat, some have proposed rigorous criteria: rights must be fundamental, universally recognized, legally enforceable, and guaranteed to everyone.[22] Others have suggested hierarchies of rights or have confined "real" rights to a narrow set of "negative liberties."[23]

In some cases, gatekeepers have used these arguments to rationalize their rejection of new claims. But, in practice, it is difficult for gatekeepers to apply the intellectuals' proposed criteria, hierarchies, or standards in a purely technical way. Shifting political currents in larger society move gatekeepers. As aggrieved groups and their champions mobilize for new rights, they sometimes succeed in altering societal values and cultural landscapes. As a result, even powerful gatekeeper NGOs may come under strong pressure to expand their agendas. To appease crucial constituencies, maintain funding, and "stay relevant," gatekeepers may embrace new causes—even if they had earlier rebuffed them as being outside their mandates or inappropriate to their methods. In this volume, cases as diverse as LGBT rights and economic rights exemplify these dynamics, with gatekeepers such as Human Rights Watch and Amnesty International rejecting such claims for decades but more recently accepting them. For their part, aggrieved groups are unlikely to be deterred by abstract assertions that they should forgo *their* rights in the interests of the human rights "core." The result in recent years has been expansion, albeit halting and contentious, in the problems considered "rights issues."

THE STATE DECISION AGENDA

The third aspect of the struggle involves consideration by states and the adoption of new norms. From the standpoint of international law, this ultimately means that a legal convention opens for signature and ratification. Constructivist scholars have done much to illuminate this process. Most important, their research has emphasized how NGOs and advocacy networks act as "norms entrepreneurs," in some cases advancing new rights. The success of this promotion hinges on a number of factors. As Joshua Busby has argued, these include a permissive international context in which state interests do not dominate the agenda; focusing events that increase the claim's saliency; credible information about the issue's gravity; low costs to accepting the norm; correspondence between the norm and existing cultural and political concerns; and supportive national policymakers.[24]

In addition, scholars should recognize the contentious nature of rights campaigns. Two aspects of conflict are noteworthy. First, while most scholarship has focused on norms entrepreneurs, their actions seldom go unopposed. As discussed earlier, movements surrounding such issues as population, environment, and development have sparked powerful countermobilizations. Similarly, opposition by NGOs, think tanks, and advocacy networks has hindered norms covering women, children, the indigenous, and many others.[25]

A second aspect of contention occurs within states. While traditional approaches to international relations portray states as unitary, there is ample justification for viewing them in more disaggregated terms. One implication is disagreement among bureaucracies or individual bureaucrats with varying sympathy for rights claims. Those in a position to block proposed norms play major roles. Long-standing U.S. refusal to ratify the Convention on the Rights of the Child exemplifies the influence of such veto players, in this case, conservative political leaders in the U.S. Senate.[26]

NATIONAL IMPLEMENTATION

International campaigns will have little impact without vigorous national enforcement. States must apply rules governing their own officials and, more problematically, members of their society. Thus a major reason for internationalizing grievances is to increase leverage at home. How might this occur? While the issue is not a focus of this volume, a few points are worth noting. First, foreign actors may encourage adherence to new rights regimes by starting programs with incentives for compliance, by attempting to shame the uncooperative, and by exerting pressure against misbehavior. But because compliance is primarily an issue of domestic politics, other mechanisms also matter. In some cases, international legitimation can increase a rights holder's political heft at home. This may occur through direct provision of outside funds, although this can open the group to criticism at home. Less problematically, the rights holder may gain if international legitimacy strengthens the group's identity, unity, and resolve. Such domestic processes present the most direct means of vindicating rights—by the rights holders themselves in national institutions.

Conclusion

This volume suggests that the rise of new rights is complex, contingent, and contentious. Of course, any group can trumpet its grievances as rights issues, but this alone has little effect. Most important in changing the group's situation is the right's implementation by governments. But in the long quest to achieve that end, adoption by gatekeeper NGOs and international organizations plays a critical initial role and is far from certain. Thus, from an aggrieved group's standpoint, it may appear that self-appointed guardians of a human rights core stonily patrol the rights frontier, admitting few new causes and favoring those conforming to the dominant rights culture. This does not mean that novel claims will always fail. This book illustrates strategies that have led to success, albeit to different degrees for various issues. But it does underline that aggrieved groups must win new rights through struggle not only with states but also with powerful nonstate actors—and that rights themselves are tools of political conflict.

Admittedly, the model presented here is an ideal type. First, in reality its parts often overlap because there are continuous interactions among local claimants, gatekeepers, and states. Second, the pattern outlined here is not inexorable. At any point, a norm may fail to advance. Third, notwithstanding the model's bottom-up nature, international champions and gatekeepers play a large role, particularly for highly repressed or legally incompetent populations. In a larger sense, the bottom-up formulation is also incomplete. Incentives offered by today's thriving international rights regime encourage the framing of local grievances as rights issues. Without widespread international acclaim for rights, problems would be portrayed in other ways, just as they were in the centuries before today's "age of rights." Nonetheless, the processes discussed in this volume—calculation of the costs and benefits of transforming domestic needs into international claims, arduous certification processes by gatekeepers, and contentious interaction between proponents and opponents—underpin the rise of new rights.

At a more conceptual level, this volume suggests that concern over rights proliferation is overblown. Human rights are political, and their precise scope will always remain disputed. In these contests, a handful of gatekeepers exerts significant influence, and a limited set of political and civil rights continues to dominate. Demands for enlargement are inevitable, however. The contemporary appeal of rights rhetoric over other expressions of grievance—and the resources devoted to ending rights abuses rather than other problems—encourage aggrieved groups to formulate particularized rights. But these will gain acceptance from the rights movement only occasionally, usually after a prolonged campaign, and often in a form less expansive than originally proposed.

Chapter 2

Orphaned Again? Children Born of Wartime Rape as a Non-Issue for the Human Rights Movement

R. CHARLI CARPENTER

In November 2005, representatives of the United Nations Children's Fund (UNICEF) country offices and a variety of independent experts met at UNICEF Headquarters in New York to discuss and assess the protection needs of children born as a result of wartime rape in conflict zones. Such children, it was clear to humanitarian practitioners, were at particular risk of human rights abuses because of community perceptions about their origin as "children of the enemy."[1] Case evidence from Bosnia, Rwanda, East Timor, and, most recently, Darfur has increasingly shown that such children are subject to stigma, discrimination, and even infanticide in postconflict settings. As described in a recent UN document, children born of rape and sexual exploitation "become the symbol of the trauma the nation as a whole went through, and society prefers not to acknowledge their needs."[2]

One of the key questions raised at the meeting was whether such children ought to be defined as a category of concern for child protection organizations operating in conflict-affected settings—and, if not, then how to meet their needs in the context of wider programming for children and for sexual violence survivors. The purpose of the meeting was, in effect, to consider whether a new category of war-affected child should be added to the growing list of issues on the agenda of the transnational network around children and armed conflict.[3] As an important gatekeeper in the international child protection network, UNICEF was trying to figure out whether and in what manner to adopt this new problem, already defined as an issue by a number of small NGOs, a growing network of academics, several donors, and the global media.

According to the outcome document of the meeting, "As with all children affected by armed conflict, children born as a result of rape may be vulnerable to violence, abuse and exploitation. . . . [T]hese children may also face increased vulnerability because they are children of survivors of violence and often children of single mothers."[4] However, the document does not call for enhanced advocacy around this category of child itself but rather situates their protection in the context of women's human rights: "The most effective way to provide assistance and care to children born as a result of rape is by supporting their mothers—the girls and women targeted for violence—and supporting family and community-based recovery and healing."[5]

This meeting, and the eventual consensus not to define children born of wartime sexual violence as a specific category around which to press specific child rights claims, raise a number of fascinating questions about the emergence of issues among human rights networks. First, why did the vulnerabilities of children born of wartime rape come relatively late to the radar screen of organizations concerned with child protection in conflict zones? Second, why do child rights advocates concerned for child protection in conflict zones balk at more aggressively advocating for the human rights of children born of rape, considering their unique vulnerabilities? Third, why has this concern taken the particular form that it has when it has been raised? That is, why has it tended to be situated under the umbrella issue of sexual violence rather than the umbrella issue of child protection, and why are these viewed as competing rather than complementary frames?

I argue that the answers to these questions lie to a large degree in the coalitional politics between the issue network around "children and armed conflict" and the issue network around "women and armed conflict." Drawing on recent work in social movement theory, I argue that the need to build a frame acceptable to both advocacy communities is driving both issue adoption decisions at UNICEF (whose mandate includes the protection of both children and women) and emerging frames within international society.[6] At the time of this writing, momentum around the issue remains stalled due to a lack of consensus between child protection experts and gender-based-violence (GBV) specialists about how to construct the issue and with what implications for the protection of the children as well as their mothers.

These findings are supported by semistructured interviews gathered between June 2002 and May 2005, five years of participant observation in the network around children and armed conflict, and preliminary results from focus group data gathered between December 2004 and March 2005.[7] I also draw on my experience as a consultant with UNICEF on two projects related to determining whether children born of war should be treated as a specific, vulnerable category in the international child rights sector. My use of such experiences is a reflective one, following critical theorists who have long argued that analysts of world politics must take explicit account of the role we play within our subject matter as we interface with the world of practice.[8]

Two general conclusions are drawn from this case. First, not all human rights problems are viewed by human rights gatekeepers as being best soluble through a rights-based approach, and such claims are particularly easy to make when the issue is promoted by champions rather than rights claimants themselves. Second, coalitional politics among gatekeepers may as easily result in new rights claims' being swept under the rug as in critical mass forming around a vulnerable category of concern.

Children of Wartime Rape as a Non-Issue for the Human Rights Network

Though the articulation of "children born of war" as an issue is very recent, grievances against this population are not. In conflict zones where sexual violence is a feature of war, babies are often born as a result of rape or sexual slavery. Anecdotal evidence and press reports have demonstrated for almost fifteen years that such children born of war are at risk of infanticide, abandonment, abuse, neglect, discrimination, and social exclusion in both conflict and postconflict settings specifically as a result of their biological origins. Oral histories of adult war children from earlier wars confirm these patterns.[9]

The number of such children worldwide has not been accurately documented, although hundreds to thousands are reported existing in nearly every war-torn society that has experienced spates of war-related sexual violence. For example, it was estimated that twenty thousand live births resulted from the rapes during Bangladesh's war of secession from West Pakistan in 1971,[10] and between two thousand and ten thousand babies were estimated born as a result of sexual violence during the Rwandan genocide.[11] A 2001 report by the War and Children Identity Project in Norway has aggregated reports such as these to estimate a population of at least five hundred thousand living "war children" worldwide.[12]

Currently there is no recognition in the international children's human rights regime that children born of wartime rape constitute a specific protected category. Yet like all other children, those conceived during wartime violence possess in theory all the rights articulated in the Universal Declaration of Human Rights (UDHR) and other major instruments, including notably the right to physical security and the right to be free from adverse discrimination. The Convention on the Rights of the Child provides for all children's right to know their parents (Article 7); to an adequate standard of living, social security, and health care (Article 6); to a nationality (Article 7); and to protection against abuse, maltreatment, or neglect (Article 19). Global human rights instruments also indicate that these and other rights be applied to all human beings without discrimination and specify a number of particular bases on which discrimination is prohibited, such as "race, colour, sex, language, religion, political or other opinion, national or social origins, property, birth or other status."[13] The UDHR in Article 25(2) specifically protects children born of nonmarital unions, a form of protection particularly relevant to children of nonmarital rape in both war and peace: "All children whether born in or out of wedlock shall enjoy the same social protection." Article 10(3) of the International Covenant on Economic, Social and Cultural Rights specifies that "special measures of protection and assistance should be taken on behalf of all children and young persons without any discrimination for reasons of parentage or other conditions." In the case of children born of wartime rape, however, a number scholars have argued that certain barriers exist to the realization of these rights, so child protection organizations operating in conflict zones might have been expected to address this shortfall within the context of their advocacy and protection initiatives.[14]

In his introductory chapter, Clifford Bob distills a model for tracing the construction of grievances as human rights issues. By the measures he describes, protection of children born of war rape would appear to be in the very early stages of issue emergence: it has been defined by issue entrepreneurs or champions but not (at the time of this writing) adopted as such by gatekeepers. The best example of such a champion is the previously mentioned Norwegian NGO, the War and Children Identity Project (WCIP), established in 2001 to raise awareness of the human rights of war children as a global constituency. The WCIP formed on the heels of a successful campaign by Norwegian *kriegsbarn* (war children) conceived by German fathers during the World War II occupation by Germany who sued the Norwegian government for failing to protect them from discrimination in the war's aftermath. Interested in situating Norway's *kriegsbarn* in a broader context and perhaps exporting their model of suing home states for compensation, WCIP became the first organization to argue that war children should be protected by a global treaty. Other agenda-setting efforts include five international documents that have called on organizations engaged in child protection in conflict zones to provide greater advocacy and programmatic attention to children born of wartime sexual violence.[15] Human rights intellectuals, including this author, have been active in defining this population as a category of concern in workshops, published articles, and international fora and might therefore be considered entrepreneurs.[16] The global media has also paid attention to this population, generating numerous reports of "rape babies" from Bosnia to Rwanda to East Timor to the Sudan.[17]

Yet despite media and donor concern for children of wartime rape, awareness of their particular vulnerabilities by GBV specialists, and the presence of a few small organizations lobbying specifically for their rights, major organizations in the growing advocacy network around "children and armed conflict"—what Bob would define as "gatekeepers" for this issue area[18]—have not adopted these children as a category of concern. In other words, the issue has not reached stage two in the agenda-setting process.[19] No major organization within this issue area has published a study or advocacy document addressing these children's concerns specifically. A content analysis of the online advocacy discourse for thirty-three major advocacy organizations' websites in 2005 found no references to stigma against children born of wartime rape.[20] That war children as a category are absent from the formal network agenda is confirmed by in-depth interviews and focus groups with humanitarian practitioners.[21] As recently as 2004, while attention to other categories of war-affected children burgeoned in transnational civil society, a UNICEF child protection officer told me, "I can't think of any organization that has dealt with [children born of wartime rape] specifically."[22]

In 2005, the situation began to change slightly, and greater interest was expressed particularly by UNICEF and the child protection unit at Human Rights Watch.[23] The change may be explained in part by the presence of organized issue entrepreneurs described earlier.[24] However, the shift seems likely to have been more greatly influenced by two trigger events occurring between 2003 and 2005.

First, media coverage of the humanitarian crisis in Darfur stressed genocidal rape by Janjaweed forces against ethnic Fur women, portraying such forced pregnancy campaigns in language reminiscent of the Bosnian war.[25] This widespread publicity regarding stigma and maltreatment of "Janjaweed babies" caught the attention of advocates as well as donors and the public, and in 2004 UNICEF child protection officials began receiving questions from field officers about how to protect these babies.[26] The importance of developing a rights-based language with which to articulate the issue was particularly evident to advocates in an era where the media and donors were already setting the agenda on the issue, at times in ways perceived by UNICEF as unhelpful to the promotion of children's rights.

Second, questions were raised within the UN system during this period about UN responsibility for children born of local women raped or sexually exploited by UN peacekeepers, particularly in West Africa and the Democratic Republic of Congo. After the initial scandal broke in 2003, the UN Office for the Coordination of Humanitarian Affairs

(OCHA) established an interagency task force to create a policy to end sexual exploitation by UN personnel. Originally aimed at prevention, better articulation of standards, and training of personnel, the interagency task force included a sub–working group on victim assistance that considered UN responsibilities not only to exploited women but also to the children born as a result of such unions. In his 2005 report to the secretary general, which was passed to the Security Council on March 24, Prince Zeid Al-Hussein of Jordan specifically referred to "children fathered and abandoned by peacekeeping personnel" as a category in need of assistance in their own right. By April 2005 the idea was circulating at UN headquarters that the United Nations might owe compensation, including child support, to the women, as well as particular attention to children stigmatized or abandoned as a result.[27]

These events, and the new language they engendered, provided a context in which child protection experts at UNICEF were encouraged to reconsider their previous inattention to children of rape as a category of concern. In 2004, UNICEF headquarters began considering guidelines for protecting children of genocidal rape, to inform its field offices in Darfur. In the same summer, the Bosnia-Herzegovina UNICEF country office in Sarajevo piloted a fact-finding study to follow up on children born of mass rape during the war in ex-Yugoslavia and now growing up in Bosnia-Herzegovina.

News of this pilot study was picked up at UNICEF's Innocenti Research Center in Florence. By 2000 certain individuals at Innocenti had helped introduce language about children born of war into the five-year-review document that followed up on Graca Machel's original 1995 report to the UN secretary general on children and armed conflict. The idea began to be floated at Innocenti and at UNICEF Headquarters in New York that UNICEF should spearhead the multicountry study called for in that document, one that would link the issue of enemy rape to the issue of rape/exploitation by peacekeepers and foreign occupation troops. Gender specialists in the Child Protection Office in New York, several of whom were also involved with the Sexual Exploitation Task Force, took the lead in securing funding for a meeting aiming to aggregate existing knowledge about the issue, determine whether a global study was necessary, and discuss UNICEF's role in promoting this issue within the human rights sector.

However, these efforts and this dialogue ultimately did not result in the articulation of children of rape as a separate category of human rights concern. Instead, UNICEF concluded by late 2005 that the children's needs should be addressed in the context of programming for their mothers and that the subject of "children born of war" should be subsumed not under UNICEF's child protection mandate but under its

emerging work in the area of gender-based-violence.[28] The Bosnian
country office elected not to release the 2004 study, which was criticized
internally and by local women's organizations as focusing on the babies
to the exclusion of rape survivors themselves.[29] At the November 23,
2005, meeting in New York, participants were split as to whether
UNICEF should spearhead promotion of this specific issue. In particular, some advocates emphasized that constructing a stigmatized group as
a category of concern might increase the stigma against them, and it
was suggested that dealing with these children's rights should be a subordinate goal to protecting and empowering their mothers who had survived conflict-related violence. The outcome document of that meeting
expressed a consensus that "children born of sexual violence in armed
conflict zones should be addressed within the context and framework of
gender-based violence (GBV)."[30] This strategy mirrored the way in
which the issue was increasingly being constructed in the wider humanitarian community.[31]

Theorizing Variation in Issue Adoption

The history of this floundering issue raises a number of interesting
questions about human rights issue adoption. First, how do advocacy
networks engaged in a particular issue area define the range of specific
issues or categories of concern constitutive of that issue area? In the case
under discussion, why were children of rape largely a non-issue for gatekeeping human rights organizations engaged in the area of children
and armed conflict in the 1990s? The very hesitant steps taken with respect to this population are in stark contrast to the attention paid since
the early 1990s to child soldiers, girls in armed conflict, displaced children, HIV/AIDS orphans, trafficked children, exploited children, and a
laundry list of other categories of concern within the network around
children and armed conflict.[32]

Second, what explains resistance of particular gatekeepers such as
UNICEF to adopting specific issues when they are promoted by norm
entrepreneurs? As advocates for a more comprehensive approach to
children of wartime rape argued in focus group settings, "If you don't
classify, if you don't identify, if you don't know, then how do you plan
the policy and the programs and how do you do the advocacy?" and
"There's no public policy without some sort of information that says,
you know, here is a problem."[33] Nonetheless, voices arguing against such
categorization have predominated in this debate so far: "Categorization
may be helpful in leveraging funds and in advocacy but categorization
can also be risky as it can lead to stigmatization or other negative impacts."[34] In fact, the argument that advocacy on behalf of a population

could actually jeopardize their human rights was made repeatedly by interviewees and focus group participants.[35] What is interesting about this rhetorical argument is that rights-based language itself can be used to justify the non-adoption of human rights problems within gatekeepers' advocacy arenas as easily as to draw attention to new problems.

Third, what drives the specific framing decisions around issues when they are eventually adopted? In our case, for example, why are child rights advocates so much readier to situate this issue strictly as a subset of GBV work rather than child-protection work? From a strictly child rights perspective, this is hardly an intuitive conclusion. To be sure, effective responses to survivors of wartime sexual violence could do much to reduce attachment difficulties these children may face with their birth mothers, as well as stigma from the women's families and socioeconomic deprivation, and such initiatives are, of course, vital in their own right. However, programming aimed at birth mothers would by itself not address the range of rights violations experienced by these children, such as the right of older war children to information about their identities. Nor would a trickle-down approach to meeting mothers' needs be likely to reach abandoned, adopted, or institutionalized children. Moreover, a mother-centered approach to protecting these babies' rights might forestall an effective response in cases where it is the traumatized mother who perpetrates abuse, neglect, or infanticide against the child or contributes to the stigma against the child through discriminatory naming practices.[36] Without conceptualizing the children as a specific population in their own right, it will be impossible to follow up on how effectively the programming for mothers is actually addressing the babies' needs. In short, situating the issue of children born of rape in the context of women's rights rather than that of child protection was not inevitable nor without implications for the way in which such children's "rights" will be constructed. Why has UNICEF largely been willing to limit discussions of the issue in this way?

As I have argued elsewhere, existing literature on transnational advocacy networks provides little help in explaining the kinds of questions raised by the politics of this case.[37] In fact, this particular absence from the child rights agenda is quite interesting theoretically, given what the extant literature on advocacy networks tells us about the correlates of advocacy campaigns. For example, Keck and Sikkink's landmark study emphasized the importance of "issue attributes" in explaining the emergence and success of specific campaigns.[38] The attributes most helpful in terms of framing issues are causes that can be "assigned to the deliberate . . . actions of identifiable individuals"; "issues involving bodily harm to vulnerable individuals, especially when there is a short and clear causal chain . . . assigning responsibility"; and "issues involving legal equality of opportunity."[39] Given the predictions of this issue attributes hypothesis, these children should be likelier to be on the agenda than child soldiers, for example, because as infants they should be perceived as highly vulnerable and innocent and because the rights violations they experience include bodily harm and discrimination.

A second common theme in the literature on advocacy networks is the importance of specific altruistically motivated individuals who initiate a campaign and lobby to draw awareness to an issue.[40] It has also been suggested that the promotion of new issues is most likely to succeed if these can be "grafted" onto preexisting norms and categories of concern.[41] But these cannot be explanations for issue non-adoption, as there are numerous international legal standards that should be easily applicable to the kinds of rights abuses these children face; and as noted earlier, champions do exist for this group. UNICEF's consensus, and the lack of attention within the child rights network to this population generally despite the presence of what have been described as permissive conditions for issue adoption, beg the question of which other factors may figure prominently in gatekeepers' decisions about adopting new issues.

My data support two arguments that may account better for the outcome in this case than do the hypotheses in the extant literature. First, human rights gatekeepers deny rights claims for rights-based reasons, and they are more likely to do so if the issue is raised by champions than if it is promoted by the rights claimants themselves. While champions may have better resources, mobility, or access to gatekeepers than rights claimants, they may lack credibility in accurately representing the rights of the aggrieved. Second, gatekeepers deny rights claims for tactical reasons having to with the organizational and coalitional politics as much as with normative concerns.

Those who see themselves as working closely with vulnerable populations value rights-based arguments more if they originate within the community itself. Participants in focus groups repeatedly stressed the importance of dealing with an issue such as this in a way that "builds local capacities," "engages the local community," and is "culturally appropriate." Similarly, the emphasis on participatory programming and planning suggests a norm to allow recipient populations to speak for their own needs rather than imposing classifications on them based on outside understandings. If a concern is not expressed as such by the population involved, then champions may be viewed as simply out of touch with events on the ground in conflict zones, and the perception of naïveté may undermine their credibility with gatekeepers. Many respondents in my data set argued, for example, that the media blows out of proportion the issue of stigma against war babies and that many of these children are doing just fine with their mothers or within their communities. Others admit that the stories one hears are "horrifying" but worry that classifying these babies as a specific group will do more harm than good, drawing jealousy from other groups, increasing stigma, and perhaps forcing an identity on a child unnecessarily.

In both cases, the implicit argument is that outsider champions (intellectuals, donors, journalists, non-operational NGOs) often sensationalize issues and lack a field practitioner's understanding of context. This engenders skepticism about whether an advocacy frame on offer by an issue champion approximates the actual needs of the population itself or simply reflects a narrow and sensationalist view.[42] As one respondent explained in reference to a workshop organized by an academic interested in children born of war, "We as practitioners in child protection have had a particularly difficult history, going back ten years, with interfacing with the academic world. . . academics that become interested in our issues, our work. . . . Some of the earliest tense interactions around that were around psychologists getting interested in the issue but wanting to come into a field situation, interview kids about traumatic experiences, and fly away. . . . Unintended things can happen if we come in and focus on this subcategory of children in need of a protection response, creating stigma instead of helping it."[43]

Yet practitioners' well-founded discomfort with classifying certain categories of concern is not always an impediment to issue adoption (and therefore cannot in itself explain non-adoption decisions). The consequences of targeted rights-based programming—creating jealousies or backlash from other recipient groups, identifying people as victims, exacerbating stigma—exist around programming for many vulnerable populations in conflict zones whose cause is very much on the international agenda, including HIV/AIDS victims, rape survivors, and demobilized child soldiers. In many of these cases, such fallout is managed creatively by practitioners in the field while the problem is discussed openly at the global level and in planning and resource allocation. A focus group participant articulated such an approach: "What we found [when we undertook a sexual violence study] is that women actually were surprisingly open about what had happened to them and the phrase we kept hearing was: tell people what you want but just don't tell my neighbors. Tell the people in the larger global context but don't tell the people I live with."[44]

Whether it is empirically or normatively valid in this case, the argument that the risks of issue advocacy cannot be managed and that advocacy is therefore best minimized does function as a rights-based rhetorical strategy for justifying issue non-adoption.[45] I hypothesize that this justification is likely to be given where the risks and costs of adopting an issue are perceived to be high and that it is a particularly effective mechanism when self-appointed issue entrepreneurs are speaking on behalf, rather than as part, of an aggrieved population.

So what accounts for gatekeepers' perceptions of "risks" or "costs"? And how do they determine whether an issue can be fitted to their mandate? This case suggests that the relationship between human rights issue networks perceived to have a stake in a particular issue is of critical importance in gatekeeper adoption decisions even when other permissive conditions exist for issue emergence. While the human rights network is often referred to as a single community of ideas and practice, in fact it encompasses numerous smaller issue networks, each with specific agendas, interests, and influence, but often highly interdependent in terms of staffing, resources, and division of labor.[46] Because these separate networks take different sets of victims as their frame of reference, issues that span network agendas but invite dissimilar understandings of a problem may cause tension between otherwise allied networks.

This tension in itself, and the transaction costs associated with negotiating it, may provide a barrier to issue adoption, which then encourages activists to approach the issue as if it could be addressed without formal attention to a category of concern. As Ann Mische argues, "Important problems (as well as opportunities) are posed by the overlap between multiple types of ties and affiliations, and the diverse projects and practices actors bring with them into cross-network interactions."[47] Sidney Tarrow has pointed out that coalitions, often described as a key factor in the success of advocacy networks, can complicate the development of advocacy frames.[48]

The pattern emerging from interviews and focus groups conducted within the humanitarian sector between 2003 and 2006 suggests that inter-network dynamics can matter for issue adoption in particular in at least three ways. First, the assumption within one network that another network for which the issue is salient may or should already be addressing it may create a disincentive to expend resources on advocacy. Notable in the interviews I have collected is a tendency toward issue-related buck-passing. Some respondents expressed the expectation that the issue was being or probably ought to be addressed by some other set of actors in an adjacent issue area but not by organizations with a mandate similar to those in which the respondent was embedded. For instance, an International Committee of the Red Cross (ICRC) staff member from its children and war unit stated: "I will tell you that we are not really considering specific projects on this, and if anything were to be done it would be done in conjunction with the protection of the mothers, with these women who have been raped. And in this case, our 'Women and War' project is definitely . . . in a better position to know what . . .

we do to protect the woman and the newborn child."[49] But a staff person from the Women's Commission for Refugee Women and Children stated, "There is no data on this that I know of. . . . I never tried to compile those numbers. But you should talk to UNICEF; child protection organizations must keep track of these things."[50]

Second, the necessity of strategic social construction across networks complicates the possibility of advocacy because a suitable cross-network advocacy frame may in fact be difficult to negotiate.[51] There was considerable disagreement among advocates about whether this issue was appropriately conceptualized as a child protection issue directly or dealt with in the context of programming to support mothers. For example, if advocates raised the issue of infanticide within conflict settings, as a specific child protection issue, would this constitute blaming the female victim or, in cases of genocide, the targeted group?[52] Because many transnational advocates occupy professional positions or affiliations in several related networks over the course of their careers, potential issue adopters' identities may be bound up in identifying issues that avoid normative conflicts between the multiple communities in which they are embedded.[53] One interview respondent described the complexity of addressing an issue such as this one because it requires "straddling" two different and in some ways competing lenses: "I don't know; it's complicated. . . . I've been sitting on that fence for the past year as a gender-based-violence officer in a child protection unit. . . . Child protection maybe still has a little controversy to it, but sexual violence has a lot. Senior managers get uncomfortable when you tell them a 13 year old is raped. . . . So they're very much inter-linked, very much multi-sectoral . . . the children born of this population as well; you can't separate it out."[54]

Third, because gatekeepers will weigh the value of the new issue against the impact that such advocacy will have on their ability to continue pursuing existing issues, inter-network overlap raises the bar for a new issue complementing, rather than clashing with, the existing advocacy agenda. One of the key concerns raised by both child protection and GBV specialists about advocating for children of rape is the potential that such an agenda might siphon attention from the already limited programming and advocacy for survivors of sexual violence themselves: "The issue of sexual violence itself was under the carpet for a long time. Certainly we should look at the children too; that's a good point. Much more information on this issue is required. . . . But right now we're still fighting to get recognition for rape survivors, let alone their babies."[55]

A combination of these factors, previously underappreciated by the literature on transnational advocacy networks (TANs), may account for failures in issue adoption within international society. Whether this hypothesis is generalizable should be tested on a wider set of cases.[56] It does, however, provide much insight into the case presented here. Activists within UNICEF sympathetic to the idea of adopting "children born of war" as an issue were critically aware of the importance of framing the issue in such a way as to build consensus between those working on infant health and those dealing with GBV. This needed consensus among gatekeepers turned out to be difficult to forge, at least in terms of constructing the issue with a child-centered focus.

By comparison, incorporating a concern with the sequelae of rape-related pregnancy into existing programming for survivors of wartime sexual violence was much less controversial for two reasons. First, it resolved the concerns that women's programming would be obfuscated by a focus only on their babies. By situating "children born of war" as a consequence and subset of the problem of GBV, advocacy on their behalf stood to strengthen and mainstream, rather than isolate, GBV programming. Second, it was much more difficult to make the case for silence as a protection mechanism when it came to mothers than to small children. Many advocates argued that children born of war might not be well served by being defined in this way operationally, a claim impossible to falsify because the children were too young to interview. By contrast, advocates could agree that given certain safeguards, programming for and fact finding on rape survivors could be reasonably participatory. Although the frame is quite different from that sought by the original champions of the issue, it better fits the intersubjective understandings among advocates concerned with both child protection and women's rights.

Conclusion

This chapter has investigated why the transnational network around children and armed conflict has been hesitant to adopt "children born of wartime rape" as a population of concern around which to gather data, develop programmatic initiatives, or advocate at the global level. I have argued that this issue has not been adopted by gatekeepers in this area largely due to intersubjective understandings among advocates about the relationship of this issue to a different issue already on the international human rights agenda: gender-based violence. UNICEF in particular has been concerned that constructing such children as a category of concern not exacerbate stigma against the children or their mothers or distract attention from programming for rape survivors.

In short, little attention was given to babies born of rape by child protection specialists in the 1990s because those advocates imagined this issue to be a subset not of child protection but of sexual violence, an area in which the "women and armed conflict" network was assumed to have primacy. At the same time, activists focusing on women were more likely to view the issue through the lens of the rape survivor's needs than those of her child and to oppose advocacy discourse that might situate rape survivors or their persecuted communities as perpetrators of child abuse. From this perspective, the emphasis tended to be on prevention of rape and of rape-related pregnancy in the first place rather than responding to the needs of the child-as-human-rights-subject afterward.

Awareness of the specific needs of children born of such violence began to grow as child protection organizations better mainstreamed awareness of GBV in its own right and when the issue of sexual violence and exploitation by UN personnel came to light. The latter provided a politically acceptable perpetrator against whom children, as well as women, might press feasible claims of redress, inviting a coalition between GBV and child protection experts rather than presenting a source of tension between them. Nonetheless, GBV specialists and sympathetic members of the child protection community were concerned about the effects of circumventing a women's rights frame to focus on the needs of children. Given strategic concerns over the impacts of advocacy for children born of war on attention, funding, and advocacy space for preexisting issues, these advocates chose a frame that would bring some attention to the children's vulnerabilities while reinforcing, rather than threatening, advocacy around GBV. This involved subsuming the issue under GBV rather than constructing it as a child rights problem directly—a setback for those issue entrepreneurs who hoped for a broad articulation of the human rights of children born as a result of war.

These insights confirm a number of hypotheses from existing literature on TANs but cast doubt on others. In particular, evidence from this case does not support the hypotheses that the inherent merit of issues, their ability to be grafted onto existing international norms, or the presence of political entrepreneurs are the key factors driving the emergence of new issues on the international agenda. At best, these are permissive conditions, confirming the argument in this volume that the role played by gatekeeping organizations in popularizing an issue is crucially important and that such organizations may strategically avoid adopting even issues that appear on the surface highly conducive to transnational advocacy.

The question then becomes what explains gatekeepers' reluctance to adopt such an issue. My analysis suggests, first, that even when the previously mentioned conditions are met, issues may fail to be adopted by gatekeepers precisely because it is sometimes perceived by human rights advocates that advocacy is inimical to the actual protection of human rights. In short, human rights gatekeepers sometimes attempt to promote a rights-based culture in ways that fall short of advocacy campaigns around particular problems. This "harmful side-effects" argument for issue non-adoption is probably particularly likely to be made (whether as a genuine rationale or a justification) when the issue is promoted by champions rather than by rights claimants themselves. This suggests that the distinction between rights claimants and champions as the drivers of the issue definition stage is not, as Bob puts it, "less important than it appears" but actually fundamental to the sorts of arguments that gatekeepers may make against adopting a new right onto their issue agenda.

More attention needs to be given by independent researchers to whether strategic inattention to a specific population necessarily serves or undermines the protection of that population—or whether this is simply a convenient justification when the political economy of ideas mitigates against issue adoption. If advocacy attention can compromise rather than promote human rights, then serious ethical considerations must take place among human rights intellectuals as well as activists. If such arguments are simply excuses for inaction, then what empirical, rhetorical, or political resources might provide leverage for issue champions in their negotiations with gatekeepers on behalf of rights claimants who might otherwise never be heard? Fascinating and policy-relevant research could be done around these sorts of questions.

Second, the idea that one can fall back on protecting human rights without specific attention to a particular category of concern is particularly attractive to advocates in cases where advocacy itself is perceived to be difficult or risky. But the risks and difficulties involved can have as much to do with the landscape of the advocacy networks themselves as with the local political environments in which they operate. A particular aspect of this environment highlighted by this case study is the importance of consensus with adjacent issue networks with whom a given set of gatekeepers has a preexisting institutional or ideational affiliation. Such a consensus has not been forthcoming between child protection and GBV advocates because of disagreements over whether to categorize these children in this way: that is, how to frame the issue and what terminology to adopt in so doing.

This suggests that the optimism of early literature on human rights networks about the value of network density for issue promotion may be misplaced. It has long been emphasized that coalitions between networks can be an important factor in successful international agenda setting.[57] Keck and Sikkink argue that "network density" is a factor promoting advocacy success;[58] and, as Meyer and Whittier document, "spillover" effects between networks can provide a means of amplifying advocacy frames.[59] But given such spillover, can the same effects pose disincentives for the selection of issues that do not neatly fit multiple network agendas? If so, perhaps failures to create common ground across networks of gatekeepers in conversational settings where new issues are broached may contribute to and explain substantive gaps in the human rights agenda.

Chapter 3
"Dalit Rights Are Human Rights": Untouchables, NGOs, and the Indian State

CLIFFORD BOB

This chapter explores recent mobilization by groups representing India's Dalits (Untouchables) aimed at transforming age-old caste-based discrimination into an international human rights issue.[1] Until the late 1990s, the daily violence, exclusion, and humiliation suffered by millions of Dalits were not treated as human rights issues by UN organs or nongovernmental organizations (NGOs). Despite decades of over-seas activism by Dalit organizations, recognition of the Untouchables' plight remained minimal. No international conventions specifically covered problems of Untouchability, human rights treaty bodies did not recognize caste-based discrimination as a human rights violation, and major human rights NGOs had not taken up the issue.

From a number of standpoints, this long-standing gap in international human rights law and practice is puzzling. First and most important is the magnitude of human rights violations associated with caste discrimination. While precise numbers are uncertain, reliable estimates indicate that there are more than 160 million Untouchables in India.[2] Many continue to endure harsh discrimination and violence because of their subordinate position in the Hindu caste system. Outside India, approximately 90 million people face similar abuse.[3] Much of this mal-treatment is concentrated in South Asian countries including Pakistan, Bangladesh, Nepal, and Sri Lanka, where it affects both Hindus and re-cent converts from Hinduism to other religions.[4] In addition, caste discrimination stretches worldwide, across the large South Asian diaspora in East Africa, Europe, North America, and other far-flung sites of South Asian migration. Finally, even outside the Hindu cultural sphere, there are parallel forms of discrimination based on work and descent. Japan's small Buraku community is probably best known internationally, but in East and West Africa other populations endure similar degradation and prejudice.[5] In sum, given the scope of Untouchability, the world community has been surprisingly slow to acknowledge caste discrimination as a "human rights" issue.

Second, and more abstractly, Untouchability might have been expected to attract greater international concern because caste hierarchies hinge on beliefs and practices inimical to basic tenets of the modern human rights movement. Across the world, whether in Hindu-based or other caste systems, Untouchability involves the ritual subordination of one group by another, often with the imprimatur of religious scripture.[6] More fundamentally, caste hinges on the idea that some groups deserve less respect and fewer rights than others. This is not because those with privilege have somehow "earned" such status but simply a result of their birth into a particular social stratum. As such, caste stands as a direct challenge to a fundamental underpinning of the human rights ideal—that all human beings are equal and deserve the same respect, dignity, and rights.

Despite these reasons that the plight of the Dalits might have been expected to attract significant attention early on, the human rights movement became concerned with the Dalits only in the late 1990s. Spearheaded by organizational development and activism among Dalits in India and the Indian diaspora, there were a number of important milestones along three distinct but interrelated tracks. As discussed later, these include actions among various UN organs, which, starting in 1996, took steps to recognize Untouchables' special human rights issues; among international human rights NGOs, which devoted increasing resources to Dalit problems and formed a transnational advocacy network (TAN) around domestic Indian activists later in the decade;[7] and among select governments, especially in Europe, which began pressuring India for action at the beginning of the twenty-first century. These achievements have not brought an end to caste-based discrimination nor have they fulfilled all the goals of Dalit activists. Nonetheless, they represent significant successes in an ongoing process.

This chapter seeks to explain both the caste's long absence from human rights discourse and these recent successes. After a brief background discussion about India's Dalits, I outline recent changes in international recognition of Untouchability and caste-based discrimination as a human rights issue. On this basis, I analyze what has changed to lead to these advances. Finally, I draw out the implications for theories of human rights and international politics.

Before proceeding, it is useful to discuss one skeptical critique of this chapter. This claim would hold that caste discrimination has always been a subject of human rights concern. To prove this, some might point to the broad language of such international instruments as the Universal Declaration of Human Rights (UDHR), International Covenant on Civil and Political Rights (ICCPR), International Covenant on Economic, Social and Cultural Rights (ICESCR), and International Convention on the Elimination of All Forms of Racial Discrimination (ICERD).[8] Indeed, Dalits have used this expansive language as a basis on which to make their more specific claims. Yet for Dalit activists, such implicit coverage was insufficient. Failing to name Dalit problems expressly meant that they went relatively unnoticed on the international stage. All-encompassing human rights language does not recognize the caste basis on which Dalits are abused and therefore makes it difficult to identify appropriate remedies. Finally, many Dalit activists, like those in other aggrieved communities, have political agendas that go beyond ending abuses and protecting rights. International recognition of "rights" can help solidify group identity, facilitate mobilization, and enhance group power among aggrieved communities such as India's Dalits.[9]

Background: Who Are the Dalits?

Traditionally, Untouchables stood outside and beneath the four main Hindu castes (*varnas*) that ranked all elements of Indian society by ritual purity and pollution.[10] Associated historically (and often today) with work deemed unclean, Untouchables were seen as permanently and hereditarily defiled.[11] Today Untouchables are a diverse group living throughout the Indian subcontinent and comprising about 16 percent of the country's approximately 1 billion people.[12] Among Untouchable populations, as within the four main castes, there are additional hierarchies among occupationally based subcastes (known as *jatis*). Historically in northern India's "Hindi Belt," *jati* rankings have been particularly strong, while in southern India the caste system has been less rigid.[13] There is further geographic variation, with *jatis* confined to particular regions and with substantial ethnic and linguistic differences among them. While most Untouchables live in rural areas, many have migrated to cities seeking economic opportunity and fleeing the rigidities of village life.[14] Dalits have sought escape from Untouchability using other methods too, among them conversion from Hinduism to Islam, Christianity, Sikhism, and Buddhism.[15] Thus today's Dalit population, while predominantly Hindu, is religiously mixed.[16] Given this diversity, viewing Untouchables as a single cohesive group is sociologically problematic. Indeed, there are conflicts among Untouchable communities, often based on occupational hierarchies within the broader group. Yet, as a social and political category, Untouchability has long been and continues to be a touchstone for political activity both inside and outside India.

The situation of the Untouchables was an important issue in India's independence struggle, and key conflicts from the 1930s and 1940s still resound in Dalit politics today. For the Congress Party, Mohandas K. Gandhi (not an Untouchable) sought to champion the group. Gandhi, a staunch defender of Hinduism, saw Untouchability as a perversion of Hindu doctrine and sought to reform the religion by urging Hindus to treat all people equally regardless of caste.[17] But for Untouchable leaders of the time, particularly B. R. Ambedkar, Gandhi's renaming of the group as *"Harijans"* was paternalistic, his view of Hindu doctrine wrongheaded, his faith in upper caste Hindus' renunciation of the hierarchy naïve, and his overall strategy—subordinating the problems of the Untouchables to the struggle for independence—misconceived.[18] Ambedkar, the most prominent Untouchable in the independence struggle, rejected the view that Hinduism could be purged of caste.[19] Instead, he argued that caste hierarchies irredeemably pervaded the religion, prompting his vow not to die a Hindu and his 1956 conversion, with tens of thousands of followers, to Buddhism. In the late colonial period, Dr. Ambedkar exploited Hindu-Muslim divisions in the independence movement and the continuing influence of the British to demand that an independent India include a separate electorate under which only Untouchables would be permitted to vote for Untouchable members of the national legislature. Under tremendous pressure from Gandhi, who believed that separate electorates would undermine Indian unity, Ambedkar eventually accepted the Poona Pact, which reserved seats in the national legislature for candidates from the "depressed classes."[20]

Since Indian independence the group as a whole has made some progress. India's constitution, much of it written by Ambedkar, formally abolished Untouchability; prohibited caste discrimination; expanded the colonial system of "scheduled caste" reservations in educational institutions, government jobs, and state and national legislatures; and established a commission to gauge and report on the group's status in independent India.[21] Under pressure from growing numbers of educated Dalits, India also passed numerous laws and constitutional amendments strengthening protections and expanding reservations for Untouchables. These measures have helped a growing but still small percentage of Dalits gain education, become affluent, and rise to high government office. Despite these policies, however, the majority of India's Untouchables continue to face significant disadvantages, discrimination, and violence. As a result, Dalit activists blame the state and major political parties, both dominated by caste Hindus, for doing too little to implement Indian laws. One key problem is continued social discrimination by higher caste Hindus. In rural India, where the bulk of India's population continues to live, Dalits are excluded from village wells, temples, and tea shops; forced to subordinate themselves before upper-caste neighbors; discriminated against in land and housing allocation; and prevented from participating in local government institutions. Throughout India, Dalits continue to occupy the lowest rungs of the economic system, often living in dire poverty. Most have little or no land. Frequently they work demeaning jobs, most notoriously as "manual scavengers" who clean the country's ubiquitous dry latrines by hand. Despite the reservation system, large numbers of Dalit children do not attend schools, remaining illiterates with few economic prospects.[22] Moreover, as Dalits have sought to improve their position, resist daily humiliations, or vindicate their constitutionally granted rights, they have frequently suffered assault, rape, or murder from upper caste groups threatened by their rise. While these so-called Dalit atrocities have won press coverage in India, in many regions government officials appear unable or unwilling to stop the violence.[23]

Dalits have responded to these abiding problems in diverse ways. As affirmative action programs have grown and development has occurred, more have become politically aware, active, and dissatisfied with existing government policy toward the group. In certain states, strong Untouchable political parties have formed and sought power, sometimes pragmatically allying with parties dominated by middle and upper castes.[24] In the huge northern state of Uttar Pradesh, Kanshi Ram's Bahujan Samaj Party (BSP) has held power under the ministership of Mayawati, a Dalit woman.[25] Dalit politicians also have held prominent roles in other Indian political parties. India has recently had a Dalit president (a largely ceremonial position), and members of recent national Cabinets have been Dalits. It bears emphasis, however, that there is no single political leadership of this vast and diverse group across India.

At the grassroots level, Dalit activism has also grown in recent years, often with little linkage to Dalit politicians in India's most powerful parties. Indeed, in many cases, civic activists condemn politicians for opportunism in allying with non-Dalit parties while doing little to help their constituencies. While it is difficult to generalize about these nonparty organizations, there appear to be several general types. First, in some rural regions, especially Bihar, Dalits have formed armed self-help groups (*senas*) to protect themselves against upper caste violence.[26] Naxalite rebels have been involved in caste warfare for years in some regions.[27] Violence grew both because of increasing Dalit resistance to ritual subordination and because of growing upper caste aggression aimed at maintaining age-old hierarchies and economic inequalities.

Second, and more relevant to recent efforts to internationalize caste discrimination and violence as human rights issues, there are a large number of nonviolent Dalit civil society organizations. These organizations seek to raise Dalit consciousness, support individuals and communities in their day-to-day socioeconomic struggles, and encourage attempts to vindicate constitutional and legal rights. Many are small NGOs founded by Dalit professionals such as schoolteachers, lawyers, and civil servants, working to improve the lives of poorer Dalits. Their tactics include using lawsuits, the media, and nonviolent civil disobedience to achieve their goals. For the most part, however, this activism has been decentralized, with little coordination among the growing number of Dalit civil society organizations sprinkled across India. Until recently, Dalit organizations in India had limited international contacts. Dalit converts to Christianity and Buddhism received support from religiously based organizations overseas.[28] In addition, transnational development NGOs with no blood, religious, or cultural ties to the Dalits operated programs to ameliorate such broad Indian social problems as poverty, landlessness, child labor, bonded labor, and violence against women. These programs benefited many Untouchables (as well as poor people from other castes), but from the perspective of Dalit civil society organizations, such aid treated the diverse symptoms of a single underlying disease, caste-based discrimination, while failing to address the cause itself.

Dalits on the International Stage

EARLY ACTIVISM, 1980–96

In this context, a small number of Dalit civil society activists located both within India and in the South Asian diaspora took steps to internationalize their grievances as human rights issues beginning in the early 1980s. Although their precise goals varied, Dalit activists had several general objectives. First, they sought to raise awareness of the continuing impact of caste-based discrimination by talking to the international media, human rights organizations, and foreign government officials. Second, activists sought allies who would pressure the Indian government to implement existing policies to curb discrimination and violence against Untouchables. Whether states, NGOs, or international organizations, such supporters might shame India into action that would improve the situation facing Dalits. Finally, Dalit activists sought recognition of the group's plight as a distinct human rights violation under international law.

Notably, the Indian state strongly opposed these Dalit efforts. First, the government claimed that the problems Dalits face were overstated.[29] While admitting that Dalits continued to face discrimination and in some cases violence, officials downplayed the scope of violations. Second, the Indian government argued that Dalit problems stem from private social customs and that the Indian state was taking strong action to end all vestiges of Untouchability. Here officials pointed to the large number of special laws for scheduled castes banning discrimination, punishing atrocities, and reserving educational, employment, and political opportunities. Finally, the government maintained that caste is a uniquely Indian social institution and therefore an internal matter not subject to outside oversight.[30]

Notwithstanding this government opposition, Dalit civil society activists made their case internationally in a variety of forums starting in the early 1980s.[31] As discussed later, the response was at first minimal. While Dalit activists gained access to NGOs and international organizations, they had only limited success in convincing these groups to adopt caste-based discrimination as a human rights issue, a situation that began to change only in the late 1990s. In this section, I provide a brief account of early Dalit failures and later successes on the international stage. Based on this discussion, the following section analyzes reasons for these contrasting patterns.

Three small organizations carried on the bulk of overseas Dalit activism in the 1980s. One of these, the Chennai (Madras)-based Dalit Liberation Education Trust, was led by an Indian with substantial experience in the United Nations; two other groups were headed by expatriate Dalits, Volunteers in Service to India's Oppressed and Neglected (VISION) based in Washington, D.C., and the Ambedkar Center for Justice and Peace (ACJP) of Toronto.[32] These groups conducted a number of activities outside India. First they sought support from potentially receptive NGOs, succeeding in the early 1980s in interesting the London-based Minority Rights Group (MRG), which established a working group on Untouchables. Made up of Dalit activists and scholars, the working group sought to "inform and influence public opinion" and act as "an international forum for all issues involving Untouchables."[33] As one of its major activities, MRG held a 1983 conference on racism and Untouchability, publishing a book based thereon three years later.[34] But Dalit activists failed to attract the support of major gatekeeper NGOs in the human rights field, in particular Amnesty International and Human Rights Watch (HRW). These NGOs are important because, given their credibility and access to the media and governmental institutions, their support for a new human rights issue can have tremendous impact on its international recognition.[35] Aware of the influence of such NGOs, Dalit activists made repeated efforts through written appeals, telephone calls, and personal visits to convince Amnesty International and HRW to adopt the caste-discrimination issue.[36] Until the late 1990s, however, these NGOs turned down Dalit appeals.

In addition to tapping NGOs, Dalit organizations sought action from UN bodies and other international organizations. For years, they failed to gain this. Beginning in 1982, however, activists were able to present their case before a variety of international bodies. In that year, VISION's president, Dr. Laxmi Berwa, speaking before the United Nations Subcommission on Human Rights, characterized the Dalits' "constant state of terror and humiliation" as similar to the "condition of Jewish people in Hitler's time."[37] More specifically, Berwa described both recent massacres of Dalits seeking to vindicate their rights and the government's rejection of his group's demands for change. From the subcommission Berwa sought action, arguing that "slavery, bonded labour, violation of civil and human rights and atrocities on harmless people" are not "internal problem[s]."[38] These Dalit organizations made similar pleas at other international conferences including the 1982 Osaka International Conference against Discrimination and the 1984 Nairobi World Conference on Religion and Peace. As other examples, ACJP's director met with representatives of the World Health Organization, as well as foreign affairs officers in Canada, the United States, and European countries. He also attended various UN-sponsored meetings including the Vienna World Conference on Human Rights in 1993, the Beijing World Conference on Women's Rights, and regular meetings of the UN Commission on Human Rights, the UN Committee on the Rights of the Child, and the UN Working Group on Indigenous Populations.[39]

At these and other international meetings, Dalit activists raised awareness of their group's plight among overseas audiences. But despite access to various international organizations, Dalit efforts to win official recognition of caste discrimination as an international human rights issue did not bear fruit until the late 1990s. The first milestone occurred in the UN Committee on the Elimination of Racial Discrimination (CERD), which is charged with analyzing periodic reports submitted by states party to ICERD. ICERD Article 1, defines "racial discrimination" as "any distinction, exclusion, restriction or preference based on race, colour, *descent*, or national or ethnic origin which has the purpose or effect of nullifying or impairing the recognition, enjoyment or exercise, on an equal footing, of human rights and fundamental freedoms in the political, economic, social, cultural or any other field of public life."[40] Reading this passage narrowly, the Indian government had long argued that ICERD did not cover caste-based discrimination, that Article 1's "descent" terminology referred only to racial descent, and that caste was a social or class category "unique to Indian society."[41] Moreover, the government pointed to its laws abolishing Untouchability, banning caste-based discrimination, and providing reservations to Untouchables.[42]

In 1996, however, CERD responded to Dalit activists' years of lobbying by holding in its concluding observations to India's decennial report that "the situation of the scheduled castes and scheduled tribes" was covered under the treaty's "descent" term, which "does not solely refer to race."[43] On this basis and bearing in mind the convention's requirement that signatories take action to eliminate all private or nongovernmental discrimination in their territories, the committee went on to criticize India for failing to provide sufficient information on the implementation and effectiveness of the country's measures to aid the scheduled castes.[44] Although this CERD opinion was in some ways paradoxical— holding that the "descent" prong of CERD's definition of racial discrimination "does not solely refer to race"—it set the stage for subsequent UN consideration of caste-based discrimination.

INDIAN AND INTERNATIONAL NGO ACTIVITY SINCE THE LATE 1990s

In 1997 another key development occurred. HRW decided to prepare a major report on caste-based discrimination—something which activists had sought for years. In part, this reversal of policy rested on the Dalits' repeated requests over the previous decade, which raised HRW's awareness of a major human rights problem in India. Other reasons for the decision included the recent CERD finding and rising attention to violence against Dalits (especially Dalit Christians) in India in the 1990s.[45] A final reason was HRW's finding the "right person" to do this groundbreaking report, a young, Harvard-educated lawyer, Smita Narula.[46] As discussed later, her 1999 report *Broken People: Caste Violence against India's "Untouchables"* attracted significant international attention and helped fuel a sustained upsurge of mobilization both internationally and within India. For this reason, it is important to go into detail about the report's preparation and aftermath.

Realizing that a report on caste discrimination would be a major undertaking, HRW approached the Ford Foundation seeking a grant to underwrite the report. The Ford Foundation, long involved in India through a variety of poverty reduction programs, many of which supported Dalit organizations, was interested in HRW's report—but also in several larger issues. First, Ford's India program officer had long hoped to nurture more effective national coordination among Dalit organizations. Second, and more broadly, Ford hoped to deepen the impact of a major human rights report. According to the Ford program officer: "Very often what happens is that Human Rights Watch decides on 'X' issue, does a report on it, raises lots of attention about that issue. But there is very little collaboration or strategic thinking that goes on with groups on the ground. One of the results . . . is that issues kind of become flash in the pan. . . . But it's very difficult to sustain that kind of advocacy work over a period of time or for local NGOs to use whatever that international group has done and move it to the next level."[47] To achieve a more lasting impact, the foundation first gave HRW a small planning grant with the promise of a larger one if HRW "identified their issues and their agenda with the participation of groups on the ground."[48] When HRW demonstrated that it had done this in 1998, by convening a national meeting of Dalit organizations to advise it on major issues to cover in the report, the Ford Foundation provided a large grant. This aimed at underwriting both HRW's report and promoting Dalit organizing on a national and international level.[49]

The Ford grant and the HRW meeting helped give rise to a new India-based organizational network, the National Campaign on Dalit Human Rights (NCDHR). Officially launched on World Human Rights Day, December 10, 1998, the NCDHR linked dozens of formerly isolated Dalit civil society organizations in fourteen Indian states. Martin Macwan, an Untouchable who headed a Gujarat-based Dalit protection organization called the Navsarjan (New Creation) Trust, was elected its president. As its first goals, the NCDHR opened a yearlong signature drive to "cast out caste in the new millennium" and began preparing a "black paper" on the contemporary situation of Dalits in India.[50] The petition, demanding "freedom from caste bondage" for 240 million Dalits in India and 260 million in Asia, called on the Indian government to "implement in letter, spirit and action" the constitution's abolition of Untouchability and the Atrocities Act, aimed at punishing violence against Untouchables.[51] As such, the petition's main focus was not a change in law but in practice. The petition also called on the United Nations "to recognize untouchability as a *Crime Against Humanity*, to include caste discrimination within the ambit of the Convention on the Elimination of All Forms of Racial Discrimination (1966) and to appoint a *Special Rapporteur* on the practice of untouchability in Asia."[52] More broadly, the campaign called on the "international human rights community" to recognize that "Dalit Rights are Human Rights" and to support Dalit demands before UN bodies. In particular, it called on this community to begin a "global effort to abolish untouchability in Asia," to consider its practice a "heinous crime against humanity," and to concern itself with "any form of discrimination and violations against Dalits, by both State and Civil Society."[53]

As part of their international agenda, Dalit activists held the First World Dalit Convention in Kuala Lumpur, Malaysia in October 1998. The convention, sponsored by Malaysia's Indian Progressive Front, gathered Dalit activists from India, other South Asian countries, and the South Asian diaspora; powerful Indian Dalit politicians; advocates for Japan's Buraku community; and international NGOs active in the emerging Dalit support network. The convention established an international Dalit secretariat and issued a declaration calling on the United Nations to recognize "caste discrimination" as a problem "far worse" than "South African or American Apartheid" affecting "300 million Dal-its through India and the world."[54] In March 2000, Dalit leaders and key overseas supporters formally established the International Dalit Soli-darity Network (IDSN) to provide loose coordination and information sharing among overseas organizations promoting the Dalit cause. To-day IDSN's core leadership consists of four national federations, the NCDHR, Nepal's Dalit NGO Federation (DNF), Sri Lanka's Human De-velopment Organisation (HDO), and Japan's Buraku Liberation League (BLL).[55] In addition, IDSN comprises twelve "international associates" including human rights, development, and religious NGOs, as well as seven national solidarity networks. The latter networks campaign prima-rily within their own countries to raise awareness about Dalit issues and promote government policy that would help eliminate caste discrimina-tion.[56]

Release of HRW's *Broken People* report occurred in March 1999. The report received significant media coverage internationally and in India, where it was translated into several local languages. The report inspired a number of national conferences in India and gave further impetus to the NCDHR's petition drive. In December 1999, the NCDHR released its own black paper, *Broken Promises and Dalits Betrayed*, during a week of promotional activities in New Delhi.[57] Attending these events were sev-eral hundred Dalit civil society activists from around India, key Dalit politicians, and sympathetic non-Dalit politicians including members of the country's National Human Rights Commission. During the week, Dalit leaders met with India's prime minister, presenting him with the black paper and a sample of the 2.5 million signatures collected during the yearlong petition drive.[58]

Outside India, HRW worked closely with its wealth of contacts to en-sure further publicity for the *Broken People* report and the Dalit cause. In a New York ceremony on November 14, 2000, for example, HRW granted NCDHR leader Martin Macwan an award as one of five out-standing human rights defenders worldwide. Thanks to a nomination by HRW and another international NGO long active with Dalit popula-tions, the Unitarian Universalist Holdeen Fund, Macwan also received the 2000 Robert F. Kennedy Memorial Center's Human Rights Award in a ceremony on November 21, 2000.[59] Both these events drew audiences of human rights advocates, policymakers, journalists, and celebrities. The twin awards also won substantial press attention in the United States and in Europe, placing the Dalit cause in the public eye interna-tionally.[60] Moreover, the Kennedy award included not only $25,000 in cash but also lobbying and promotional services by the Memorial Cen-ter's small but well-connected Washington staff during the year that Macwan was the organization's laureate. Macwan employed these services and the Memorial Center's contacts to gain entrée to powerful American politicians, State Department staff, and UN officials. In addition, he was particularly interested in meeting American civil rights leaders, and he established strong ties with several of them.

UNITED NATIONS ACTIONS SINCE THE LATE 1990s

In August 2000, the Dalits scored another important success when the UN Human Rights Commission's Sub-commission for the Promotion and Protection of Human Rights issued a resolution declaring that "discrimination based on work and descent is a form of discrimination prohibited by international human rights law."[61] While not specifically addressing caste-based discrimination, this broader terminology clearly covered it. Based on the encompassing language of the UDHR and the widespread existence of discrimination based on work and descent, the resolution called on all governments to pass, implement, and enforce measures, including affirmative action programs, to end such discrimination.[62] The resolution also explicitly urged governments to move beyond action in the political sphere and to use legal sanctions, both civil and criminal, against "all persons or entities" within their jurisdictions who discriminated on the basis of work and descent.[63] Finally, the subcommission charged Rajendra Kalidas Wimala Goonesekere with preparing a working paper that would identify communities worldwide affected by such discrimination, examine existing governmental measures to abolish it, and recommend further measures to achieve this goal in practice.[64]

This resolution and the resulting working paper (hereafter the Goonesekere Report) launched a process of discussion and report production that continues in the Human Rights Commission today. The Goonesekere Report, issued on June 14, 2001, was an important milestone in several respects.[65] It argued that discrimination based on "work and descent" violates international human rights law.[66] In addition, it documented such discrimination among "a large portion of the world's population," in South Asian countries and Japan, focusing particularly on discrimination against scheduled castes in India.[67] Thus, despite some Dalit activists' misgivings over the absence of the specific term "caste-based discrimination" in the subcommission's original resolution, the working paper clarified that the broader term encompassed the narrower one. Moreover, the report emphasized the unique aspects of discrimination based on "work and descent," in which "victims . . . are singled out, not because of a difference in physical appearance or race, but rather by their membership in an endogamous social group that has been isolated socially and occupationally from other groups in society."[68] Important as well, at the start of its lengthy discussion on India, the working paper discussed Dalit arguments about the religious basis for caste discrimination, contrasting Ambedkar's view that Hindu scriptures created the caste system against Gandhi's claim that caste is not intrinsic to the Hindu religion.[69] Without taking a stand on this issue, Goonesekere thereby underlined Dalit criticisms of Hinduism—an important goal of many in the Dalit movement. Finally, the Goonesekere Report recommended further study of the issue, particularly of the existence of discrimination based on work and descent in Africa and "perhaps in South America."[70]

Two years later, a second working paper undertook this task, focusing on groups in various parts of Africa and Yemen. This working paper again highlighted the "combination of causal factors and expressions" that made discrimination based on work and descent different from forms of discrimination previously examined by the subcommission.[71] It also held that there is "no doubt that social institutions in respect of which the term 'caste' is applicable" are covered by the term "descent" and therefore that discrimination arising therefrom constitutes racial discrimination under CERD.[72] At the same time, the working paper held that the term "descent" also covered situations other than those related to caste.[73] In July 2004, an expanded working paper covered three topics: legal, judicial, administrative, and educational measures taken by states party to CERD; an account of additional groups affected by work-and-descent-based discrimination (focusing primarily on diaspora communities); and a proposed framework for eliminating such discrimination.[74] Based on this report, the subcommission appointed two special rapporteurs to prepare a comprehensive report on discrimination based on work and descent worldwide.[75] In April 2005 the commission adopted this resolution by consensus.[76]

These developments at the Human Rights Commission overlapped with activists' efforts to have the Dalit cause discussed at the UN's September 2001 World Conference against Racism, Racial Discrimination, Xenophobia, and Related Intolerance (WCAR), a major international conference in Durban, South Africa. According to the NCDHR, the WCAR was a "rare opportunity to raise the visibility of India's 'hidden apartheid' at the international level. Increased visibility [together with a] strong international commitment [would] significantly enhance the ability of Dalit activists to pressurize and influence the Indian Government to implement its national and international human rights obligations."[77]

The WCAR process involved a series of international preparatory committee meetings (PrepComs) open to NGOs as well as states. The NCDHR and IDSN, as well as HRW and other supportive NGOs, participated in several of these PrepComs, seeking to have caste-based discrimination included in the WCAR's Draft Programme of Action. Not surprisingly, the Indian government strongly opposed these efforts. As one measure, it blocked foreign activists from entering India to attend a WCAR organizational meeting in 2000; as another, it sponsored attendance at the PrepComs by Untouchables who backed the government position and minimized India's problems of caste discrimination.[78] Despite these tactics, which in any case probably increased media attention to the caste issue, members of the IDSN convinced state delegations from the Netherlands and Denmark to sponsor language supportive of the activists' positions.[79] Thus the key preparatory document for the WCAR, the Draft Programme of Action, included paragraph 73, urging governments "to ensure that all necessary constitutional, legislative, and administrative measures, including appropriate forms of affirmative action, are in place to prohibit and redress discrimination on the basis of work and descent, and that such measures are respected and implemented by all State authorities at all levels."[80]

At the WCAR itself, however, the government of India exercised its considerable power to block consideration of paragraph 73. Although UN secretary general Kofi Annan spoke of descent-based discrimination at the WCAR's opening plenary and although several states had earlier appeared responsive toward paragraph 73, Indian pressure succeeded in keeping mention of such discrimination out of the conference's final Programme of Action. The WCAR foundered on a number of issues unrelated to caste discrimination, but in public and private the Indian government worked hard to delay consideration of the caste issue. Thus, according to India's minister of state for external affairs, Omar Abdullah, "In the run up to the world Conference, there has been propaganda, highly exaggerated and misleading, often based on anecdotal evidence, regarding caste-based discrimination in India. We in India have faced this evil squarely. We unequivocally condemn this and, indeed, any other form of discrimination. The issue has remained at the top of our national agenda. . . . It is neither legitimate nor feasible nor practical for this World Conference or, for that matter, even the UN to legislate, let alone police, individual behaviour in our societies."[81]

One of India's top priorities at the WCAR was keeping paragraph 73 out of the final declaration. No other state supported its inclusion with equal zeal. As a result, despite extensive mobilization by members of the Dalit network, paragraph 73 never came up for debate.

In spite of this setback, the network succeeded in other important goals. Hundreds of Dalits attended the parallel NGO and youth conferences, and the former devoted twenty paragraphs of its final declaration to caste discrimination. Dalit protests and consciousness-raising events at the conference also attracted substantial press coverage. International awareness of Dalit issues undoubtedly increased as a result. More concretely, Dalit organizations forged new linkages with human rights NGOs in the United States and Europe, as well as with organizations representing racial and indigenous minorities worldwide.

In the wake of WCAR, CERD held a special thematic discussion on descent-based discrimination in August 2002. Attended by representatives of Dalit organizations and the state of India, the discussion debated both the dimensions of caste discrimination and its inclusion under CERD. Despite Indian government opposition, CERD upheld its interpretation of descent-based discrimination as including "forms of social stratification such as caste and analogous systems of inherited status which nullify or impair [the] equal enjoyment of human rights."[82] In its General Recommendation 29, it "strongly condemn[ed] descent-based discrimination . . . as a violation of the Convention."[83] Underlining the international dimensions of the problem, CERD recommended that state parties identify communities suffering from descent-based discrimination, pass and implement legislation outlawing it, monitor and curb segregation and hate speech based on such discrimination, and ensure that all communities enjoy equal administration of justice, education rights, civil and political rights, and economic and social rights.[84]

OTHER INSTANCES OF INTERNATIONAL ACTIVISM

Beyond UN bodies, the Dalit movement has also been active in several other international venues where IDSN solidarity organizations are located. As one example, the Dutch organization has convinced its government to give prominence to the issue of caste discrimination. For instance, the country's human rights ambassador has declared that "the Netherlands cares about the plight of the Dalits. Offering equal opportunities for outcastes, tribals and minorities is one of the main objectives the Netherlands is pursuing in the international context."[85] In European Union (EU) organs, Dalit progress has been mixed. In a 2003 resolution, the European Parliament urged the European Commission and other EU organs to include discussion of caste discrimination in its human rights reports, to promote the "fight against caste discrimination" in the United Nations, to support appointment of a UN special rapporteur on the issue, and to take concrete measures on the issue in "political dialogues and in European Union development and trade cooperation" with India and other countries.[86] Notwithstanding such rhetorical support, Dalit activists have been disappointed in more concrete actions by the European Union.

Dalits also reached out to the global justice (antiglobalization) movement, particularly around the World Social Forum (WSF) held in Mumbai in January 2004. This linkage hinged on Dalit concerns about the effects of privatization and liberalization in India in the 1990s. These policies were framed by the government as a way of boosting the Indian economy with benefits for all Indians. Dalit activists, however, believed the policies would result in major job losses in the public sector, where Dalits had made considerable progress thanks to long-standing occupational reservations. With no reservations policies covering the private sector, rollbacks in public sector employment appeared to menace opportunities for Dalits. Within India, one response has been a call for expanding scheduled caste reservations to the private sector. Internationally, the NCDHR and IDSN played a major role in establishing linkages with the global justice movement, many of whose members have opposed economic liberalization policies. At the Mumbai WSF, the NCDHR mobilized large numbers and conducted seminars on issues affecting Dalits, thereby forging linkages with sympathetic activists from around the world. To attract further attention, particularly within India, organizers conducted mass marches across the country in the days leading up to the WSF.

Grievances into Rights: Sources of Dalit Successes on the International Stage

One should not exaggerate the impact of these international developments. Caste discrimination remains rampant in India, other South Asian countries, and elsewhere. Moreover, given the limited power of international law, there is no guarantee that even full accomplishment of the Dalits' global agenda will affect policy in these countries. Nonetheless, it is clear that Dalit activists have made significant progress on the international plane since they began their human rights campaign in the early 1980s.

How did they do so? In this section, I discuss factors that kept caste-based discrimination off the international human rights agenda for years and the changes starting in the late 1990s that brought the issue to unprecedented (if still limited) prominence by the early years of the twenty-first century. Some of these factors relate to the changing international context, others to the organizational basis for Dalit action, and still others to the strategic aspects of Dalit activism.

Undoubtedly, the end of the Cold War coincided with a rise of interest in and concern for human rights issues among international organizations and NGOs. Some scholars and policymakers decried the "proliferation" of rights,[87] but aggrieved groups in a variety of national settings seized on the rights "master frame" to project their causes overseas.[88]

Thus the 1990s saw unprecedented activism by groups such as indigenous peoples, the physically disabled, the mentally disabled, and many other groups that sought to frame their long-standing grievances as internationally recognized human rights abuses. Such attempts were not always or immediately successful, as international organizations and even human rights NGOs proved less receptive to such claims than many aggrieved groups had anticipated. Nonetheless, in the 1990s, Dalit activists likely benefitted from a more receptive international environment than in previous decades. Alone, however, this broad development is insufficient to explain Dalit successes at particular times and in specific venues. Organizational and rhetorical factors played a key role as well.

ORGANIZATIONAL FACTORS

Dalit activism expanded substantially in the late 1990s, both at home and abroad. At the domestic level, there had been no prior nationwide group promoting the Dalit cause as a human rights issue. It is true, however, that several small NGOs based both within and outside India had taken the issue to the international level starting in the early 1980s. The CERD's 1996 holding that ICERD covered the scheduled castes demonstrates that, after years of intensive lobbying, these small but highly motivated groups had some success. But the lack of a nationwide Dalit organization within India appears to have limited the impact of the lobbying efforts both inside and outside the county. The foundation of the NCDHR in 1998 broadened the base of domestic Indian mobilization, while the group's nationwide signature campaign and black paper energized activists. As other scholars have shown, the existence of a cohesive national movement can play an important role in attracting international support, grounding formation of a transnational advocacy network, and ultimately pressuring home states to change policy.[89]

Internationally, the Dalits' organizational capacity also increased substantially in the last years of the century. Soon after its own formation, the NCDHR moved to the international arena, forming the IDSN in 2000. This network is far larger in size and resources than the three small NGOs that pioneered international activism in the early 1980s. In addition, the network has transcended earlier limitations in thinking about issues affecting Dalits. Previously, most development and religious organizations had aided India's poor with programs aimed at solving the disparate problems they faced, from poverty to illiteracy to forced labor. These programs continue today, but the NCDHR and IDSN now promote an approach that frames the Dalits' many problems in comprehensive terms—as outgrowths of caste-based discrimination endemic to Indian society.

It is worth underlining that in their early days both the NCDHR and IDSN worked closely with HRW and various development and religious NGOs long active in India. Publication of the *Broken People* report and international prizes for Martin Macwan, orchestrated by HRW and allied NGOs, added domestic and international legitimacy to the Dalit cause. In addition, these events brought increased publicity to arguments that individual Dalit activists had been making for years. It is impossible to know whether the Dalits would have advanced as rapidly without the support of these overseas NGOs, but this aid appears to have played a key role in the early days of the NCDHR and IDSN. More recently, the latter organizations are clearly at the fore of international Dalit activism. The vibrant and increasingly dense transnational advocacy network around them has made its presence known through persistent, sometimes vociferous, lobbying of international organizations and states, preparation of high quality reports on Dalit issues, and activism aimed at gaining media coverage.

RHETORICAL FACTORS

In addition to these organizational developments, Dalits changed the rhetoric surrounding caste-based discrimination. For one thing, the transnational Dalit network has continually emphasized the scale of human rights violations against Untouchables. The *Broken People* report presented the most comprehensive and internationally prominent account of these abuses. In addition, the NCDHR and IDSN used protest marches, manifestos, and web pages to continually emphasize the magnitude of human rights violations both in India and abroad. For example, in its initial campaign manifesto, the NCDHR states, "Every hour 2 Dalits are assaulted, every day 3 Dalit women are raped, every day 2 Dalits are murdered, every day 2 Dalit houses are burnt down."[90] Important as well, the diverse abuses Dalits suffer are discussed not in the piecemeal terms of the past but in holistic ways. Thus activists pinpoint caste-based discrimination as the source of their degradation and victimization. As an NCDHR document states, Dalit activism "threaten[s] the vested interests, privileges of the hitherto dominant non-dalit castes. Raising consciousness of Dalits and resistance on a wide range of issues such as distribution of surplus land, minimum wages, dignity, justice have led to brutal caste violence against Dalits and Dalit women in particular."[91]

Dalit activists have also taken steps to counter government claims that the problem is primarily one of social custom, rather than governmental inaction. Human rights scholars have long suggested that it is easier to spark international action around de jure discrimination and violations by state authorities than de facto discrimination by private actors.[92]

This would seem particularly true in a democratic state such as India where numerous laws formally prohibit such discrimination. In the Dalit case, activists sought to overcome these problems by emphasizing two arguments: the Indian state's lassitude in enforcing its long-standing laws protecting Untouchables; and, in some cases, state officials' complicity in violations.

The former claim is more common, with numerous NCDHR campaign documents criticizing Indian officials, particularly at the local level, as indifferent to the plight of Dalits. Emphasis is often placed on the fact that despite laws abolishing manual scavenging, local and state governments continue to employ people at these jobs. More broadly, Dalit activists accuse the government on local, state, and national levels of being insufficiently diligent in implementing its constitutional and legal obligations to protect Dalits from discrimination and violence. Recent reports from the government's own National Commission on Human Rights confirm these accusations.[93] Dalits also fault the state for failing to improve their economic standing. As the Indian state has moved to privatize the economy since the 1990s, Dalits have argued that their opportunities for employment under the reservation system have declined.

The second argument aims to show that despite national and state law prohibiting caste discrimination, state actors, particularly at the local level, are actuated by caste prejudice. Dalit activists argue that police forces, composed of higher caste Hindus, have failed to prevent atrocities against them and, in many cases, have condoned or participated in such violence. The slogan "hidden Apartheid," which activists and supporters used to describe caste-based discrimination especially in the run-up to the WCAR in Durban, South Africa, had similar overtones. Its implication was that, as in the case of South African apartheid, caste discrimination had official sanction even though the Indian Constitution and many laws abolished Untouchability and provide benefits to Dalits. ("Hidden apartheid" also serves as an inspirational message for international mobilization, suggesting that, as in the case of South African apartheid, international pressure can leverage change in India and elsewhere.)

Finally, the international campaign has addressed the Indian government's claim that the Dalits' situation is unique to Indian society. The campaign did so in two ways: first, by accepting that caste-based discrimination is framed within the broader terminology of work-and-descent-based discrimination, and second, by identifying populations outside India and the Hindu cultural sphere who suffered this form of discrimination. With respect to the first move, it is worth noting that this terminological change, although seemingly minor, represented an important compromise on the part of Dalit activists. For decades within India, one of the primary targets of Untouchable activism has been the Hindu caste system and Hinduism itself.[94] By contrast, discrimination based on work and descent includes no special focus on Hinduism or the Indian caste system. While some UN reports include significant discussion of India's caste system, the primary means by which Dalit problems have entered official UN human rights discourse is through the terminology of work-and-descent-based discrimination. Notably, Dalit activists have pragmatically accepted this approach, especially after the Goonesekere Report's mention of the Gandhi-Ambedkar debate over Hinduism's role in creating Untouchability.[95] Meanwhile, however, outside the official UN context, both at home and abroad, Dalit activists continue to emphasize the term "caste discrimination."[96] For example, the April 2005 UN Commission on Human Rights vote appointing two special rapporteurs on work-and-descent-based discrimination was made pursuant to a resolution that included no specific mention of the term "caste-based discrimination." But in reporting on this vote to its members and the broader public, the IDSN website avoided the work-and-descent term, instead stating that the commission had voted to appoint rapporteurs to "tackle the entrenched problem of caste-based discrimination."[97] In doing so, the IDSN maintains strong support among an Indian base most concerned about the Hindu caste system, even while folding itself within the broader category of work-and-descent-based discrimination used in the United Nations.

In addition to repositioning its cause within the work-and-descent category, the Dalit network also sought to identify and forge ties with other populations worldwide suffering similar forms of discrimination. By so doing, activists hoped both to underline the problem's scope and to attract broader support from international actors, some of whom might otherwise be reluctant to offend the Indian government.[98] Notably, early NCDHR documents, even those directed at the international community, had highlighted the Dalits' problems in India with only general references to similar problems in Asia.[99] Within a few years, however, Dalit activists had learned the importance of internationalizing their issues. For instance, during preparation of the Goonesekere Report, key NGOs urged others in the network to provide Goonesekere with information on caste-based discrimination around the world. The purpose, as one campaigner stated, was "to demonstrate that addressing caste-based discrimination is not just a politically-motivated attack on India, but a genuine and under-recognized human rights issue affecting a number of different societies (for example, the Burakumin of Japan and various groups in west Africa, as well as the Dalits of several different countries in south Asia including India)."[100] Today, the IDSN website

prominently notes that 260 million people worldwide suffer caste discrimination, highlighting problems in Sahelian Africa, West Africa,
Ethiopia, and Somalia as well as South Asian countries and Japan.[101]
With the continuing series of UN subcommission working papers on
caste discrimination worldwide and the recent appointment of special
rapporteurs, these measures appear to have succeeded.

Conclusion

Contemporary human rights law and institutions provide an expansive
terrain on which individuals and groups suffering a variety of grievances
may stake their claims. The language of the UDHR and many other
human rights instruments is broad, and NGOs and international organizations are often willing at least to hear the claims of groups suffering
abuses. But for many aggrieved groups, the general coverage provided
by international human rights instruments may be insufficient. For adequate remedies to be found, it may be necessary to pinpoint violations
in a more specific sense. Naming an abuse specifically may make it possible to target perpetrators and shame institutions into corrective action.

Yet even for domestic populations suffering significant human rights
violations, international attention and support are far from assured.
This chapter has chronicled a lengthy period of neglect toward Dalit issues—as well as a more recent surge of attention to them among NGOs,
international organizations, and foreign states. This pattern suggests
that substantial grievances and major violations may sometimes have difficulty breaking through to key actors within the international human
rights movement. In the Dalit case, the identity of the target state appears to have played an important role in creating difficulties. When
abuses occur within countries like India—democratic states having
laws that formally prohibit such abuses—convincing international actors to look beyond the law to the realities of discrimination is difficult. More generally, human rights campaigns face greater difficulty
mobilizing against a democratic state than against a highly repressive
"pariah" state.[102]

Beyond these contextual issues, however, the eventual successes of
Dalit activists highlight the relevance of organizational and rhetorical
factors, over which aggrieved groups exercise significant control. In projecting the Dalit cause overseas, the formation of a national coalition of
formerly disparate Indian NGOs played a key role, as did the rapid creation of an international network of solidarity NGOs. These provided an
ongoing organizational basis for consciousness raising, lobbying, and
other activism in a variety of international forums. On a rhetorical level,
Dalit activists advanced their cause internationally by strategically adapt-

ing to the needs of international actors. Most important, they reframed caste-based discrimination within the broader rubric of work-and-descent-based discrimination. In addition, Dalit activists uncovered, publicized, and linked themselves to victims of similar abuses outside India and the Hindu cultural zone. Notably, international NGOs and foundations played an assistive role in these processes, providing resources, ideas, legitimacy, and publicity to the long-term efforts of small groups of Indian and expatriate activists.

Today, much remains to be done to help India's Dalits and victims of similar discrimination worldwide. In contrast to the recent past, however, there has been real progress on the international stage. The evils of caste-based discrimination are today far better known, and major human rights organizations, both nongovernmental and intergovernmental, have placed the issues on their agendas. The key to ending abuses must come from domestic political and social processes, but to the extent that international attention and resources can help, Dalits have significantly advanced their cause in recent years.

Chapter 4

Applying the Gatekeeper Model of Human Rights Activism: The U.S.-Based Movement for LGBT Rights

JULIE MERTUS

Introduction

In recent years, many groups representing people who are lesbian, gay, bisexual, and transgendered (LGBT) have framed their grievances as international human rights claims. In so doing, many of these advocates have fought to add their cause to the human rights movement and to place a new right to sexuality on the international agenda. This chapter explores application of the "gatekeeper thesis" to the LGBT case by examining the relationship of Amnesty International and Human Rights Watch to LGBT concerns. Discussing each organization in turn, the first half of the chapter shows how the organizations responded to both internal and external pressures exerted by LGBT activists. Although the chapter does not attempt to prove causal connections, it does suggest a relationship between the gatekeeper organizations and smaller human rights groups that entered the debate on LGBT rights after the gatekeepers. The second half of the chapter sheds further light on the validity of the gatekeeper thesis by analyzing the associated efforts of LGBT groups to raise their concerns themselves, without gatekeeper support.

Convincing the Gatekeepers

The two most important gatekeeper organizations for LGBT activists have long been Amnesty International (AI) and Human Rights Watch (HRW), both of which operate worldwide in situations of severe repression. Both AI (founded in 1961) and HRW (founded in 1978) wield considerable influence over human rights standard setting, institutionalization, monitoring, and enforcement. There are many similarities between the organizations. Both enjoy strong reputations for professionalism. Both started as small entities with limited mandates based on widely respected international human rights norms. And both later ballooned in size and scope of work. Beyond these similarities, however, the organizational structures and institutional mandates of AI and HRW differ in several important respects.

From its founding, AI has been a mass organization with a complex governing structure comprising an international secretariat (based in London) and loosely affiliated national chapters. As Wendy Wong observes, the particular networking structure of AI "allowed only a few nodes the ability to set the agenda, and indeed, often exclude certain rights from consideration."[1] Granting agenda-setting authority to central nodes is particularly important for organizations driven by a normative agenda. At AI, LGBT advocates faced an uphill struggle in attempting to convince the central nodes to enlarge AI's mandate to address their concerns. Nonetheless, even as they devoted attention to the AI decision makers at the center, LGBT advocates could not neglect the broad AI membership at the margins. While AI members generally do not determine policy directly, they do wield influence both through their willingness (or resistance) to pay annual dues and their participation in AI's central advocacy tactic, letter-writing campaigns on behalf of abuse victims.[2] LGBT advocates seeking to place their issues on AI's agenda thus have had to negotiate norm development with both the national and international management and the mass membership.

By contrast, HRW was founded as an advocacy organization without a mass membership, albeit with a generally knowledgeable and devoted core membership. HRW's principal advocacy strategy is monitoring and reporting: naming abuses as rights violations; blaming violators for their actions; and shaming them into change by generating press, diplomatic, and economic pressures. LGBT advocates aiming at HRW's acceptance thus had to find a way to influence organizational priorities and to reorient organizational focus within the boundaries set by a less than transparent and participatory process.

AMNESTY INTERNATIONAL

AI is an unusual organization, not only because of its enormous size and complex relationship with its membership but also because of its steadfast claim to moral authority. Political analyst and AI "biographer" Stephen Hopgood explains that it is this broad desire to act on the side of morality that unites AI staff and volunteers.[3] AI has "no entry requirements in terms of values, beliefs, identity, or experiences. It is not organized around a shared interest (like a labor union) or a shared identity (like a woman's rights group), or a common god (as in a formal religion), or a shared ideology (like a political party)."[4] Individuals working as staff and as volunteers are dissimilar in more respects than they are similar, drawn together primarily by "the concept of witnessing, exposing truths, and taking action."[5]

In exercising its claim to moral authority, AI has come a long way from its modest beginning in 1961, when it emerged with a letter-writing campaign for the release of "prisoners of conscience" (POCs), people imprisoned for their political beliefs.[6] Since then, AI has expanded both its constituency and methodology. Today, it is a multifaceted network consisting of sections, affiliated groups, and international members.[7] The mandates driving the AI International Secretariat and AI country offices, which traditionally have focused narrowly on certain issues, have also expanded considerably. This occurred, however, only after contentious debate between the "guardians" of AI's core mission in the International Secretariat's Research Department, who opposed expansion as undercutting AI's moral authority, and the larger membership that was more likely to support expansionist goals. Ultimately the expansionists won out, and today AI web pages are likely to paint AI's vision in broad terms, advocating for "a world in which every person enjoys all of the human rights enshrined in the Universal Declaration of Human Rights and other international human rights standards."[8] In pursuit of this vision, AI's mission today is—to quote one of the many AI sites—to "undertake research and action focused on preventing and ending grave abuses of the rights to physical and mental integrity, freedom of conscience and expression, and freedom from discrimination, within the context of its work to promote all human rights."[9]

Fitting sexual orientation into even an expanded AI mandate has been extremely challenging. To some extent, the opposition to LGBT concerns reflects a reluctance to expand the AI mandate for any group and for any issues. But the weight of the opposition has come from arguments particular to LGBT cases. Opponents to LGBT concerns (often located in the AI Research Department) have expressed a concern over a lack of universality of opinion on sexual behavior. The AI Research Department at the International Secretariat in 1986 admonished: "For AI to get into the field of sexual behavior would be to enter into matters so different from those we work on now that it would make people question our other activities."[10] According to this argument, the claims of LGBT advocates conflict with the standard AI model of POCs.[11] POCs receive AI attention generally because they act with principle in the face of persecution. Specifically, POCs knowingly and willingly violate the iniquitous laws of authoritarian governments. In the case of sexual orientation, this model does not always apply. The debate in such a case would center on whether "homosexual behavior" is considered to be "genetic" or a "question of choice."[12]

Even if homosexual behavior were considered volitional, the AI mandate problem would not be resolved because the acts in question may be illegal under the laws of many countries otherwise considered to be respecting human rights. For instance, ages of consent and rules for heterosexual behavior vary considerably from state to state, and these laws are generally thought to be within the sovereign jurisdiction of the state. Following this reasoning, the best that AI's decision-making body, the International Council Meeting (ICM), could do when it passed a resolution on homosexuality in 1978 was to state that POC status may be granted to those imprisoned for advocating homosexuality but not for those imprisoned for engaging in such activity.[13] Although a step in the right direction, this was no solution for LGBT advocates who wanted sexual orientation in the AI mandate and who were concerned that persons imprisoned for sexual offenses alone did not fall within the AI terms of reference.

Despite the International Secretariat's opposition to embracing LGBT issues, the demand for inclusion of LGBT issues, which began as a faint cry in the 1970s, grew stronger and became more vocal in the early 1980s within the larger AI structure as well as outside it.[14] Within AI, the U.S. office was among the leading supporters of LGBT rights, with a few key activists (such as Alice Miller, Cynthia Rothschild, and Michael Schelew) playing key roles in pushing the membership and staff along on the matter. Outside of AI, the International Gay and Lesbian Human Rights Commission (IGLHRC) launched an "Amnesty campaign" that encouraged AI's membership and staff to lobby itself.

One significant attempted compromise occurred in 1979, when AI recognized that "the persecution of persons for their homosexuality is a violation of their fundamental rights."[15] This enabled AI to conduct letter-writing campaigns for LGBT people on the grounds that their imprisonment (and treatment prior to their imprisonment) constituted a violation of their fundamental rights. Sexual orientation itself was still not a ground for AI action, however, and attempts to inject it formally and openly into the AI mandate remained highly divisive within the organization.[16] Throughout the 1980s, the issue of sexual orientation continued to arise at the AI biannual general meeting, an important decision-making forum for AI. The International Lesbian and Gay Association (ILGA) and IGLHRC became increasingly involved in advocacy directed at the AI-International Secretariat.[17] Neither side walked away entirely satisfied.

A new review of AI policies on LGBT-related concerns was spearheaded by the work of a Mandate Review Committee (MRC). Established in 1988, the MRC was tasked with wide consideration of consistency in mandate application and impartiality in interpretation.[18] The debate grew so heated in the 1980s that the MRC chairman resigned in protest over what he perceived to be the AI International Secretariat's (largely the Research Department's) trying to impress its "personal views" on the MRC to block the addition of sexual orientation to the mandate.[19] Finally, in the early 1990s, AI explicitly began recognizing sexual orientation as a ground for protecting LGBT POCs.[20] Instead of altering the AI mandate to insert a new term, AI agreed to interpret the word "sex" that was already present in its mandate to include sexual orientation. The new policy opened the door for AI chapters to undertake letter-writing campaigns for LGBT prisoners in a wide range of countries, including Cameroon, Uganda, Guatemala, the United States, Turkey, Nepal, Saudi Arabia, South Korea, and China.[21]

The degree to which country offices devoted attention to LGBT concerns has varied significantly, however, with the U.S., Canada, and U.K. offices engaging most actively in support of LGBT issues.[22] A milestone occurred in 1994, when AI-USA became the first mainstream human rights organization to publish a widely circulated monograph on gay and lesbian rights as human rights. The slim volume, aptly titled *Breaking the Silence*, did not unveil any information that was not already well-known by governments and NGOs alike. Yet its framing of LGBT issues in human rights terms—naming wrongs as human rights violations—provided a kind of template for other groups to do the same. The very existence of the report signaled that it was time for all human rights NGOs to break their own silence on LGBT issues—and as described later, HRW and other NGOs soon took steps to deepen their involvement with LGBT rights.[23] With an easily identifiable pink triangle prominently displayed on the front cover along with the AI logo of the burning candle, even reading the report in public became an act of disclosure—not about the sexual orientation of the reader but about AI's concern for the human rights of lesbians, gay men, and transsexuals.

Another milestone occurred in June 2001, when AI released its first study on torture and ill-treatment of LGBT persons. "Crimes of Hate, Conspiracy of Silence: Torture and Ill-Treatment Based on Sexual Identity" drew attention to many cases previously neglected by human rights advocates.[24] The report documented cases in Uganda, Pakistan, Argentina, Russia, and the United States. Among them were cases in which people were harassed while in custody, physically and sexually assaulted, subjected to unnecessary medical or psychiatric treatment, and forced to flee their countries because of persecution based on their sexual identity.[25] As with *Breaking the Silence*, the significance of this report rested in more than the cases covered. The report provided an example of how standard human rights methodology—namely, the identification of victims and perpetrators—could be applied to the lives of LGBT persons.

In addition to letter writing for POCs and report writing aimed at shaming public officials, AI representatives have lobbied UN bodies addressing human rights to pay greater attention to human rights violations based on sexual orientation.[26] To support these efforts, AI' s International Secretariat and AI-USA created new organizations to energize and involve their membership. The most prominent of these are the former's Amnesty International Lesbian, Gay, Bisexual and Transgender Network (AILGBTN)[27] and the latter's OUTfront.[28] The AILGBTN seeks to provide a focal point for volunteer activism on LGBT issues and to help facilitate national networks to share materials, skills, or experiences with each other in order to foster greater AILGBTN presence and visibility.[29] While the AILGBTN engages in international-level advocacy, OUTfront works within the United States for similar goals: promoting human rights standards that protect the basic human rights of LGBT people; increasing public awareness of human rights abuses based on sexual orientation and gender identity; and working in coalition with LGBT, religious, youth, and other groups to develop community-based responses to human rights issues facing the LGBT community.[30]

In sum, the new LGBT focus within AI was instigated from within and made possible through its mandate reform initiatives.[31] In a less than perfect process, AI transformed itself from its beginnings as a mass membership organization with a narrow "prisoner of conscience" mandate to a dynamic membership-based organization with a broad mission addressing many forms of persecution, including persecution based on sexual orientation.[32]

HUMAN RIGHTS WATCH

HRW is the largest U.S.-based international nongovernmental human rights organization. It began in 1978 as Helsinki Watch, with the goal of monitoring Soviet bloc countries' compliance with the human rights provisions of the Helsinki Accords.[33] Helsinki Watch adherents were both liberals and conservatives. Liberals applauded the civil freedoms it supported, embracing them as part of a larger liberal agenda. At the same time, conservatives used Helsinki Watch reporting on abuses in the Soviet bloc to support their own agenda in the Cold War.

Helsinki Watch was deeply criticized during these early days for focusing too narrowly on human rights abuses in the Soviet bloc while paying scant attention to human rights abuses elsewhere, including those committed in the Americas with the support or acquiescence of the United

58   Julie Mertus

States. The founders of Helsinki Watch responded to criticism about its limited focus by creating a new division, Americas Watch. The organization grew rapidly to cover other regions of the world, thus spawning Africa Watch and Asia Watch. In 1988, the separate watch committees were united to form Human Rights Watch. Thus the structure of HRW today is both geographical and topical. The earlier geographically separate "Watch" projects each continue to have their own different directors and staff, with centralized oversight, and HRW follows specific issues through its distinct projects.

In contrast to AI, the campaign to bring LGBT concerns to HRW was not determined by the ability of LGBT rights supporters to infiltrate HRW and to educate sympathetic colleagues to support their causes. HRW, like AI, engaged very little in LGBT issues in the early 1990s. "We don't have *those people* [LGBT] in Africa," one HRW staffer remarked in 1993 to the then only openly gay researcher in the organization.[34] The staffer encountered a range of curious questions and remarks, such as "How do you ever find *those people*?" and "Did they know you had these special interests [i.e., being gay] when they hired you?"[35] These conversations did not represent an official HRW position, and indeed most of the senior staff would have been aghast had they realized the hurt they caused with their naïve questioning. Nonetheless the statements were important indicators of a work environment woefully unsupportive of LGBT concerns.

Even as sexual orientation remained neglected in much of HRW's work in the 1980s and early 1990s, three factors pushed HRW into committing itself on a policy level to LGBT rights. First, the early to mid-1990s was a heyday of human rights organizing. The optimism unleashed by the end of the Cold War ushered in a period of expansion in human rights organizing. Human rights groups appeared ready to take on a longer list of individuals and wrongs, including sensitive issues brought by LGBT communities.[36]

Second, the 1990s were also a time of UN human rights conferences, and these conferences were a perfect outlet for the new energy and ideas arising out of post–Cold War optimism. In particular, as explained later in this chapter, LGBT organizing at the 1993 Vienna World Conference on Human Rights and the 1995 Beijing World Conference on Women highlighted LGBT human rights issues, making them impossible for supporters of human rights to ignore. The HRW Women's Rights Division was one of the influential participants in these joint efforts. [37]

Third, the 1991 decision of AI to recognize and work on LGBT concerns, and the 1994 release of AI-USA's report *Breaking the Silence* put pressure on HRW to examine its own policies. While there is no conclusive proof that a "keeping up with the neighbors" syndrome was in play, the timing between AI's entry into LGBT issues and HRW's acceptance was very close, both in time and in similarity of content. In 1994, HRW issued a policy on sexual orientation that read as follows: "Human Rights Watch opposes state-sponsored and state-tolerated violence, detention, and prosecution of individuals because of their sexual identity, sexual orientation, or private sexual practices. Human Rights Watch derives this policy from the rights to life, liberty, and security of the person (Universal Declaration of Human Rights [UDHR], Article 3; International Covenant on Civil and Political Rights [ICCPR], Articles 6 and 9); rights of freedom of expression and association (UDHR Articles 19 and 22; ICCPR Articles 19 and 22); the right against arbitrary detention (UDHR Article 9; ICCPR Article 9); the right to privacy (UDHR Article 12; ICCPR Article 17); and the prohibition of discrimination on the basis of status (UDHR Article 2; ICCPR Articles 2, 26)."[38]

Translating this HRW policy into action depended greatly on the individual researchers charged with implementing it and the advocacy staff supervising it. HRW advocacy director Widney Brown was a potent force within the HRW bureaucracy, actively pushing for these changes over many years. She was aided in her struggles by a seemingly unrelated phenomenon: HRW's decision to rent office space to smaller NGOs, including the tiny UN lobbying arm of the IGLHRC, a U.S.-based group that made its mark with its strong asylum project and its professional monitoring of human rights abuses against LGBT communities around the world.[39] In the beginning, IGLHRC rented a cubical in HRW on a monthly basis, largely for the purpose of stationing a temporary San Francisco staff person to work on the yearly IGLHRC award ceremony in New York. Each year the IGLHRC presence within HRW expanded and, by the time of Julie Dorf's resignation from IGLHRC in 1998, IGLHRC had a permanent presence in HRW.

The presence of the IGLHRC had a distinct opening effect on HRW, although it is unclear whether this was the former's intent. One IGLHRC staff member sent to work at HRW, Scott Long, had already worked on a joint HRW-IGLHRC report on sexual orientation and criminal law in Romania.[40] This time he was not officially being asked to work with HRW; he was just using office space. Yet his physical presence was for many at HRW a constant reminder of their need to devote greater attention to LGBT concerns.

Three years after he had moved into IGLHRC office space inside HRW, Long left IGLHRC to accept a post as the first director of the HRW LGBT project.[41] Almost immediately after he took the new post in 2003, Long observed, his abilities to exert influence in international human rights circles grew substantially. Long remembers that the same people who never had time for him as an IGLHRC representative responded to his new name tag. By combining HRW respectability with an informed stance on LGBT issues, the new HRW project has been able to influence a range of issues using a variety of techniques, from press releases and letter writing to report writing and support of legal actions.

Interventions by the LGBT project at HRW have included, for example, a letter to the Netherlands minister of alien affairs and integration protesting that official's proposal to resume expulsions of gay and lesbian asylum seekers to Iran;[42] a letter to the Guatemalan president urging his government to take immediate steps to stop a pattern of deadly attacks and possible police violence against transgender women and gay men;[43] a report documenting and condemning violence against lesbians in South Africa;[44] and press releases condemning the city of Moscow for attempting to ban a gay pride parade.[45] In addition, the HRW LGBT project has published substantial reports on Egypt (which resulted in the release of many men arrested and tortured in a three-year crackdown against gays in Egypt) and Jamaica (which inaugurated a nationwide debate about sodomy laws, homophobic violence, and HIV).[46]

The fact-finding and reporting on LGBT concerns under the HRW label has helped to elevate them to the attention of the human rights mainstream, forcing both states and NGOs to respond. Not only has HRW become a player in the campaign to elevate LGBT human rights causes to international attention, but it has also encouraged other, smaller organizations in their efforts to do the same.

In sum, it took years of intense pressure by staff and LGBT activists for AI and HRW to take on what were widely viewed as unpopular, niche-group concerns. Once identified, however, the gatekeepers' green light on LGBT issues was enough to spur other, smaller, yet influential human rights organization to follow suit. While the smaller groups were loath to admit that they had waited for AI and HRW to adopt the issue, the timing of their engagement is highly suggestive.

Some of the organizations entering the new area with reports issued after AI and HRW were the Lawyers' Committee for Human Rights (renamed Human Rights First), the International Human Rights Law Group (renamed Global Rights), the International Commission of Jurists, and the Center for Women's Global Leadership. Human Rights First, for example, included LGBT hate crimes in its influential publication *Everyday Fears: A Survey of Violent Hate Crimes in Europe and Latin America*,[47] and Global Rights referred to the human rights of gay men and lesbians in its "Report on the Regional Preparatory Conferences for the Conference on the Americas."[48] But perhaps the strongest example of LGBT issues having "arrived" on the human rights scene was Global Rights' creation of a separate shadow report on lesbian, gay, bisexual, transgender, and intersex rights in the United States. Coordinated by

Global Rights, the report was endorsed by eleven advocacy organizations. These included non-LGBT-specific organizations such as AI-USA, Immigration Equality, and the Law and Policy Program of the Columbia School of Public Health. They also included LGBT-specific advocacy groups such as the Human Rights Campaign Fund, the National Center for Lesbian Rights, and the LAMDA Legal Defense Fund.[49] Also significant was the March 2007 publication of the Yogyakarta Principles, an authoritative statement by human rights experts on the application of international human rights law in relation to sexual orientation and gender identity.[50] Although signed by individuals and not by organizations, the document did include a number of prominent human rights experts serving as staff at well-respected regional and international human rights organizations.

Changing the International Agenda

International LGBT advocacy groups such as ILGA and IGLHCR have not only sought to have their concerns brought to international attention through gatekeeper NGOs but also sought to raise their own issues before international bodies. Instead of attempting to survey all LGBT work with international bodies, which is growing increasingly intensive and varied, this discussion concentrates on two illustrative efforts: the nearly fifteen-year campaign of the International Lesbian and Gay Association to win one of the flags of international acceptability, that is, attaining UN consultative status; and the efforts to use "the right to sexuality" to bridge the emerging area of women's human rights with LGBT concerns.

ILGA's UN CAMPAIGN

Currently more than two thousand NGOs enjoy consultative status at the United Nations, which enables them to make a contribution to the work, programs, and goals of the UN by attending the meetings of the Economic and Social Council (ECOSOC) and its various subsidiary bodies. In some instances, these NGOs may also make oral interventions; submit written statements on agenda items; and serve as technical experts, advisers, and consultants to governments and the UN Secretariat. The main requirements for this entry card to the United Nations include that (a) the organization's activities must be relevant to the work of ECOSOC; (b) the NGO must have a democratic decision-making mechanism; (c) the NGO must be in existence and officially registered with the appropriate government authorities as an NGO/ nonprofit for at least two years prior to application; and (d) the basic resources of the organization must be derived in the main from contributions of the national affiliates, individual members, or other nongovernmental components.[51]

Even after these requirements are met, NGOs focusing on LGBT issues have faced additional obstacles to seeking admission into the UN circle. For nearly fifteen years, the leader of the campaign to change this cycle has been ILGA, a self-described "world federation" bringing together more than four hundred gay and lesbian organizations in eighty countries on all continents.[52]

Since its drive for UN status began in 1991, ILGA has viewed acceptance by the United Nations as central to its mission. Although ILGA was awarded consultative status in 1993, this achievement was short lived, as the United States led a successful campaign to strip ILGA of its consultative status.[53] The purported justification was the fact that some national member organizations, including the United States–based North American Man-Boy Love Association (NAMBLA), condoned intergenerational sex. ILGA attempted to make itself more appealing to the United Nations and to human rights NGOs by expelling NAMBLA from its ranks.[54] Nonetheless, the reconstituted organization was denied reaccreditation. And, as further punishment, the UN AIDS program indicated that it would not fund any project linked to ILGA.[55]

ILGA never relented in its drive for consultative status. The crucial moment for the ILGA campaign came in 2005, when it supported five LGBT advocacy groups in their application for ECOSOC status: the ILGA International Secretariat, ILGA-Europe, the Danish National Association for Gays and Lesbians (LBL), the Lesbian and Gay Federation in Germany (LSVD), and the Gay and Lesbian Coalition of Quebec (CGLQ).[56] In January 2006, the ECOSOC NGO Committee summarily rejected the applications of gay and lesbian advocacy groups—such as ILGA and LBL—without substantive debate. However, in a development that would tip public sentiment in favor of the LGBT activists for the first time, HRW and AI made a public statement in favor of the applicants, requesting that countries sitting on the ECOSOC committee accord ILGA fair treatment.[57]

With each UN defeat, the network supporting consultative status has grown. The U.S. decision to vote with Iran, Cuba, Sudan, and Zimbabwe in 2006 against admission of two of the LGBT applicants drew particular attention. In an open letter to Secretary of State Condoleezza Rice, a coalition of forty-one organizations, led by the Human Rights Campaign, HRW, the IGLHRC, and the National Gay and Lesbian Task Force, called for an explanation of the vote that aligned the United States with governments that have long repressed the rights of sexual minorities: "As the State Department's own reporting demonstrates, severe human rights violations based on sexual orientation or gender identity or expression take place in many countries around the world. Arbitrary arrest, torture, and extrajudicial killings are common. . . . We find it incomprehensible that the U.S. government would recognize these human rights abuses, while denying the people subject to them the right to make their case, alongside other respected human rights organizations, before the U.N."[58]

The open letter to Rice was followed by a petition, endorsed by more than two hundred organizations from more than sixty countries supporting LGBT groups' bids for ECOSOC status.[59] UN watch groups subsequently began reporting on the ILGA consultative status campaign as an issue that called into question the credibility of the United Nations, pointing out that a United Nations that really cared about human rights would not tolerate the selective application of human rights in any cases.[60] The support of mainstream human rights organizations galvanized ILGA to reassert the importance of consultative status. In 2006, ILGA announced a campaign to have an increasing number of LGBT groups apply for ECOSOC status.[61] This effort, billed as "gaining the right to speak in our own name at the United Nations: the ECOSOC campaign," included an effort to maintain an LGBT presence at the United Nations Human Rights Council (which in 2006 took the place of the disbanded United Nations Human Rights Commission, becoming the core UN human rights body). In addition to sending a delegation of twenty-six activists to monitor council meetings in fall 2006, ILGA staged a springtime gathering at the new UN body by holding its twenty-third world conference in Geneva, home of the council.[62]

In October 2006, ILGA attempted to make the most of the relatively open stance toward NGOs taken by the new United Nations Human Rights Council, sending a delegation of twenty-six activists to attend council meetings. In addition, the delegation of ILGA activists presented their case for ECOSOC status to Grupo Latinoamericano y del Caribe (GRULAC), a gathering of government representatives from the Latin American and Caribbean region.[63]

Finally, on December 11, 2007, ECOSOC granted consultative status to ILGA-Europe, the European Region of the International Lesbian and Gay Association, as well as the Danish and German national lesbian and gay associations, LBL and LSVD.[64] ILGA's efforts to increase the visibility of LBGT groups at the international level continue to pay off, as more such organizations received consultative status in ECOSOC. During the July 2007 substantive session, ECOSOC states members overturned an earlier ECOSOC NGO Committee decision denying consultative status to CGLQ and the Swedish Federation for Lesbian, Gay, Bisexual and Transgender Rights (RFSL), welcoming these two as the newest LBGT-related consultative organizations. ILGA declared victory as these new additions brought to seven the number of LGBT rights groups now actively participating in ECOSOC discussions and processes.[65]

"Sexual Rights" as Human Rights

In the early 1990s, LGBT concerns were also brought to the United Nations under the aegis of international NGOs working on women's human rights. In this case, the gatekeeper organization, HRW, played a considerable role, largely through its newly created Women's Rights Division, led by the lobbying work of Dorothy Thomas. Thomas shared influence with Charlotte Bunch, the head of the Center for Global Leadership (CWGL). Bunch's sensitivity to lesbian concerns was no accident—before she had been a human rights activist, Bunch was a leading lesbian rights activist. Together, Thomas and Bunch were a potent force. Thomas's cool yet persistent demeanor gave her an edge in encouraging mainstream human rights NGOs to address seemingly divisive issues, such as the rights of women in wartime and sexual and reproductive rights—both contentious topics in the 1990s. Although the term "lesbian" never made it into either the official government or NGO platforms for action emerging from the 1993 World Conference on Human Rights in Vienna, Thomas was able to make it easier for lesbian lives to be recognized by other publicly identified straight women active in international human rights organizing. By speaking authoritatively yet nonthreateningly with the vast "political middle," in governmental delegations at UN events, Thomas pried open the gates for more radical voices to be heard. Bunch was there to oblige.

By tapping into her social justice roots, Bunch was able to relate to the more radical grassroots organizations throughout the world, and in particular in Eastern Europe, where women's organizing had taken on urgency due to the exploding Balkan wars.[66] Bunch's carefully crafted intervention at the 1993 World Conference on Human Rights—an all-day "women's tribunal" in which women from around the world testified about their personal experiences—proved to be one of the first vehicles for bringing the issues of sexual violence and violence against lesbians to the attention of mainstream human rights NGOs and government representatives.[67] Although LGBT advocates faced considerable resistance at the 1993 meeting, even from their own human rights peers, they had emerged as a political force, albeit still at the margins of the human rights movement.[68] Bunch repeated the freestanding tribunal formula at several subsequent world conferences, focusing on a different issue each time but always including sexual orientation. Through the efforts of women such as Thomas and Bunch, young LGBT activists were inspired to attempt their own interventions at the UN level—a feat deemed unimaginable before.

With their own separate workshops, displays, and speakers in the main NGO halls as well as in the "lesbian tent," and a panoply of workshops and activities, being at the margins suited lesbian activists. They made a strong showing, both in numbers and in the final outcome at the World Conference on Women in Beijing in 1995. Although the language would not find its way into the final Beijing document, references to sexual orientation were prominently discussed and included in brackets (indicating failure to obtain agreement) in the draft platform for action. This was an improvement over Vienna because it recognized the existence of a constituency interested in lesbian concerns and drew attention to their issues as human rights concerns. In Beijing, as in Vienna, however, very few mainstream human rights advocates were willing to risk their own reputations by pushing for nonbracketed language.[69]

One important component of these campaigns was the attempt to raise "sexual rights" at the United Nations. For LGBT activists seeking to frame their concerns in human rights terms, the notion of "sexual rights as human rights" holds great promise because it focuses on the behavior that is being punished, prohibited, or otherwise limited (i.e., the right to marry or partner with an adult of one's own choosing) and not the categories of "homosexual," "gay," "lesbian," or "transgendered." Many sexual minorities simply do not view their identity in terms of the hetero/homo dichotomy and, rather, present a wide variety of sexual identities that resist categorization. For them, the globally exported "ideas of 'gay liberation' serve 'not as emancipatory slogans,' but impose external categories onto widely divergent peoples, thus obscuring the inherent value of fluidity and deliberation in sexual identity."[70] Not only does a "sexual rights" approach accept that gays and lesbians are different, but also it demands the end of state-condoned denial of their ability to be different.

Prior to 1993, the concept of "sexual rights" was nowhere to be found in international documents, even in bracketed language. Indeed, with the exception of provisions prohibiting discrimination on the basis of biological sex, matters of sexuality and sex practices were wholly ignored.[71] However, due to the concerted efforts of women's rights advocates, references to "sexuality" were included in the 1993 World Conference Declaration and Platform for Action and in many subsequent documents from international conferences. Initially the concept of the "right to sexuality" was incorporated only in the negative sense, as in recognition of women's rights to be free from violence related to sexuality. It was not until the 1994 International Conference on Population and Development (ICPD) that sexuality "began to sneak into international documents as something positive rather than always violent, abusive, or sanctified and hidden by heterosexual marriage and violence."[72] For example, instead of focusing solely on how women are victimized by brutal husbands, the focus was on improving women's ability—inside and outside marriage—to make their own decisions regarding their sexuality. The ICPD document also presented an additional advance for LGBT advocates in its references to "reproductive health," which it defines as requiring "that people are able to have a satisfying and safe sex life" and can decide "if, when, and how often" to reproduce.[73]

The 1995 Beijing World Conference on Women's Platform for Action further advanced the concept of sexual rights by affirming that "the human rights of women include the right to have control over and decide freely and responsibly on matters related to their sexuality, including sexual and reproductive health free of coercion, discrimination and violence."[74] Notably, in 1999, the ICPD+5 reaffirmed the principles and strategies set forth in the 1994 document, including those addressing sexual rights, creating additional language that could be used in support of LGBT advocacy.

Conclusion

International LGBT advocates have sought not only to have their concerns brought to international attention through gatekeeper NGOs but also to raise their own issues before international bodies. In so doing, LGBT activists have engaged in two very different kinds of activities. First, they have engaged in traditional human rights activism, which uses monitoring and reporting to apply existing human rights norms to LGBT lives. These include the right to privacy in the criminal law context, the right to equality, the right to family, the right to nondiscrimination, the right to freedom from torture (applicable in cases of "forcible cures" for homosexuality and psychiatric mistreatment generally), and the right of transsexuals to recognition of their new sex. Second, they have sought to promote new international human rights that are important to LGBT lives, including "the right to sexuality."

As this chapter has explained, LGBT rights as human rights were only tentatively and incrementally adopted by major gatekeepers under pressure from LGBT supporters working mainly internally but also externally. This gradual embrace of LGBT rights was shaped by the preexisting missions of the major NGOs. Over time, their adoption of LGBT issues broadened, and this in turn led to wider—though still limited—

acceptance by other human rights NGOs. At the same time, LGBT advocates working on their own and with gatekeeper assistance have sought to inject LGBT concerns directly onto the international human rights agenda. ILGA's efforts to gain consultative status and the broader attempts to advance the right to sexuality illustrate these efforts.

Chapter 5

From Resistance to Receptivity: Transforming the HIV/AIDS Crisis into a Human Rights Issue

JEREMY YOUDE

The Joint United Nations Programme on HIV/AIDS (UNAIDS) estimates that 33 million people worldwide are HIV-positive.[1] The AIDS epidemic presents one of the greatest challenges to public health systems around the world, straining national budgets and medical expertise worldwide. Not only is AIDS incurable, but it also disproportionately afflicts people in their early adult years. The very people who should be contributing to the economic, political, and social development of the state are instead falling ill and dying. This has huge social and economic costs. It also harms governance and democratization.[2]

In response, states, nongovernmental organizations (NGOs), and intergovernmental organizations have taken an active role in providing access to treatment, education, and prevention programs. Given the magnitude and effects of the AIDS epidemic, this is not surprising. What is surprising, though, is that, instead of predicating their actions simply on public health grounds, advocates for people living with HIV/AIDS (PLWHAs) increasingly argue that education programs and treatment access are matters of human rights. For example, UNAIDS declares, "The risk of HIV infection and its impact feeds on violations of human rights, including discrimination against women and marginalized groups. . . . Over the past decade the critical need for strengthening human rights to effectively respond to the epidemic and deal with its effects has become evermore clear. Protecting human rights and promoting public health are mutually reinforcing."[3] The International Federation of Red Cross and Red Crescent Societies specifically advocates human rights as a cornerstone of its AIDS prevention programs. Protecting rights, it argues, will empower vulnerable groups to

demand education, economic opportunities, and protection from violence. This, in turn, will reduce HIV transmission.[4] Amnesty International notes that human rights abuses contribute to HIV's spread and
undermine treatment efforts, and Human Rights Watch finds that such
abuses fuel transmission, which in turn leads to additional abuses and
discrimination.[5] Similarly, Physicians for Human Rights encourages
medical professionals to both treat the disease and call attention to its
underlying causes.[6] In this approach, health care workers can use their
public credibility to highlight violations of economic, social, and cultural rights and the ways in which those violations increase a person's
vulnerability to infection.

Historically, disease containment has not involved human rights strategies but has instead relied on "coercion, compulsion, and restrictions."[7]
Reciprocally, diseases have not typically been the subject of human
rights activism. Today's emphasis on human rights in HIV/AIDS treatment and prevention therefore represents a major and contentious
shift in public health policy and human rights advocacy. Why did public health officials move away from traditional strategies and turn to
human-rights-based strategies for confronting AIDS? Why did human
rights NGOs accept HIV/AIDS as a rights issue? By examining these
changes, we can see how the meaning of the area of human rights itself
has evolved and how strong advocates in critical positions can catalyze
change.

In the first section of this chapter I identify three human rights approaches to AIDS. Next I explain how advocates began promoting rights
arguments against the public health orthodoxy of the mid-1980s. This
effort started at the national level, led by public health officials and domestic AIDS activists particularly in the United States. As discussed in
the third section, similar rights-based approaches to AIDS were brought
to international organizations by a few well-placed individuals, most im-
portantly Dr. Jonathan Mann, initial director of the World Health Organization's (WHO) Global Program on AIDS (GPA). Mann's advocacy
faced stiff opposition from WHO bureaucrats imbued with traditional
public health attitudes, but the battle in this key international organization helped inform the world about the advantages of integrating
human rights into AIDS policy. In this context and under pressure from
their own AIDS advocates, key states began adopting their own rights-
based policies concerning the disease in the early 1990s, as discussed in
the following sections on Brazil and South Africa. By the mid-1990s,
conventional human rights NGOs, long reluctant to embrace AIDS as a
rights issue, also began changing their attitudes, as discussed in the
chapter's final section.

Defining a Human Rights Approach to AIDS

What does human rights mean in the HIV/AIDS context? In the early days of the epidemic, advocates invoked human rights to argue against detention and isolation of those suffering from AIDS. Later, the rights frame was expanded to include equal access both to education about AIDS transmission and to palliative and later recuperative treatments. More recently, some activists have promoted a broader rights approach, demanding reductions in poverty and social inequality, which are seen as major risk factors for HIV infection.

These three approaches to human rights in the HIV/AIDS context are not mutually exclusive, but they have different policy emphases. The first two reflect a pragmatic way of combating AIDS. Their advocates did not necessarily have an attachment to human rights per se. Instead, they saw rights norms as tools for effectively addressing the epidemic. For instance, when governments began placing HIV-positive persons into isolation and indefinite detention, advocates argued that doing so frightened people away from testing and treatment, thereby spreading the disease.[8] To support these arguments, activists also appealed to human rights principles against arbitrary detention and restrictions on free movement, which are both part of the Universal Declaration of Human Rights and the International Covenant on Civil and Political Rights. Similarly, activists invoked the rights to information and education as a basis for disseminating basic facts about the disease, its spread, and its treatment. Simple as these measures seem, implementing them often meant confronting deep aversions to openly discussing sexual practices (including homosexuality) and intravenous drug use. It also meant reaching out to marginalized communities such as commercial sex workers. Rights arguments provided an important basis for overcoming these societal taboos.

The third meaning of human rights in the AIDS context represents a further shift in thinking. Using rights language and treaties, it calls for fundamental socioeconomic changes to reduce vulnerability to exploitation and disease. For instance, instead of promoting informational campaigns about AIDS prevention and treatment, this approach seeks to alter the social conditions placing people in peril of infection. Dr. Paul Farmer, a physician and medical anthropologist who teaches and practices both at Harvard Medical School and in Haiti, is one of the most vocal advocates of this position. The NGO he founded, Partners in Health, uses human rights arguments to challenge the "structural violence" that increases individual disease risk. In this view, "HIV transmission and human rights abuses are social processes . . . embedded . . . in

... inegalitarian social structures."[9] Thus human rights norms are not just tools for reducing AIDS but a foundation for achieving health for all.

Failures of Traditional Public Health Strategies

Traditional public health strategies for containing communicable disease have relied on isolation and quarantine. Isolation refers to separating those who are exhibiting signs of illness from the rest of the population. Quarantine functions more as a preventative measure. It involves separating those exposed to a disease from the rest of the population, even though they may not be exhibiting any signs of illness. If infected or considered susceptible to infection, individuals were isolated for a period of time, then officials could prevent the disease from spreading into the general population. While such a strategy has a certain logic, its application has traditionally ignored individual rights. Fidler notes, "Historically speaking, infectious disease control measures have never been kind to individuals. Quarantine practices had long been notorious for their ill-treatment of and cruelty to travelers."[10] Quarantine strategies often reflected popular prejudices and were applied in an arbitrary manner. Dispossessed and "undesirable" groups were often blamed for the spread of disease, as they were thought to be "dirty."[11] This then gave officials license to forcibly remove groups from cities and institute discriminatory measures. Historically, for example, the spread of bubonic plague was blamed variously on Jews, Roma, Africans, and Asians.[12] As a result members of these groups were forced from their homes, had their possessions burned, lost their jobs, and were barred from traveling—all in the name of protecting public health. In one particularly egregious example, blacks were blamed for being carriers of bubonic plague during an outbreak in the early twentieth century in Cape Town, South Africa. The South African government, starting in 1901, used this as a pretext for removing blacks from urban areas and creating a sanitary corridor between whites and blacks.[13] This was the first officially sanctioned segregation by race in South Africa and a precursor of the government's later apartheid policies.

When AIDS first emerged, many states fell back on these traditional means of disease control. Quarantine, forced isolation, mandatory testing, and employment bans were commonplace. Cuba, for example, imposed a systematic quarantine on all HIV-positive persons in 1986, a strategy that remained in place until 1993.[14] Such restrictive measures were not solely the province of authoritarian states, however; many liberal democratic states adopted similar measures. The government of the southern German state of Bavaria introduced sweeping regulations requiring testing and screening of members of high-risk groups for HIV in 1987. This measure was soon expanded to include applicants for civil service posts, foreigners from non-European Community states, prisoners, prostitutes, and drug addicts. The governments of Iceland, Switzerland, the United Kingdom, some Canadian provinces, and some U.S. states all sanctioned the forced isolation and/or house arrest of HIV-positive persons during the 1980s. In perhaps the most sweeping measure, Sweden amended its Contagious Disease Law in 1985 and 1988 to include HIV/AIDS. This revision mandated that HIV-positive persons follow certain orders, such as required testing and contact tracing, or face mandatory isolation or jail time. Isolation periods could be as short as three months, but they averaged one year in length. By the mid-1990s, the Swedish government had used the Contagious Disease Law to isolate more than sixty people.[15]

During these early years, little international coordination on containing the spread of HIV existed. Most campaigns focused solely on informing the public how HIV was (and was not) transmitted. Widespread fear and misinformation inhibited international coordination, as few states were willing to take an active role on an issue that was largely framed as one of individual responsibility and morality. Human rights were not even on the agenda initially.

This changed in the mid-1980s as activists and officials started to argue that existing policies failed to stop the epidemic's spread and perhaps even exacerbated it. In this view, threats of quarantine, isolation, and discrimination made people unwilling to be tested or counseled.[16] In the United States in particular, activists took to the streets to challenge government policies that promoted stigmatization of HIV-positive persons. The AIDS Coalition to Unleash Power (ACT-UP) took the lead in these demonstrations. Founded in 1987 in New York largely by gay activists, ACT-UP channeled the frustration many HIV-positive persons felt about the lack of public education and treatment options available to them. The group took nonviolent direct actions to call attention to the plight of those with AIDS and to humanize its victims.[17] ACT-UP sought to counter American politicians such as Jesse Helms, who introduced legislation to deny funds for safer-sex education programs aimed at gay men, and journalists such as William F. Buckley, Jr., who called for tattooing the buttocks of HIV-positive gay men and the arms of HIV-positive IV drug users.[18] ACT-UP charged that government policies failing to protect rights, provide accurate information, or offer effective treatments were genocidal.[19] The group also agitated for a quicker review process for AIDS drugs.

In response to this activism, public health policies in the United States and elsewhere slowly changed, with punitive and discriminatory elements replaced by policies that respected individual rights and liberties. Notably, however, this shift occurred for pragmatic reasons—to better stem the epidemic—not because of an ideological commitment to human rights.[20] Moreover, neither the public health nor the human rights communities uniformly welcomed this new approach. Elements within both communities greeted calls for connecting AIDS and human rights with skepticism or hostility. The next two sections highlight the battles within each.

Public Health Agencies and AIDS as a Human Rights Issue

Traditional public health strategies do not emphasize respect for human rights. At the same time, though, certain public health practitioners were among the most forceful proponents of integrating human rights into AIDS prevention work. This clash led to significant discord within the public health community. These disagreements played themselves out at the international level through the experiences of Jonathan Mann and the GPA.

The international community initially reacted to AIDS with apathy. Because it was first discovered in the United States and other Western states, many observers believed that AIDS was a disease of the rich and largely confined to these states.[21] Some in the international community even expressed relief that the disease emerged in these states. An internal WHO memo from 1983 on AIDS argued that the WHO did not need to involve itself in the issue. AIDS, its author noted, "is being very well taken care of by some of the richest countries in the world where there is the manpower and know-how, and where most of the patients are to be found."[22] Between 1981 and 1985, scientists scrambled to find AIDS' causative agent and understand how the disease was transmitted, while paranoia and discrimination grew. Many public health officials saw AIDS as another infectious disease that could be addressed using traditional public health strategies for disease containment like quarantine and isolation.

Between 1985 and 1990, a shift occurred toward a period of "global mobilization."[23] The international community discovered not only how widespread the disease was but also how vital international cooperation was for effectively combating the disease. Instead of being associated with wealth, AIDS quickly became associated with poverty as more and more cases were discovered in developing states.[24] Discussions about an international response to AIDS formally began in April 1985 when the WHO held a special consultation about how to stem the spread of the disease. The following year, the WHO declared AIDS to be a global health priority and committed the agency's resources to combat AIDS.[25]

The WHO began some programs devoted to HIV and AIDS in the mid-1980s, but it quickly became obvious that an international response to the disease required a more coordinated effort. In February 1987, the WHO officially launched the GPA.[26]

The GPA's initial approach to AIDS largely followed traditional public health approaches used to fight infectious diseases such as cholera and smallpox. It encouraged states to develop national AIDS programs and sought donations from developed countries targeting nations that were especially in need of assistance. Within a year of the program's founding, 170 countries requested assistance in forming their own national AIDS programs and coordinating their activities. The GPA initially provided technical and organizational guidance and small amounts of funding (less than US$1 million) to 151 countries.[27] Starting with a small budget and one secretary, Mann eventually turned the GPA into the WHO's largest single project with a staff of more than two hundred under his leadership.[28]

The story of Dr. Jonathan Mann's tenure at GPA embodies the conflicts over how best to address the AIDS epidemic. Upon GPA's founding in 1987, Mann was appointed to lead the organization. Mann came to GPA from directing an anti-AIDS program in Zaire and was widely respected for his medical skills and charisma. His experiences in Zaire convinced him that treating AIDS required compassion and respect, not discrimination and stigma.[29] Upon joining GPA, Mann immediately started meeting with government officials and members of the press from around the world to raise the profile of GPA and encourage the active involvement of as many states as possible. Mann's personal diplomacy, for example, inspired the Swedish government to increase its voluntary donations to GPA from US$1.8 million in 1986 to US$10.5 million in 1987.[30] Mann's efforts received widespread praise not just for elevating AIDS to a high place on the international agenda but also for putting WHO back on the international map. While his actions won praise from many, Mann also inspired jealousy among his colleagues in less well-funded WHO programs.[31]

Because GPA was housed entirely within the WHO, its approach largely adopted traditional public health strategies. These were the techniques with which the WHO was familiar, and few saw any reason to deviate from them. Mann, though, started to argue publicly that any AIDS prevention efforts needed to place respect for human rights front and center—even though this might deviate from traditional strategies. Tensions rose within the organization. The original three objectives of GPA's global AIDS strategy were to prevent HIV infection, to reduce the personal and societal impacts of HIV infection, and to mobilize national

and international efforts to combat the disease. In 1991, GPA undertook an effort to assess the applicability of these objectives to the epidemic as it was then unfolding. While not rejecting its original objectives, GPA added six clarifying points: emphasizing adequate health care
coverage, expanding treatment for STDs, reducing women's vulnerability to infection through increased education, eliminating cultural and
social impediments to discussing matters of sexuality, planning for the
anticipated socioeconomic impact of AIDS, and communicating the
public health rationale for eliminating discrimination against those with
HIV.[32] This list shows the tension between traditional public health
strategies on AIDS and new strategies that emphasize human rights. Traditional strategies focusing on individual risk reduction play a prominent role, but the GPA called for access to information and socioeconomic changes that allow people to realize their full range of human
rights. The human rights framework was working into GPA's arsenal,
but it uncomfortably shared space with other strategies. Mann's personal, pragmatic interest in human rights as an AIDS prevention strategy often clashed with the WHO leaders who oversaw the program and
believed in the traditional strategies.

Tensions over the appropriateness and relevance of human rights to
AIDS increased in 1988 with the election of Dr. Hiroshi Nakajima as
WHO's director general. Nakajima had previously served as WHO's regional director for the Western Pacific and chief of WHO's Drug Policies and Management unit. He was also viewed as a more traditional
and conservative leader—a contrast to his predecessor, Dr. Halfdan
Mahler.[33] Nakajima and Mann quickly clashed over GPA's organizational autonomy vis-à-vis WHO and how best to raise and spend GPA's
funds.[34] They disagreed about the prominence given to GPA relative to
other WHO programs, GPA's embrace of nontraditional tactics, and
GPA's support of projects that fell outside traditional public health
bounds. Mann and Nakajima also clashed over access to AIDS drugs in
developing states.[35] Nakajima called for a retrenchment of GPA's
budget and activities and cut the organization's budget by US$35 mil-
lion in 1990 when donations to the program fell short. He also resisted
Mann's efforts to broaden the focus of GPA to encompass issues of
human rights and delayed or cancelled joint anti-AIDS initiatives between GPA and other UN organizations.[36] The constant squabbling un-
dercut GPA's effectiveness, as outsiders could not be certain that GPA
initiatives would actually occur.

The disagreements eventually became too much for Mann. In March
1990 he resigned as the head of GPA. In a strongly worded letter to
Nakajima, Mann noted, "There is a great variance between our positions

on a series of issues which I consider critical for the global AIDS strategy."[37] He lambasted Nakajima's attitude, stating, "Dr. Nakajima's attitude is that AIDS is not such a big problem. The figures say otherwise."[38] Mann's replacement, Dr. Michael Merson, had previously headed up the WHO's Diarrheal Disease Control and Acute Respiratory Infections Control programs. He, like Nakajima, was viewed as more of a traditionalist but was faulted for his lack of imaginative leadership.[39] His tenure at GPA's helm coincided with a period of complacency. Contributions to GPA, and AIDS programs in general, plateaued, as donor states showed little inclination to continue to support the efforts of GPA. Rumors also circulated during Merson's tenure that top WHO officials ordered GPA staffers to remove quotations from and references to Mann in its materials. The campaign, which Merson vigorously denied, sought to exorcise Mann's influence and bring the GPA back in line with other WHO programs.[40]

Many of the conflicts over the appropriate response to AIDS came to a head at the Eighth International Conference on AIDS, held in Amsterdam in 1992. Press reports noted a severe and visible fissure among competing camps. On the one hand, Merson and his allies argued that the international AIDS control regime should focus its energies on promoting condom usage and treating venereal disease. By encouraging changes in behavior, they argued, the disease could be stopped. Mann led a competing faction, arguing that the fight against AIDS required an all-out assault on discrimination and inequality because it was these two factors that gave rise to the epidemic in the first place.[41] An emphasis on behavioral change assumes that those infected with HIV have willingly entered into the behaviors that exposed them to the virus. Those advocating a human-rights-based approach countered that poverty and inequality put people in positions in which they could not freely exercise the choice to avoid putting themselves in harm's way.

In the 1990s, Mann and his followers continued their efforts, publishing, speaking, and lobbying governments for a linkage between AIDS (and other health issues) and human rights. In 1993, Mann helped launch the Francois-Xavier Bagnoud Center for Health and Human Rights at Harvard University, the first academic center with such a focus. The following year, he cofounded *Health and Human Rights*, a journal that speaks to both academics and practitioners interested in the issue. These platforms allowed Mann to maintain his public advocacy, eventually winning over some of his foes. For instance, by 1993, Merson was calling for AIDS prevention programs that recognized and respected human rights.[42] In 1998, Mann died in an airplane crash en route to Geneva to consult with UNAIDS officials. Many obituaries and remembrances highlighted Mann's efforts to call attention to human rights and public health. One noted that the Harvard School of Public Health gave its graduates a copy of the Universal Declaration of Human Rights along with their diplomas at his suggestion.[43]

Ultimately, Mann's rights-based approach to AIDS prevailed at the international level. At the 1994 World AIDS Summit in Paris, delegates agreed to disband GPA and replace it with UNAIDS. This new organization combined the resources and expertise of various organizations within the UN system to coordinate international AIDS programs, with human rights approaches as a central strategy.[44] This rights-based approach remains dominant today.

Human Rights Organizations and AIDS

WHO traditionalists were not the only ones resistant to linking AIDS and human rights. Major international human rights organizations such as Amnesty International and Human Rights Watch initially expressed skepticism at including AIDS, or any public health concern, within the pantheon of human rights issues. Gruskin and colleagues, writing in 1992, specifically chastised human rights NGOs for failing to involve themselves with HIV/AIDS issues. They argued that this undermined attempts by public health officials to encourage governments to take seriously the human rights of those with HIV. Without the public campaigns in which human rights NGOs frequently engage, international organizations lacked neutral, nongovernmental sources about country practices toward AIDS patients. Local AIDS service organizations tried to fill this gap, but they rarely had the resources or expertise to provide this information effectively.[45] Seeing little action on AIDS from established human rights NGOs, Mann called for the creation of "an Amnesty International-style organization for people who are discriminated against because they have [AIDS]."[46]

Major human rights organizations like Amnesty International and Human Rights Watch initially shied away from HIV/AIDS because it was too distant from their previous campaigns and strategies. Amnesty International's mission, for instance, largely focused on political and civil rights violations against particular individuals. Protecting human rights in the context of AIDS fell too far outside its mission. Not only did AIDS affect large numbers of people, but also its human rights implications centered primarily on social and economic rights.

It was not until 2001 that Amnesty International broadened its organizational mission to include abuses of economic, social, and cultural rights. With this change, the right to information and freedom from discrimination came under Amnesty's purview.[47] Amnesty situated its AIDS efforts within its broader campaign to promote health as a human right.

This includes instrumental efforts in linking human rights and AIDS, such as ensuring access to accurate information and expanding treatment options. It also includes broader efforts to combat social and economic disempowerment.

Human Rights Watch (HRW) has long focused its energies on major violations of established political and civil rights. Concerns about social vulnerability to disease did not fit within this framework. By 2002, though, HRW's attitude changed, and the organization established a program to document human rights violations based on HIV status, advocate for legal protections for HIV-positive persons, and produce research on AIDS-related human rights abuses.[48] Part of the motivation for instituting such a program arose from a new appreciation for the indivisibility of human rights. Though AIDS-related rights abuses generally arise from violations of economic, social, or cultural rights, HRW now holds that these rights are mutually reinforcing with the political and civil rights with which they have traditionally been concerned.[49] Violations of human rights fuel HIV infection, and a person's HIV-positive status can lead to further human rights violations. Sexual violence and lack of information can spread the virus, and those infected with the virus may then be subject to discriminatory laws and social stigma. Joseph Amon, the head of HRW's AIDS campaign, writes, "Because human rights abuses fuel the HIV epidemic, HIV/AIDS programs must explicitly address, and find ways to mitigate, these abuses."[50] By drawing on its expertise documenting and exposing human rights violations, HRW has found a role for itself in combating HIV/AIDS.

Despite their recent inclusion of AIDS within their missions, human rights organizations have faced continuing criticism. Paul Farmer has been most outspoken, excoriating NGOs such as Amnesty International and Human Rights Watch for being too conservative. He calls their approach overly legalistic, ignoring the daily realities of the vulnerable populations they are trying to help. New laws or treaties are rarely enforced, and they cannot help people find jobs, take control of their bodies, or be integrated into the larger national community. Compiling reports and holding press conferences will do little to change the fundamental economic, political, and social dislocation that makes a population vulnerable to HIV infection in the first place. These tactics, Farmer explains, are too passive and do too little to reduce "structural violence" in societies.[51] To use a medical analogy, Farmer charges human rights NGOs with constantly treating symptoms without addressing the underlying disease.

Recent developments suggest that human rights NGOs may be heeding Farmer's criticisms. For example, Larry Cox, who took over as Amnesty International USA's executive director in May 2006, has pledged to better integrate social and economic rights with the organization's traditional focus on political rights.[52] Farmer, for his part, seems cautiously optimistic about Cox's pledge, but he has also worked to empower new human rights NGOs.[53] He serves on the Board of Directors of the National Economic and Social Rights Initiative (NESRI), a new human rights organization that works to realize human rights to health and education.[54] He sees NESRI as a tool for challenging the "orthodoxy in health and human rights" by fostering the development of a more expansive human rights culture.[55] As a new organization, NESRI may also lack the institutional structures of more established human rights NGOs and therefore be in a better position to adapt its programs to integrating health and human rights.

AIDS and Human Rights at the National Level

Brazil and South Africa provide two examples in which local organizations framed national struggles against AIDS in human rights terms. In both cases, grassroots organizations rallied public support and attracted international attention by calling for their governments to respect human rights as part of the AIDS fight. Interestingly, AIDS activists in both countries had participated in national democratization movements and applied the techniques they had learned to their new cause.

BRAZIL

After years of military rule, democracy returned to Brazil with the adoption of a new constitution in 1988 and the inauguration of a democratically elected president in 1990. One of the major players in the pro-democracy movement was the "sanitary reform movement." This loose affiliation of health care workers and academics promoted health as a human right. Thanks in part to this group's activities, Brazil's 1988 democratic constitution recognized health as a fundamental individual right and charged the government with ensuring it. The constitution also called for an active and ongoing dialogue between the government and civil society groups on how best to uphold human rights.[56]

Using this legal framework and the lessons learned through the pro-democracy movement, PLWHAs have formed numerous legal aid groups. These groups ensure that HIV-positive persons know their rights, how to obtain treatment, and where to go if they experience discrimination. The legal aid groups have also pressured Brazilian public health officials to treat AIDS as a human rights issue.[57] More broadly, Brazilian AIDS policy has moved beyond a focus on individual behavior to address the larger social context in which people make decisions about sexuality.[58] Many programs now recognize that the socially vulnerable may make different decisions regarding sexuality than the privileged. Finally, some of the local NGOs have been active in international meetings and networks.[59]

The success of local AIDS activists is most apparent regarding provision of antiretroviral drugs (ARVs). ARVs have shown remarkable promise in treating HIV-positive persons, prolonging and enhancing lives. However, these drugs are expensive. When first released in the 1990s, one year's supply cost more than ten thousand dollars—too expensive for most Brazilians. Activists pressed pharmaceutical companies to reduce prices and encouraged the government to produce generic versions under a compulsory licensing scheme. Significantly, the campaign framed access to ARVs as a human right. In this view, to uphold the constitutionally guaranteed right to health, the government needed to ensure that all Brazilians had access to these drugs, regardless of their ability to pay.[60] To make this argument, activists sued the Brazilian government for free and universal treatment. They achieved their goal in 1996, and the government has remained committed to providing ARVs ever since (despite pressure from the World Bank to abandon the policy).[61] This has had broader repercussions. Free AIDS treatment demonstrates to marginalized groups that the government cares about them, increasing their use of all forms of preventative health care.[62]

SOUTH AFRICA

In South Africa too, activists, most prominently the Treatment Action Campaign (TAC) have incorporated human rights into the AIDS fight. TAC was founded on December 10, 1998, International Human Rights Day, with a mission of building a racially diverse, grassroots movement to gain greater access to ARVs. The group's founders initially believed that their primary target would be the multinational pharmaceutical companies that produce ARVs. However, after the government refused to make ARVs available despite a Constitutional Court ruling compelling it to do so, TAC began to focus its energies on changing government policies.[63]

Many TAC activists derive inspiration from their backgrounds in the antiapartheid movement. Zackie Achmat, the group's founder and chairperson, cites Nelson Mandela as his model.[64] Prior to founding TAC, Achmat directed the AIDS Law Project and established the National Coalition for Gay and Lesbian Equality (NCGLE). Working with the African National Congress (ANC) in the early 1990s, Achmat helped ensure that sexual orientation would be included in South Africa's postapartheid Bill of Rights.[65] These experiences not only provided Achmat with knowledge of the antiapartheid movement but also fostered a network of committed activists who shared these understandings.

TAC draws heavily on the antiapartheid movement, using similar language, symbols, and songs.[66] To pressure the national government, the group uses such tactics as civil disobedience, mass protests, and litigation. These public actions further TAC's mission of educating South Africans about their rights in the context of AIDS.[67] Drawing on the legacy of the antiapartheid movement also increases TAC's legitimacy and allows the group to counter accusations that it is unpatriotic or "un-African."[68]

With the ANC-led government sensitive to charges of rights abuses, TAC has brought legal cases charging violations in such venues as the Constitutional Court, Human Rights Commission, and Commission on Gender Equity. The cases are grounded in part in the human rights guarantees contained in the South African Constitution and Bill of Rights. These documents charge the government with specific positive obligations to uphold a pantheon of individual rights, including the rights to equality, dignity, and access to health care.[69] TAC also draws on international human rights treaties to justify its positions. For instance, in criticizing the government for failing to implement a comprehensive AIDS program including access to ARVs, TAC cited Article 25 of the Universal Declaration of Human Rights (on the right to an adequate standard of living for health and well-being), Article 16 of the African Charter on Human and Peoples' Rights (on the right to health and the government's responsibility to ensure it), the Rome Statute of the International Criminal Court (on crimes against humanity including the denial of medicine), and Section 27 of the South African Constitution (on the right to health care services and the government's responsibility to provide them).[70]

TAC does not limit its activities to South Africa. The organization has built alliances with AIDS service organizations (ASOs) and activist groups around the world, lending its credibility to these groups while presenting a united transnational front to the international community. Doctors without Borders, the Gay Men's Health Crisis of New York, and ACT-UP have collaborated with TAC to pressure both the South African and American governments.[71] Achmat calls on fellow activists to cajole wealthy governments around the world to provide monies for treatment and to ensure that human rights are upheld for all PLWHAs.[72]

Conclusion

The recasting of AIDS as a human rights issue, rather than simply a public health concern, is an important example of the struggle for "new" human rights. Initially, a pragmatic response to the epidemic's severity and the failures of traditional public health approaches, human rights approaches have become far more than that. Today, in fighting AIDS, access to information and treatment are central issues, underpinned by national and international human rights norms. Some advocates also raise broader human rights arguments about the pernicious effects of "structural violence" in creating social vulnerabilities to the disease.

Key players in this unprecedented transformation from disease to human rights issue include national-level AIDS activists, particularly in the United States. Well-placed individual advocates, notably Jonathan Mann, were also critical to raising international consciousness about rights-based approaches to AIDS. As a result, powerful organizations such as the GPA and UNAIDS promoted human rights approaches to AIDS, opening the door to broad acceptance of such policies internationally. In turn, this has affected local AIDS activists in the developing world, who drew on their own experience in domestic democratization movements to call attention to shortcomings in purely public health strategies to AIDS.

Major human rights NGOs such as Amnesty International and Human Rights Watch have not been leaders in promoting the link between AIDS and human rights. Issues of disease and infection were too alien to the NGOs' long-standing focus on violations of civil and political rights. However, in the 1990s, the human rights NGOs came under pressure from national and international AIDS advocates. With this lobbying and with the United Nations' embrace of human rights approaches to AIDS, the human rights NGOs have recently begun to work on limited aspects of the AIDS issue. This has not satisfied those such as Paul Farmer who believe that tackling the disease requires fundamental societal change. But it does represent a significant expansion in the cultures and missions of these organizations, one that mirrors public health institutions' earlier and equally contentious move to adopt rights-based approaches to AIDS.

Chapter 6
Disability Rights and the Human Rights Mainstream: Reluctant Gate-Crashers?

Janet E. Lord

Introduction

In the 1970s, international human rights monitors loudly condemned the Soviet Union's internment of political dissidents in "psychiatric hospitals." Nongovernmental organizations (NGOs) such as Helsinki Watch and Amnesty International (AI), along with local activists such as Andrei Sakharov and Yuri Orlov, publicized the horrors of these detentions: squalid living conditions, abusive guards, and cruel "treatments" such as forced electroshock and drugging. In some cases, the international pressure generated by these reports helped free political prisoners. But at the same time that human rights NGOs highlighted the political abuses of psychiatry, they ignored the plight of detainees with mental or physical disabilities who experienced similar conditions in the very same institutions. More recently, Human Rights Watch has continued this neglect—and thereby unwittingly condones abuses against persons with psychosocial disabilities.[1]

International human rights law is, of course, applicable to all. Until recently, however, human rights organizations and the United Nations ignored persons with disabilities. For their part, "handicapped" service organizations long embraced paternalistic, charity, or medical approaches, treating people with disabilities as pitiful victims rather than as rights-bearing individuals. In recent decades, however, people with disabilities have advocated for the reconceptualization of disability as a social construction and, more recently, have fought for rights-based approaches to disability. Even more recently, disability activists have taken this campaign for the rights of more than 600 million people worldwide to major human rights NGOs and the United Nations. In particular, activists have sought a new international convention on disability rights. In December 2006, the movement scored a major victory when the UN General Assembly adopted the Convention on the Rights of Persons with Disabilities. While much remains to be done to implement the convention, more than one hundred twenty-five countries quickly signed it, and it won twenty ratifications to trigger its entry into force in May 2008.[2]

This chapter chronicles the multifaceted struggle for disabled people's rights at the international level. First, I examine the contentious rise of rights-based approaches within the disability community itself. Second, I discuss the rights of persons with disabilities as reflected in international human rights law, highlighting gaps that led activists to promote a specialized convention on the subject. Third, I analyze the convention campaign, a major part of which entailed efforts to convince key human rights NGOs such as AI and Human Rights Watch to support it. In the fourth section, I examine broader efforts to convince these gatekeeper NGOs to address ongoing abuses against persons with disabilities.

The Framing of Disability: From Pity to Rights

Until recently, the dominant medical and charity models viewed disability as a problem localized within the individual.[3] These models reinforced the perception of persons with disabilities as "broken" people whose only hope for "normalcy" lies with medical or rehabilitation experts who might "repair" them.[4] But the medical and charity models do not reflect the perspective and experience of people with disabilities themselves. Rather, they stem from the false assumptions of the able-bodied majority, who perceive disabled people as "problems" in need of "solutions." Deliberately or not, these attitudes have served to isolate persons with disabilities and inhibit their full participation in society. Such views have done so directly through government policies restricting the social and economic options of people with disabilities. More insidiously, they have done so by damaging the self-perceptions of disabled people.

Beginning in the 1960s and 1970s, organizations of persons with disabilities began promoting a "social model" of disability. In this view, society, with its patronizing attitudes and obstructive policies, "handicapped" the individual. Once it is perceived that a range of societal impediments—from stairs to stereotypes to statutes—segregate people with disabilities, a rights-based approach becomes logical. A person with a disability, whether physical or psychosocial, becomes a rights-bearer, like all human beings. In addition, the role of people with disabilties in self-advocacy and in establishing organizations led by disabled people themselves was a core part of the emerging movement. Disability rights movements organized first in North America and Europe during the

1970s and later in Latin America and other regions during the 1980s and 1990s. These movements were far from unified, with many of them organized along impairment-specific lines and having only weak, ill-coordinated, and fractious national federations. Moreover, disabled people's organizations often faced opposition from traditional "service" organizations for the "handicapped."[5] Nonetheless, by the mid-1990s, many of these national movements had helped replace discriminatory laws with more inclusive ones, not only in the United States, Canada, Sweden, Australia, and Japan but also in the developing world, including Liberia, Yemen, Cambodia, and Uganda.[6] As a result, people with disabilities have come closer to being treated as equal citizens in many parts of the world.[7]

While the disability movement focused primarily on domestic politics, it did not ignore international institutions. Through meetings and conferences, disabled people's organizations began to make linkages regionally and internationally. As in the domestic sphere, this activism began when disabled people's organizations demanded greater power within preexisting "service NGOs." One of the earliest and most important of these struggles occurred within Rehabilitation International (RI), one of the largest international NGOs working on disability issues. RI was founded in 1922 as the International Society for Crippled Children.[8] From the start, the organization reflected a charity approach to disability, and its membership was primarily nondisabled medical and rehabilitation professionals. At the 1980 RI Congress in Winnipeg, Canada, only about three hundred of three thousand delegates were disabled. But that year members with disabilties formed a caucus and proposed a resolution (the "equality amendment") requiring the RI Delegate Assembly to include at least 50 percent disabled persons. When the resolution was defeated at the RI Assembly, these delegates declared the formation of a new organization, Disabled Peoples' International (DPI). Today, DPI is the only cross-disability, global membership organization, including approximately 130 national member assemblies. As one of the original DPI delegates recalled, "Some three hundred [disabled] delegates who gathered there from all parts of the globe had a sense of their own destiny. They wanted to proclaim their rights as citizens, to an equal voice in the decision-making of services, the policies and programs that affected them. They were no longer willing to passively accept the control of rehabilitation professionals over their lives. They demanded dignity, equality, and full participation in society. They demanded release from the yoke of paternalism and charity."[9]

Under similar pressure, other international NGOs working on disability issues have adopted a rights-based approach, particularly in their advocacy work. These include Leonard Cheshire International, the Center for International Rehabilitation, Handicap International, and Land-mine Survivors Network. Most strikingly, as a response to its participation in the UN Disability Convention negotiations, RI took steps to indicate its shift toward a more rights-based approach. In the negotiations over the convention, RI's team of human rights experts included several lawyers and activists with disabilities. At a symbolic level, the organization today "prefers to go by the abbreviation of its . . . name, and RI now stands for Rights and Inclusion as well."[10] In recent years, RI appointed as its chairman Lex Freiden, a prominent disabled activist and the former chair of the U.S. National Council on Disability, although Freiden was succeeded as RI chairman by a nondisabled person.

The Marginalization of Disability in Human Rights Law

As new international organizations such as DPI formed, and as older NGOs moved toward rights-based approaches, both became increasingly interested in using international law to promote their goals. International human rights law, however, falls short in providing adequate coverage of the rights of persons with disabilities. On its face, the International Bill of Rights, which comprises the Universal Declaration of Human Rights (UDHR),[11] the International Covenant on Civil and Political Rights,[12] and the International Covenant on Economic, Social and Cultural Rights,[13] applies to all people. This is so despite the fact that the Conventions do not explicitly prohibit discrimination on disability grounds or provide rights to persons with disabilities.[14] In practice, however, explicit mention in an international convention encourages action, while implicit coverage discourages it.[15] Thus activists working for women's rights, child rights, migrant worker rights, and many others have pressed for specialized human rights conventions to fight discrimination and monitor human rights. Beginning in the 1980s, people with disabilities and their allies sought to do the same.

Before examining these efforts, several earlier developments need to be discussed. First, in the early 1970s, the United Nations adopted the 1971 Declaration on the Rights of Mentally Retarded Persons and the Declaration on the Rights of Disabled Persons.[16] While these documents recognized disability as a human rights concern, the disability community soon discredited them as reflecting medical and charity models. Thus, for example, the 1971 declaration employs the now offensive term "mentally retarded" in its title, qualifies the scope of rights for people with intellectual disabilities in providing that "the mentally retarded person has, *to the maximum degree of feasibility,* the same rights as other human beings,"[17] and sets as its goal "their [disabled people's] integration as far as possible in *normal* life."[18]

The 1980s saw the launching of the UN Decade of Disabled Persons (1982–93) and the adoption of the World Programme of Action Concerning Disabled Persons.[19] In 1987, the Global Meeting of Experts to review the World Programme recommended that the United Nations draft an international convention on discrimination against disabled persons, but draft agreements prepared by Italy in 1987 and Sweden in 1989 were rejected by the UN General Assembly at its forty-second and forty-fourth sessions.[20] Both efforts were initiated by European disability activists, but there was little in the way of broader international support for the drafting of a legally binding instrument, and these fledgling efforts gave way to lesser initiatives to develop nonbinding documents pertaining to disability. The decade culminated in the adoption of the UN Standard Rules on the Equalization of Opportunities of Persons with Disabilities (UN Standard Rules) and the Principles for the Protection of Persons with Mental Illness (MI Principles).[21] These documents add specificity to the general framework of international human rights protections but leave significant gaps and do not fully reflect a rights-based approach to disability. The UN Standard Rules is by no means a comprehensive account of rights-based issues relevant to persons with disabilities and is drafted in programmatic language rather than terminology reflecting human rights obligations. The MI Principles refer to patients rather than persons with psychosocial disabilities or consumers. Moreover, for many in the psychosocial disability community, the MI Principles seem to legitimize institutional care models as opposed to community integration, self-empowerment, and self-determined living. More important, the two documents are not part of a legally binding human rights convention. In the mid-1990s, as disabled people's organizations themselves became more involved in international advocacy, activists began arguing that the MI Principles reinforced the status quo, perpetuating human rights abuses against people with mental disabilities.[22]

In a related development, a small but important NGO, Mental Disability Rights International (MDRI), formed in 1993. Its founder, Eric Rosenthal, a staff person at Human Rights Watch (HRW), had sought for years to stimulate the interest of the NGO in the rights of persons with mental disabilities. These efforts failed, however, for several reasons. First, HRW leaders argued that they did not have the resources to devote to a division or program on the issue. More significantly, HRW staffers, unfamiliar with disability rights issues, failed to see the connection between their work and that of disability rights activists. As one well-known human rights activist and former HRW staff member acknowledged as late as 2000, "It's a poor reflection on the well-funded human rights community that [disability rights] issues have been invisible to us."[23]

Springing from the mainstream human rights movement, MDRI focuses on the civil and political rights of people with disabilities, such as due process rights and freedom from cruel, inhuman, and degrading treatment. Moreover, its methodology mirrors that of the major human rights gatekeepers: lengthy investigations, public reports meticulously detailing abuses, and campaigns to shame authorities into improving treatment of psychiatric patients around the world. With this familiar organizational profile, MDRI has been more successful than other disability organizations in winning grants from well-established human rights funders such as the Ford Foundation and Open Society Institute.

While MDRI's efforts have been tightly focused, a number of disabled people's organizations took a broader approach to international advocacy. Seven groups are most powerful, forming a loose-knit network, the International Disability Alliance (IDA).[24] These seven were the first to gain ECOSOC consultative status and, more significantly, a seat on the expert panel established in 1992 to monitor the implementation of the nonbinding UN Standard Rules on the Equalization of All Forms of Opportunities for Persons with Disabilities. All NGOs in the IDA are membership groups or federations of membership groups devoted solely to disabled issues. Excluded from the IDA are nonmembership advocacy organizations, national level membership organizations, and international development organizations with disability activities. Within the IDA there are also power asymmetries based primarily on the groups' status as "disabled people's organizations." Two members, RI and Inclusion International (II), founded by parents of people with intellectual disabilities, do not have this status and therefore remain suspect to other IDA members. Accordingly, both RI and II have taken a secondary role in efforts to internationalize the issues, even while seeking to boost their disability credentials with delegations composed of leading disabled advocates.

In the mid-1990s, the international disability community began to discuss in earnest the merits of pressing for an international convention on the rights of persons with disabilities. Some leaders in the community, such as the UN special rapporteur on disability, former Swedish parliamentarian Bengt Lindqvist, questioned the utility of such a convention, asking in particular whether, if passed, it would in fact be implemented by states. Moreover, they held that in a context of limited resources for people with disabilities, a convention would divert time and effort from activities more directly beneficial to the disabled. Such activities include organizing the disabled politically, advocating on concrete and particularized issues, and strengthening existing national, regional, and international legal frameworks. Proponents of a convention, however, such as Theresia Degener of Germany, a frequent consultant to the United

Nations on disability issues, argued that it would be beneficial, given the failures of the United Nations' previous nonbinding agreements. In addition, pointing to the contemporary International Campaign to Ban Landmines, supporters noted that the drive for a convention could itself raise awareness, thereby helping the disabled. In 1998 and 1999, the UN Disability Programme convened expert meetings, each of which resulted in a report advocating a new convention addressing the rights of disabled people.[25] The 1999 Hong Kong meeting was particularly important, convening grassroots disability activists and international human rights lawyers and advocates from around the world. In a weeklong session, the group reviewed the implementation of international standards on disability and their potential future, concluding that the existing framework fell short.[26]

Soon after the 1999 conference, some members of IDA started to issue calls for an international convention on the rights of persons with disabilities. During March 2000, participants at the World NGO Summit on Disability convened in Beijing to discuss the language of a possible treaty.[27] In a concluding declaration, the World Summit urged the international community "to immediately initiate the process for an international convention."[28]

In fall 2001, the nascent campaign received a major and unexpected boost when Mexico, a country with no prior record of supporting disability advocacy internationally, introduced a resolution to the UN General Assembly calling for an ad hoc committee to draft an international disability convention. This proposal, vigorously promoted by President Vicente Fox's disability advisor, a former presidential candidate himself and a disabled activist, took the international disability movement by surprise. But key activists quickly worked to exploit this opportunity for advancing their agenda.

One strategy supported by the Convention Development Group (CDG), a loose network of Washington, D.C.-based disability organizations, was enlisting the support of powerful human rights organizations, in particular HRW and AI.[29] While HRW had expressly rejected work on mental disability rights in the early 1990s, CDG members, including MDRI, believed participation by the human rights gatekeepers to be essential. According to this view, the gatekeepers' expertise in rights work and in UN treaty processes would help advance the convention. In addition, their participation in the campaign would provide legitimacy that might help attract broader support to the cause.[30] Other disability activists, however, cautioned against consorting with the human rights mainstream, arguing that only the disabled could adequately articulate the issues. In addition, some feared that "professionalization" of the campaign would lead to participation by doctors, psychiatrists, and rehabilitation experts, all anathema to important wings of the disability movement.[31]

Notwithstanding this contention, the CDG approached the mainstream human rights organizations and convinced them to attend an April 2002 "summit." The meeting included disability advocates and leading figures in the human rights movement, such as Aryeh Neier of Open Society Institute, Kenneth Roth of HRW, and representatives of AI, and Physicians for Human Rights (PHR). During the meeting, both communities noted the human rights movement's long-standing disregard of the rights of people with disabilities.[32] More affirmatively, disability activists promoted the idea of an international convention, presenting a white paper detailing a rationale for its development.[33] This effort succeeded, convincing major human rights NGOs, including AI, HRW, and PHR, to support the treaty process.[34]

Beyond attendance at the summit and rhetorical support for the convention, the major rights NGOs provided strategic backing for the campaign, although they did not initiate their own programs on disability rights or on the convention.[35] For one thing, disability activists could draw on the experience of human rights campaigners who had succeeded in promoting the Mine Ban Treaty, the Convention on the Rights of the Child, and other international conventions. Just as important, HRW, AI, and the International Service for Human Rights sporadically attended sessions of the ad hoc committee, as well as briefings and conferences related to the convention. At the 2003 ad hoc committee session, HRW and International Service for Human Rights issued a joint statement strongly supporting the convention, while AI followed in subsequent sessions with oral interventions. Their participation, however, remained marginal throughout the negotiation process, and these organizations did not engage in meetings and joint lobbying efforts of the International Disability Caucus, which was the main voice of the process and was controlled by disabled people's organizations. Finally, the Open Society Institute (OSI) provided substantial financial support to the campaign. This came in the form of a grant to the Landmine Survivors Network (LSN), a disability organization known to OSI through LSN's work on the landmines campaign. The grant underwrote LSN's major role at the UN Disability Convention negotiations in 2004, where it proposed draft language, lobbied delegates, and promoted the convention in the media.

With the imprimatur of HRW, AI, and other human rights gatekeepers, with funding from OSI, and with strong backing from Mexico and other states, the disability convention moved through the United Nations. The mainstream human rights groups, however, remained marginal within the coalition of NGOs that comprised what came to be known as the International Disability Caucus (IDC). The IDC leadership was wholly dominated by disabled people's organizations, and the leadership of disabled people themselves was a fundamental principle of its lobbying and communication operations during the process. Following the 2003 meeting of the ad hoc committee, a working group, composed of twenty-seven states, twelve NGOs, and one national human rights institution, developed a draft text that formed the basis for formal negotiations. In August 2006, a final text was adopted by the ad hoc committee, and then by the whole UN General Assembly in December 2006. The Convention on the Rights of Persons with Disabilities embraces a social model of disability and articulates the full range of civil, political, economic, social, and cultural rights with specific application to disability.[36] An optional protocol to the convention was likewise adopted at the same time, allowing states to opt into a procedural mechanism whereby the treaty-monitoring body established within the framework of the convention can hear individual and group communications alleging violations of the convention.[37]

While galvanizing international attention and support for the rights of persons with disabilities, the campaign and the convention itself have also affected the international disability community. Thus a number of disability organizations have established programs based on the substantive and methodological models used by powerful human rights NGOs. For example, the Center for International Rehabilitation has modeled its International Disability Rights Monitor, a global reporting scheme to analyze compliance with the convention, on HRW's Landmine Monitor.[38] In 2002, a rival monitoring project, Disability Rights Promotion International, was also launched by the former UN special rapporteur on disability, Bengt Lindqvist, and international disability expert Marcia Rioux.[39] Notwithstanding these recent efforts to mirror the human rights NGOs' methods, the only significant long-term partnerships between a disability rights NGO and a mainstream human rights funder are those of MDRI and a smaller Hungarian group, Mental Disability Advocacy Center, both funded by OSI and each focusing on monitoring the rights of persons with psychosocial disabilities according to traditional monitoring and reporting methods.[40]

Conclusion

The adoption of the Convention on the Rights of Persons with Disabilities represents an important victory for the international disability movement. But questions remain about the potential of the convention to protect the rights of persons with disabilities. Long-term partnerships between disability rights organizations and powerful human rights NGOs remain scant. Only Mental Disability Rights International, with its roots in the human rights movement, has done this by working collaboratively with HRW, as in the case of its work in Kosovo, which HRW helped to publicize. By contrast, HRW has rejected DPI's repeated appeals to support human rights capacity building among disabled people's organizations in the developing world. AI has not embraced disability rights in its long-term planning nor has it included disability rights in its prominent human rights education program.[41]

More broadly, to the extent that disability organizations are now conforming themselves to the methods and concerns of the convention, for instance by forming international monitoring programs, it is appropriate to question whether this is a good use of scarce resources. Given that most countries have weak and fragmented disability communities with little or no advocacy experience, such top-down monitoring and reporting projects may have little impact and may indeed be ineffective given the capacity needed to do first-rate monitoring and reporting work. Advocacy may be more effective where it creates participatory linkages between disabled people's organizations and government decision makers, giving people with disabilities a greater voice in policymaking. Such efforts might include lobbying the World Bank, facilitating the participation of disabled people's organizations in elections, and increasing their employment in government ministries. Even more effective may be programs to help disabled persons directly, through education, job training, and capacity building, which would help them assume leadership positions in mainstream civil society and politics.

In sum, disability rights organizations are perhaps best characterized as reluctantly gate-crashing on the human rights movement. Throughout the UN Disability Convention campaign and the broader effort to advance disability rights internationally, disabled people's organizations have sought to do so on their own terms and under their own leadership. The international disability community—to the extent that we may speak in such terms about such a fragmented group—holds the mainstream human rights movement at arm's length. It demands recognition as a legitimate human rights player but asks the gatekeepers to remain marginal to the disability movement. It is also important to recognize that the human rights gatekeepers are not the only actors from whom the international disability community demands respect. They also demand it of state and foundation donors, international development banks, and humanitarian assistance organizations—all of whom have largely ignored disability issues and/or failed to address disability in rights-based terms.

Chapter 7

New Rights for Private Wrongs: Female Genital Mutilation and Global Framing Dialogues

MADELINE BAER AND ALISON BRYSK

International human rights conventions and foundational documents do not mention a number of long-standing cultural practices that affect the health of women and children, and mainstream human rights organizations have not typically included these issues in their international campaigns. In the past generation, however, a transnational coalition politicized a number of these traditional practices, including female genital "cutting" or "modification." This practice has become increasingly contentious and is now widely referred to as female genital mutilation (FGM).

Particularly in African countries, women have organized against the practice primarily because of its significant health risks. Facing opposition within their own societies, some of these women sought support abroad from international and nongovernmental organizations (NGOs). Early efforts by local advocates did not resonate with international organizations deterred by concerns about cultural autonomy and national sovereignty. But by the early 1970s, heightened international awareness sparked activism by Western feminists. They added a women's rights frame to the earlier discourse that focused mainly on health consequences.

Using this new framing and their own greater influence in Western societies, feminists put female genital cutting (renamed female genital mutilation) onto the agenda of international organizations and human rights NGOs by the early 1990s. Initially this newfound institutional focus on FGM had little human rights component. By the mid-1990s, however, there was broad consensus within the international rights community that FGM violated a number of core human rights: the right of women to be free from discrimination on the basis of gender; the right to life and physical integrity, including freedom from violence; the rights of the child; and the right to health.[1] The rights of people to participate in their culture and the right to religious freedom are also invoked in discussions about FGM and human rights.

However, feminist groups, international organizations, and human rights NGOs encountered unexpected opposition from the very people they aimed to assist—African women, including many who opposed the practice. For some, rights claims did not resonate, and others felt insufficiently consulted in the transnational campaign. Worse yet, women's rights claims, with their connotations of cultural imperialism, were seen as ineffective or even counterproductive in actually ending the practice. Since the late 1990s, these tensions have been reduced somewhat through the rise of a new and less controversial combined "health rights" framing for the issue, which appeals internationally but does not alienate locally.

Acceptance of FGM as a human rights issue is an example of how abuses are no longer perceived as only the work of state actors. Nonstate actors are increasingly recognized as sources of human rights violations. "Private wrongs" such as FGM require traditional human rights standards to incorporate new claimants, new targets of advocacy, and new roles for global civil society.[2] Eradication of the practice of FGM relies not only on advocacy and framing processes from the domestic to the international level but also on convincing local communities to end the practice. In this way, FGM is a new rights issue on the international level, and on the local level as well, as many communities are resistant to accepting new interpretations of a previously accepted and culturally important practice.

This chapter analyzes the contentious rise of FGM as a rights issue. In the first section of the chapter, we provide background information on FGM. We then explore efforts to end the practice, focusing on the distinctive approaches of local and international activists prior to about 2000. We find that FGM has been framed as a health issue, a human rights issue, and a mixture of the two. We also examine framing back to the local level, where rights language does not always resonate with communities where FGM is practiced.

Cultural Practice and Health Consequences

FGM is one of the terms used to describe a variety of practices that involve the partial or complete removal or cutting of the female external genitalia for the fulfillment of cultural, religious, or other nonmedically therapeutic purposes.[3] The World Health Organization (WHO) estimates that 100 million to 140 million living women and girls worldwide have undergone some form of the procedure, while an additional 2 million girls are at risk each year.[4] FGM is practiced primarily by certain cultures in twenty-eight sub-Saharan and northeast African countries but also occurs in parts of Asia and the Middle East. It also is practiced among migrants from these areas now living elsewhere.

The custom has religious and cultural significance as a rite of passage from childhood to adulthood. The practice is often done with the intent of ensuring the woman's virginity, which is a requisite for marriage.[5] In communities where it is routinely practiced, FGM is associated with positive female attributes such as physical cleanliness and sexual chastity. Most communities that perform FGM are Muslim, although the practice predates Islam (and Christianity), is not called for in the Qur'an, and is not practiced by most Muslims outside Africa.[6] A small number of Christian, Jewish, and animist groups also perform FGM.

The health consequences of the practice vary depending on the form of FGM and the conditions under which it is performed. Short-term consequences can include extreme pain, shock, bleeding, tetanus or sepsis, and infection. Long-term complications can include scarring, damage to the urethra, chronic infections, infertility, and infant and mother mortality during childbirth. In recent decades, the procedures have become a conduit for the transmission of HIV from unsanitary instruments used on multiple girls.

Campaigns against FGM

In this section, we present a brief history of anti-FGM campaigns, focusing on the different ways in which activists have framed the issue. Two frames have been particularly prominent. Indigenous activists, cognizant of the issue's cultural sensitivity and anxious to use the most effective means to end the practice, have long preferred a "health frame," which highlights the dire short- and long-term consequences of the procedure for women. By contrast, outsiders, starting with Christian missionaries in the 1920s, have used other frames in addition to highlighting the health consequences of the practice. Of particular interest to this chapter, beginning in the 1970s, Western feminists campaigned against FGM using a "rights frame." This approach highlighted issues of violence against women, women's control over their own bodies, and women's social and sexual empowerment.

THE COLONIAL PERIOD

Efforts by Westerners to prevent FGM began in the 1920s, with Protestant missionaries in Kenya prohibiting the custom among their converts. For the missionaries, the practice was unchristian and unhealthy.[7] For Kenyans, however, the missionaries' campaign quickly came to symbolize the imposition of outside values on their communities. Thus, FGM became associated with nationalism, particularly among Kenya's dominant Kikuyu (Gikuyu) ethnic group, among whom the anti-FGM campaign was centered.[8] For example, Jomo Kenyatta, Kenya's anticolonial leader and first president, defended the practice in his 1938 book *Facing Mount Kenya*. Kenyatta described FGM (referred to by Kenyatta as "clitoridectomy") as the most important component of the initiation custom that helped maintain Kikuyu identity. Therefore, "the abolition of the surgical element in this custom means to the Gikuyu the abolition of the whole institution [of initiation]."[9] Similarly, in colonial Sudan, a 1943 British policy to outlaw infibulation (the most severe form of FGM) was deeply resented and led to the secret and rapid circumcision of some girls.[10]

THE HEALTH FRAME IN THE 1960s TO THE 1980s

These contentious early attempts to end FGM foreshadow analogous conflicts over the practice since the decolonization period in the 1960s. In independent African countries, local women's groups began opposing the practice early on, primarily on health grounds. Rather than campaign for controversial national anti-FGM laws, these organizations focused instead on educating women and families about health risks in hopes of convincing people to abandon the practice. One such organization, Les Femmes Voltaiques (The Women of Upper Volta) held radio broadcasts against FGM in 1975.[11] Domestic NGOs working on FGM in Egypt, Burkina Faso, Kenya, and Sudan began working with international groups in the 1970s.[12]

In 1984, African women attending a seminar in Dakar, Senegal, formed the Inter-African Committee on Traditional Practices Affecting the Health of Women and Children (IAC) to share information and help coordinate activities of national NGOs fighting FGM on the local level.[13] Notwithstanding this trans-African networking, the overall progress of these local civil society efforts was slow, and few African states had the capacity, will, or resources to support the campaigns.

In the face of these problems, a number of African and Middle Eastern women began publicizing FGM internationally in the 1970s and 1980s. Nawal El Saadawi, an Egyptian scholar, medical doctor, and writer, published *The Hidden Face of Eve* in 1977, which covered topics related to the lives of Arab women including marriage and sexuality, aggression against female children, and FGM.[14] In 1994, Dr. Nahid Toubia, Sudan's first woman surgeon, founded Rainbo: Health and Rights for

African Women, an organization working to eradicate FGM.[15] In Ghana in 1983, Efua Dorkenoo established the Foundation for Women's Health, Research and Development (FORWARD), whose primary focus is ending FGM. In their activism and writings, these women discussed their personal histories of circumcision, and their testimonies have been instrumental in drawing international attention to the issue (as well as other issues pertaining to the lives of African and Middle Eastern women).

Despite these diffuse efforts to publicize FGM and the health consequences of the practice, major international organizations were reluctant to take up the issue. Before the predominance of rights frames in the international system in the 1990s, international organizations viewed FGM as a domestic cultural matter, not a question of international relations. For instance, when the Economic and Social Council of the United Nations asked the WHO to study FGM in 1958, WHO leadership refused because FGM was seen as a cultural matter, not as an international medical issue.[16] FGM was not discussed at the first UN World Conference on Women in 1975 due to the widespread belief that FGM was not an appropriate matter for the international system.[17]

By the late 1970s and early 1980s, UN subcommittees began to study FGM and began providing outlets for national governments and NGOs to discuss the health issues related to FGM.[18] One such forum was the WHO-sponsored Seminar on Harmful Traditional Practices Affecting the Health of Women and Children in Sudan in 1979. This was one of the first international conferences where FGM was discussed.

While the health frame was widely used and accepted in some venues, there were also problems with this approach to FGM. Descriptions of long-term pain and suffering as a result of FGM did not ring true for some African women who had undergone less extreme forms of the procedure or did not experience the health problems described by activists.[19] In addition, basing opposition to FGM on health consequences opened the door to medicalization (rather than eradication) of the procedure, including milder forms of circumcision conducted under hygienic conditions and using anesthesia.[20]

THE RIGHTS FRAME

Notwithstanding these problems with the health frame, heightened international awareness around FGM in the 1970s mobilized one important audience, the burgeoning women's movement in Western countries, particularly the United States. For feminist leaders, FGM was a "tool of patriarchy and a symbol of women's subordination."[21] In the name of women's rights, according to these Western activists, the practice must be ended everywhere. Thus, in the 1970s and 1980s, Gloria Steinem, Mary Daly, Fran Hosken, and other feminist leaders condemned FGM and urged international organizations and NGOs to take up the cause.[22] As an important step toward globalizing the issue, feminist organizations renamed it, from the relatively neutral "genital cutting" or "female circumcision" to the far more emotive "female genital mutilation."[23]

Robin Morgan and Gloria Steinem's article "The International Crime of Genital Mutilation," published in *Ms.* magazine in 1980, was an early example of Western campaigning against FGM. Hosken's later *Genital and Sexual Mutilation of Females* educated many Westerners about the practice, while her rhetoric sparked debate over the appropriate way to approach the issue.[24] Similarly, the documentary film *Warrior Marks* by Pratibha Parmar and Alice Walker also brought the issue to American audiences,[25] as did Walker's 1992 fictional account of the life of a genitally mutilated woman, *Possessing the Secret of Joy.*[26]

Western feminists working on FGM in the 1980s and 1990s published on that topic and raised the issue at international conferences. During this time, women's rights were increasingly becoming accepted as human rights, which opened space for the discussion of FGM as a rights issue on the international level.[27] For example, UN adoption of the Convention on the Elimination of All Forms of Discrimination against Women (CEDAW) in 1979 was a critical step toward international recognition of human rights abuses taking place within the private realm, such as FGM. CEDAW incorporated feminist arguments about state obligations to protect women and girls from private abuse of human rights.[28]

While rights-based feminist mobilizing scored some successes internationally, for many years this framing was handicapped by the emphasis on national sovereignty within international organizations. This hindered attempts to persuade international organizations and NGOs to view FGM as a rights issue. In the 1980s international organizations such as UNICEF and WHO struggled to reach consensus on how to approach FGM, due to the diversity of member states' positions on the subject.[29] Some African states resisted international pressure to eradicate FGM and objected to women's rights framing. African leaders cited higher national priorities, such as dealing with underdevelopment, as reasons not to embark on FGM eradication campaigns. While restricted by these factors, international organizations provided a forum for discussion of the issue by hosting conferences and funding national civil society efforts to eradicate FGM.[30]

In the early 1990s, UN attention had diffused to professional medical organizations such as the Sudanese Obstetrical and Gynecological Society, Doctors without Borders, and International Planned Parenthood Federation.[31] More broadly, international reluctance to view FGM as a rights issue began to change in the 1990s, with the post–Cold War strengthening of human rights discourse.[32] By the mid-1990s international bodies had shifted from an emphasis only on the medical consequences of FGM to a human rights-based model.[33] In 1990, the UN Committee on the Elimination of Discrimination against Women adopted General Recommendation No. 14, which expressed the committee's concern over the continued practice of FGM and urged governments to support efforts to eradicate the custom.[34] A 1993 UN Declaration on the Elimination of Violence against Women explicitly included FGM within the category of violence against women, which also includes marital rape, dowry-related violence, and sexual abuse of female children.[35] These international declarations placed FGM squarely within the rights framework, whereas previous international attention to FGM focused on the medical aspects of the practice.

The 1993 UN World Conference on Human Rights in Vienna, a milestone in making FGM a human rights issue, called for the elimination of violence against women, including traditional practices that take place in the private sphere.[36] The International Conference on Population and Development (ICPD) held in Cairo in 1994 also highlighted the interconnections between women's health and human rights regarding FGM. The Programme of Action adopted at the ICPD set twenty-year goals in four related areas, including access to reproductive and sexual health services, where FGM is mentioned.[37] This Programme of Action represented "a shift at the international level away from thinking about female genital mutilation primarily as a health issue and towards considering it as an issue of women's health and rights."[38]

In a 1998 joint statement by the WHO, UNICEF, and the United Nations Population Fund, the organizations took a strong stand against FGM, calling it a violation of the rights of women and girls to the highest attainable standard of health.[39] UNICEF now supports partner programs that work on the local level to educate communities about both the health and human rights consequences of FGM.

Major human rights organizations such as Amnesty International and Human Rights Watch did not begin working on FGM until the late 1990s, mainly because issues of violence against women were outside the scope of their organizational focus. Prior to the early 1990s, Amnesty International was concerned primarily with state violations of individual civil and political rights.[40] Feminist activists and scholars pushed for the inclusion of women's rights as human rights in the 1970s and 1980s, leading Amnesty International to decide to begin working on violence against women as a human rights issue in 1989.[41] Despite this shift to include women's rights in their work, Amnesty's work on women's human rights remained limited by their focus on abuses by state actors and by the distinction between the public and private realms.[42] This distinction prevented action on abuses of women and girls that took place within the family, such as domestic abuse and FGM. The early prioritization of human rights abuses by government forces is reflected in Amnesty's 1991 report *Women in the Front Line*.[43] The report documents human rights abuses of women by the state but does not mention FGM or other types of abuse against women and girls by nonstate actors.

Following active debates within the organization about the false distinction between public, political rights (the traditional focus of Amnesty's work) and private rights abuses that were mostly affecting women, Amnesty International began to view abuse in the private realm as having public aspects.[44] For example, Amnesty noted that discrimination against women is often officially sanctioned by the state and that the abuses against women in the private realm are similar to other abuses that Amnesty had traditionally worked on, such as violations of the rights to physical integrity and to nondiscrimination.[45] Amnesty's 1995 report *Human Rights Are Women's Right* reflects this new interpretation of human rights, stating that government sponsored discrimination against women directly contributes to private violations of human rights.[46] Despite this shift toward recognizing private abuses of women, this report only mentions FGM in the appendix.[47]

Amnesty International officially decided to include FGM in its work in 1995 as part of a broader attempt to address human rights violations by nonstate actors and to strengthen the organization's work on abuses against women and girls. Amnesty "recognized the urgency of taking a position against this widespread form of violence against women prior to the Fourth UN World Conference on Women held in Beijing in September 1995."[48] FGM was on the international agenda by this time, and it had been discussed at a number of international conferences. Thus, international organizations had already accepted FGM as an international human rights issue before Amnesty accepted it.

Amnesty International has increasingly incorporated FGM into its work since the late 1990s. Amnesty's 2004 report *It's in Our Hands: Stop Violence against Women* discusses FGM as an example of violence against women that is supported by cultural values. In this report, Amnesty admits that the human rights movement was "slow to come to the defense of women" and that it has "taken a long time to overcome the false division between violations in the public arena and violations in the private sphere."[49] Amnesty describes its initial work on FGM as "modest but encouraging" and the decision to include the issue in their work as challenging because it involved a reconceptualization of human rights and of Amnesty's role in promoting human rights internationally.[50]

RIGHTS AND HEALTH FRAMING

Notably, the rise of FGM as an international human rights issue occurred without displacing the prior health frame. What has emerged at the international level is a mixture of the health frame, which highlights the medical consequences of FGM, with arguments about the human rights of women and girls. International health organizations such as the WHO continue to use the health frame as well as a rights frame.[51] Doctors without Borders strongly opposes FGM as a human rights violation and as a threat to health and identifies medical staff involvement in the practice as a breach of ethical and professional standards.[52] The World Medical Association condemns the participation of physicians in any form of female genital circumcision and encourages national medical associations to oppose the practice in keeping with international efforts by the WHO and the UN Commission on Human Rights.[53]

Although the rights framing used by Western feminists was beneficial in gaining a place for FGM on the international human rights agenda, this approach to FGM created tensions with indigenous women's organizations in Africa when it emerged in the 1970s and 1980s. Many African women's organizations that had been working to ban FGM for decades were alienated by the Western discourse that denied them agency and misunderstood their intentions toward their daughters.[54] Some Western feminists at this time portrayed African women as either voiceless victims of male domination or as cruel torturers of their daughters.[55] Western feminists such as Hosken launched scathing attacks on those who supported FGM and called for immediate global action to eradicate all forms of FGM. In one of her detailed reports on FGM, Hosken asserted: "The politics of genital mutilation are first of all the patriarchal politics of controlling the production and reproduction of the wholly-owned female labor force—the primary resources of male power and wealth."[56] Her gender-based critique and call for immediate action were met with resistance by some Africans who promoted slow change from below rather than rapid international action.[57] Some African advocates dismissed the international human rights framework entirely as an ineffective tool for changing local practices.[58]

These tensions between Western feminists and local activists working on FGM emerged at a number of international forums on women's rights. During the 1980 UN Conference on Women in Copenhagen, African women boycotted an FGM panel sponsored by Western women because of the perceived insensitivity to African perspectives by Western feminists.[59] At this conference, four African women presented their own panel discussion on FGM at an NGO forum that ran parallel to the official UN conference.[60] The African women accused Western feminists of being condescending and confrontational in their work on FGM. Fazwia Asaad, wife of an Egyptian doctor associated with the WHO, noted after the conference: "In France it has become quite fashionable to talk about circumcision, but these women, these white collar intellectuals, know nothing of these things. Why do they want always to talk about circumcision? Women in these regions have many more serious problems. I wonder about their priorities."[61] A statement by the Association of African Women for Research and Development made after the conference warned paricipants in "this new crusade of the West" against engaging in "ill-timed interference, maternalism, ethnocentrism, and misuse of power" in their work on FGM.[62]

Bringing the Frame Home: What Kind of Rights?

The foregoing tensions point to the fact that transnational campaigns to eradicate FGM involve more than framing the issue from the local to the global level. Effective framing back to the local level to communities where FGM is practiced and supported is also necessary. As recent survey research by Elizabeth Heger Boyle and Kristin Carbone-Lopez shows, Western and non-Western opponents of FGM sometimes differ in their reasons for opposing the practice.[63] The survey finds that African and Middle Eastern women who oppose FGM more frequently cite moral, religious, or medical reasons for their opposition than the reasons cited by many Western activists, such as human rights and women's rights. This need for framing back to the local level is a subsequent stage of new rights formation not covered in Bob's general model of new rights development.

Given the entrenched nature of FGM and its ties to religion and culture, NGOs and international groups face challenges in finding ways to talk about the practice that will resonate at the local level. Locally appropriate frames are not necessarily the same frames that are used at the international level and with national governments, and local understandings of the issues can influence international approaches to anti-FGM efforts. As Shareen Hertel's work on transnational advocacy reveals, international networks are not the only actors setting the agenda and framing the claims made by international human rights campaigns. Local activists on the receiving end of international rights advocacy can also influence and alter the way claims are made within transnational campaigns.[64] While campaigns aimed at eradicating FGM at the local level have traditionally used the health frame, local efforts are also increasingly incorporating the rights frame in their work. The result is a general trend toward a health rights framing of the issue that combines both education about the health consequences of FGM and the human rights component.

Prior to the international acceptance of rights framing of FGM, domestic campaigns and efforts at the village level in parts of Africa and the Middle East appealed to parents and community leaders mainly by emphasizing the health risks of FGM as the primary issue. During the 1980s in particular, health education programs for men and women at the local level were effective, as they were not culturally biased and were easier to accept than campaigns that were perceived to attack religious or cultural norms.[65] These efforts also often involved educating people in Muslim communities about the absence of a call for FGM within Islam.

Partners of UNICEF point to several important elements for successful anti-FGM work on the local level. These include a noncoercive and nonjudgmental approach, educating communities about the harmfulness of FGM to women's health, encouraging collective commitments and public declarations to abandon the practice, and spreading the message of abandonment to communities.[66] This approach is based on the belief that "the most effective approaches to this issue have been found not by punishing perpetrators but through encouraging and supporting healthy choices."[67]

The Sabiny Elders, a council of clan leaders in Uganda, chose to abandon FGM in the late 1990s and now works to change the minds of parents through discussion of the health consequences associated with the practice, such as complications during childbirth and HIV.[68] Changing attitudes at the village level often involves convincing those who make their living as circumcisers to abandon the practice and helping them find alternative employment. Health-focused arguments are the most persuasive in convincing them to stop performing FGM.[69] Attempts to enforce a partial ban on female circumcision in Egypt focused on educational programs sponsored by the Health Ministry to explain the health dangers to villagers.[70]

In cases where gender-based violence is defended as part of local culture, human rights language may not resonate as strongly as other types of arguments. In his work with communities in Sierra Leone, Melron Nicol-Wilson found that avoiding cultural and religious rationales of the practice and focusing instead on the health risks was easier and more successful than using a women's-rights-based approach.[71]

Although the health frame alone is successful in some local communities, many NGOs and anti-FGM programs now use a mixture of health

and women's rights frames in their advocacy. The relief and development agency CARE International shifted from a needs-based to a rights-
based approach in its programs in the early 1990s.[72] This resulted in a
reframing of FGM as a traditional practice with serious health consequences to one that violates the human rights of women and girls to
health, bodily integrity, and security of the person. In their work with So-
malis living in Kenyan refugee camps, CARE workers found that refugees
who had been exposed to ideas and norms from other cultures, including the human rights dialogue used in the refugee camps by international workers, were open to rights-based discussions of FGM. In this
context, FGM was discussed and approached as both a women's rights
and health rights issue. Through discussions of rights and health consequences, many people in the camps concluded that FGM was a violation
of these rights and should be abandoned. Following another CARE project in eastern Ethiopia, clan leaders from seventy villages met and declared an end to the practice of FGM. They cited the lack of religious
support for FGM and referred to the practice as a violation of human
rights that causes severe health complications for women and girls.

Tostan, an NGO created in 1991 to foster community development
and respect for human rights in Africa, has worked to educate communities about both the human rights and health consequences of FGM.
The NGO's programs use local languages and emphasize respect for
African culture while challenging the practice of FGM.[73] Tostan programs in Senegal teach local people about human rights, women's
rights, and the health risks of FGM, leaving the decision to abandon the
practice to the collective will of each community. Since 1997, 2,336 villages in Senegal, 298 in Guinea, and 23 in Burkina Faso have chosen to
abandon FGM as a result of these education programs. Prior to programs like these, many men in these villages claimed that they did not
know what FGM was, how it was performed, or the links between FGM
and health problems in women. Once they learned about these connections and understood why some of their daughters had died, they became active participants in campaigns to eradicate the practice.[74]

National legislation, where it exists, frequently cites a mixture of
health- and rights-based reasons for outlawing FGM. Politicians supporting a 2001 law banning FGM in Kenya cited the grave health risks, including the spread of HIV, as well as the need to protect children according to international human rights norms.[75] National anti-FGM
efforts in Ethiopia focus on educating villagers about the brutality of the
practice and on the public health dangers such as the spread of HIV.
This campaign advocates a holistic approach to FGM that not only edu-
cates about health and human rights but also works to improve the situation of girls and women in general.[76]

International pressure has played a role in the adoption of anti-FGM policies on the national level.[77] Fourteen African nations have criminalized the practice, and others have legislation in process.[78] Egypt banned female circumcision in June 2007 following the death of a twelve-year-old girl who was undergoing the procedure in a private medical clinic. The new ban prohibits all forms of female circumcision including procedures carried out by medical professionals, which were previously permitted by Egyptian law.[79]

Many states where FGM is practiced have not yet passed legislation against the custom, and compliance with national laws is low in those states that have passed legislation.[80] Prosecutions and arrests in countries that have criminalized the practice are extremely rare.[81] As with many human rights abuses, enforcement by national governments and international bodies is weak. For example, nearly all women and girls in Egypt (97%), Mali (93.7%), and Sudan (89%) report having undergone some form of FGM despite formal opposition to FGM by all three governments.[82]

The passage of state legislation may not always be the most effective tool for eradication of FGM. As in many areas of policy change, implementation on the ground can be the missing link. In order for campaigns to be implemented, local women and their families must be part of efforts to abandon the practice. This can be difficult, as cultural change takes time, and communities are reluctant to give up a practice that is tied to religious beliefs and cultural pride.[83] Legislation also can have the unwanted effect of pushing the practice further underground, which can increase the health risks.[84] Criminalization is further complicated by cultural norms that view prosecuting women for crimes as abnormal and by situations where placing fathers in jail can leave families vulnerable to economic hardship without their primary breadwinners.[85]

Conclusion: FGM as a New Rights Issue

FGM is a new rights issue in the sense that it does not appear in the major human rights conventions, and attention to it as a human rights issue is fairly recent. In this vacuum, advocates have drawn from extant rights such as the right to health, the rights of women, and the rights of children to construct an argument against the practice. Organizing against FGM is a case of the power of the health frame; both the right to health (a positive right, i.e., the right to have the highest standard of health) as well as the negative right to not be subjected to medically unnecessary, dangerous, and inhumane physical harm by medical personnel or members of one's community. Although the right to health is not as widely recognized or valued as some core civil/political rights, it can be a powerful tool for approaching human rights issues in a neutral way, where other approaches may not resonate with local cultural values.

International and local campaigns that frame FGM as a human rights issue follow many aspects of the process of new rights development that Clifford Bob describes in the introduction to this volume. Politicized groups frame long-felt grievances as rights claims, and they attempt to place these rights on the international agenda. This process began with calls from African women for support in challenging this deeply entrenched practice in their communities. Although their appeals to international actors regarding the painful and detrimental health consequences of FGM were met with sympathy, norms about national sovereignty and the unwillingness by international actors to confront cultural and religious practices prevented FGM from reaching the international human rights agenda for decades. This reluctance by international actors to take on the issue was partly rooted in an understanding of FGM as both a private matter and a part of local culture.

Western women who took up the cause in the 1970s and 1980s framed the issue as a violation of the rights of women and girls and as a symptom of patriarchy. Their calls for treating FGM as a human rights violation ran up against the sanctity of the private realm of the family, fears of cultural imperialism, and a general disregard for issues affecting only women that only began to change during the 1990s.

Multiple frames were used by advocacy groups in different contexts and with varying levels of success. While the health frame avoided issues of cultural and religious imperialism, it also led to medicalization of the practice in some cases, which left the underlying gender discrimination issue unchallenged. Women's and children's rights frames resonated on the international level following the acceptance of these rights into mainstream human rights discourse, but they were not as useful in convincing people on the local level to abandon the practice.

Many advocates approach human rights gatekeepers in NGOs and international organizations for assistance in placing their grievances on the international agenda. In the FGM case, however, Amnesty International, UNICEF, and the WHO initially resisted such appeals. The omission of the practice in major human rights documents combined with conflicting norms of national sovereignty, and the public/private split problematized its emergence as a new right and instead relegated it to the jurisdiction of local decision making and the family. Instead of the gatekeepers' leading the way to its acceptance as a human rights issue, local and regional NGOs from Africa as well as Western feminists persistently raised the issue at international conferences. Various UN conferences in the 1980s and 1990s on women's issues and subsequent involvement by UN agencies were the catalysts for increased action on FGM rather than actions by traditional human rights gatekeepers.

The third stage in new rights development occurs after the right has been accepted and NGOs and transnational advocacy networks promote the issue to states and international bodies. International pressure has been somewhat successful in pressuring a number of national governments to enact legislation against FGM. However, international attention, support, and resources for stopping FGM have not been sufficient to eradicate this deeply entrenched practice. While international and governmental actions are necessary to confront FGM, the women and families who practice FGM hold the power to abandon it in their communities. Anti-FGM work on the local level requires NGOs and advocates to frame FGM in appropriate ways, and positive changes stem more from education than law enforcement. Arguments against FGM are not always rights based, and the framing of the issue is still contested across local and international levels.

The shifting venues and contested frames of the campaign against FGM have implications for our broader understanding of the meaning as well as the process of human rights mobilization. While this book's model of the rise of new rights draws our attention to the power of transnational intermediaries to influence which rights are recognized, we must also be aware of the unresolved competition over who decides. At the national level, procedural democracy and citizenship provide representation and adjudication for new rights claims in the public sphere. But in a globalized world, the most private possible personal space is a zone of contention among communities pursuing norms and control of their members, distant strangers linked by identity politics, international institutions seeking to manage the global commons of reproductive health, and states juggling each of these. A generation of rights claims over FGM has helped to deepen understanding of the right to health, broadened appreciation of the gendered nature of private wrongs, modestly reduced some of the more egregious practices, and fostered some programs for women's education in Africa. Yet none of these struggles has fully established self-determination over basic bodily integrity for tens of millions of women and girls, in the private sphere still unreached by the global rise of rights.

Chapter 8
Economic Rights and Extreme Poverty: Moving toward Subsistence

DANIEL CHONG

Introduction

Economic and social rights have long been part of the human rights movement. Indeed, the Universal Declaration of Human Rights (UDHR) gives them equal status with civil and political rights.[1] In practice, however, for most of the period since the UDHR's adoption by the UN General Assembly in 1948, economic and social rights have held a secondary place in the human rights movement. Most obviously, the international treaties deriving from the broad statements of the nonbinding UDHR divided sharply between civil and political rights, on the one hand, and economic, social, and cultural rights, on the other. The International Covenant on Civil and Political Rights (ICCPR) included rights protecting individuals from abuses such as torture, slavery, and arbitrary detention, as well as political rights such as freedom of expression, association, and religion, upon which states might infringe only under narrow circumstances.[2] However, economic and social rights, which are arguably the most relevant to those in extreme poverty, were set forth in Article 2 of the International Covenant on Economic, Social and Cultural Rights (ICESCR) to be realized only "progressively" and to the extent of a country's "available resources."[3] Along with this sharp distinction in international legal status went a major practical difference. Leading members of the international human rights movement, in particular major nongovernmental organizations (NGOs) such as Amnesty International and Human Rights Watch, focused most of their work until the mid-1990s on civil and political rights, indeed on a narrow range of such rights.

Notably, however, while human rights practitioners neglected economic and social rights, many of the underlying goals embodied in such rights were pursued by other organizations, albeit under different labels. To be specific, the alleviation of poverty, chiefly through development aid and various antipoverty programs, was an important element in the foreign policies of many countries in the period after World War II. In addition, numerous private organizations, including humanitarian, development, and social justice NGOs, acted against poverty and disease even if they did not frame their causes in human rights terms.

Since the mid-1990s, there have been distinct though interconnected changes in both of these situations. First, the leading human rights organizations have devoted increasing resources and personnel to economic and social rights. As discussed in detail later, both Amnesty International and Human Rights Watch have moved to adopt economic and social rights in some form. In addition, the International Commission of Jurists was one of the first human rights organizations to devote significant attention to economic and social rights, convening a meeting of international experts as early as 1986 that led to the Limburg Principles, which seek to clarify and elaborate economic and social rights law.[4] The World Organization against Torture has retained its focus on preventing torture but in recent years has established a program on economic and social rights that seeks to link extreme poverty to an increased vulnerability to cruel and degrading treatment.[5] The International Federation for Human Rights, a network of more than 140 French organizations, expanded its mandate in 2001 to include a focus on making economic and social rights law applicable to international trade and the activities of transnational corporations.[6] Likewise, new human rights organizations have been created specifically to address subsistence rights. These include issue-specific organizations, such as the FoodFirst Information and Action Network (FIAN, formed in 1986) and the Centre on Housing Rights and Evictions (COHRE, formed in 1994), which advocate for rights related to basic subsistence. It also includes new organizations created to promote economic and social rights more broadly, such as the Center for Economic and Social Rights (formed in 1993), the National Economic and Social Rights Initiative (formed in 2004), and many more.[7] While limited in their scope, these developments represent an important change in the human rights movement that may presage further receptivity to economic and social rights.

Second, key antipoverty organizations have begun framing their long-standing goals in rights terms. For one thing, social justice groups are employing human rights language to mobilize their constituencies to fight extreme poverty. American organizations that have used human rights discourse to campaign against poverty include Public Citizen, the Bank Information Center, the Center for Economic Justice, the Women's International Coalition for Economic Justice, the Coalition of Immokalee Workers, Bread for the World, the Center of Concern, the One Campaign, the Kensington Welfare Rights Union, and the Women's

Economic Agenda Project. In addition, humanitarian organizations are increasingly using rights-based approaches in implementing basic subsistence projects among the poor throughout the world. Most of the major international development NGOs have adopted a rights-based approach, including CARE, Oxfam, Save the Children, ActionAid, World Vision, and dozens of others. Thus they have begun to argue that fighting extreme poverty is not merely a matter of voluntary charity but of vindicating the rights of the poor.

Finally, a number of other developments confirm the rise of economic and social rights:

- international conferences relating to economic and social rights, such as the UN World Conference on Human Rights in Vienna (1993), the World Summit for Social Development in Copenhagen (1995), and the World Summit on Sustainable Development in Johannesburg (2002), among others;
- the mainstreaming of human rights approaches within UN development agencies such as the UN Development Program, the UN Children's Fund, and the World Health Organization;
- an increase in national legislation and institutions (such as human rights commissions) that explicitly incorporate economic and social rights concerns; and
- an increase in funding for economic and social rights from private foundations and bilateral state donors.

What explains the recent rise of these long-neglected rights? This chapter identifies two broad causes. First, since the end of the Cold War, the international political environment has become increasingly receptive to economic and social rights. This increasing openness, discussed in detail later, has created more permissive conditions for adoption of these rights by NGOs. It has also strengthened long-standing demands for greater attention to economic and social rights, particularly among social movements in the developing world. Second, to explain why some gatekeeper NGOs have adopted economic and social rights (while similar ones have not) one must closely examine internal organizational, ideational, and strategic factors. For certain NGOs, these factors make adoption of economic and social rights sensible, while for others they do not.

Defining Subsistence Rights

To make this argument, this chapter focuses on a core set of economic and social rights, or "subsistence rights," which relate to the basis of nutrition, shelter, and health care.[8] Among other sources, Article 25 of the UDHR enshrines subsistence rights: "Everyone has the right to a standard of living adequate for the health and well-being of himself and of his family, including food, clothing, housing and medical care and necessary social services." Similar wording has been included in the ICESCR and several other legally binding international treaties, which "recognize the right of everyone to an adequate standard of living."[9] These, according to Henry Shue, are some of the most basic human rights, whose "enjoyment is essential to all other rights."[10] Subsistence rights are arguably preconditions for all economic and social rights, as well as civil and political rights, because people can exercise no other rights if their time and energy are consumed by the need to acquire basic resources to survive. As the United Nations Development Programme (UNDP) states simply, "Poverty limits human freedoms and deprives a person of dignity."[11] "Indeed," as the UN high commissioner on human rights notes, "no social phenomenon is as comprehensive in its assault on human rights as poverty. Poverty erodes or nullifies economic and social rights such as the right to health, adequate housing, food and safe water, and the right to education."[12]

Despite the rhetorical embrace of subsistence rights, almost 1.4 billion people live in extreme poverty, with almost 700 million lacking adequate nutrition and 1.2 billion lacking clean water.[13] Tens of thousands of people in these conditions die each day, largely from preventable diseases. It is true that in the past fifty years tremendous progress has been made in reducing the proportion of the world's people living in extreme poverty, thanks in large part to economic growth in East Asia.[14] But progress toward reducing the absolute number of people in extreme poverty has slowed to a near halt in the past two decades.[15]

At first glance it is puzzling that subsistence rights were so long neglected, given the scope of global poverty in the decades after promulgation of the UDHR. Equally puzzling in that historical context is their rise since the early 1990s. In the following sections, I first discuss the changing political context that provided permissive conditions for these developments. Next, I focus on organizational factors internal to NGOs, which provide a more fine-grained explanation for the long period of neglect and more recent trend toward adoption of subsistence rights.

The Changing Political Context

A Cold War Chill on Subsistence Rights

The broadest reason for the historical neglect of economic and social rights is the Cold War, which led ideological differences over rights to be linked to ongoing geopolitical conflict. In the West, economic and social rights became victims of these battles by becoming associated with governments and policies in the socialist East. Shortly after the UN General Assembly's adoption of the UDHR, which spelled out all rights as indivisible and equal, the United States led an almost single-handed campaign to assign a secondary status to economic and social rights. In 1951, the U.S. ambassador to the United Nations, Walter Kotschnig, argued that "civil and political rights were of such a nature as to be given legal effect promptly by the adoption of such legislation or other measures as might be necessary. The economic, social and cultural rights while spoken of as 'rights' were, however, to be treated as *objectives* toward which States adhering to the Covenant would within their resources undertake to strive, by the creation of conditions which would be conducive to the exercise of private as well as public action, for their progressive achievement."[16]

In the context of the Cold War, the philosophical arguments marshaled by the United States against subsistence rights typically took the following form. Human rights must be legally enforceable and justiciable (i.e., subject to review in courts and quasi-judicial arenas) to be legitimately defined as rights. States are only legally accountable for their negative obligations—obligations not to interfere with personal liberty—and these were associated exclusively with civil and political rights. Issues of basic material subsistence such as adequate housing, food, and health care were therefore understood as "goals and aspirations" to be implemented voluntarily within the private sphere but not subject to public scrutiny. As such, individuals should be held responsible for their own material well-being. While the state was empowered to provide benefits to its vulnerable populations, it was not legally required to do so as a matter of right.[17] Subsistence rights, according to the predominant line of thinking in the West, required fundamental economic redistribution generated through massive governmental interference in the economy. This would not only compromise other individual freedoms but also be impossible to monitor through the judicial process. In other words, economic and social rights were perceived as essentially different from civil and political rights—a difference that involved extensive and expensive positive duties that were inherently nonjusticiable.[18]

As a result of U.S. pressure, the planned UN covenant that would codify all human rights was subsequently divided in two, with more concrete normative obligations and stronger monitoring mechanisms reserved for civil and political rights. For example, the ICCPR envisioned the immediate enforcement of civil and political rights, creating a dedicated UN committee to monitor compliance (Article 28), while the ICESCR merely required states to "take steps" with their "available resources" to "progressively" realize these rights. Civil and political rights were adopted into dozens of national constitutions as enforceable, justiciable rights, while economic and social rights were either ignored or down-graded in national constitutions as more vague "directive principles."[19] Economic and social rights were therefore in practice relegated to sec-ond-class status in the field of international human rights.

NGOs that attempted to pursue subsistence rights during the Cold War era ran into strong opposition, particularly in the United States. Be-cause these rights were associated with the socialist policies and rhetoric of the Soviet bloc during the Cold War, there was little political and cul-tural space for human rights organizations to advocate for them. Social movements such as the American civil rights movement in the 1960s that attempted to move the rights debate into issues of economic subsis-tence "got attacked for being Commies and red-baited to death" and therefore abandoned this approach.[20] As Carol Anderson notes:

The struggle [for African American economic rights] was ultimately destroyed . . . by the Cold War and the anti-Communist witch hunts, which compromised the integrity of the black leadership, twisted the definition of human rights into the hammer and sickle, and forced the NAACP to take its eyes off the prize of [all] human rights. . . . The Cold War had obviously transformed human rights into an ideological battlefield between the Soviet Union and the United States and engulfed the struggle for black equality. The Cold War identified in stark, pejorative terms entire categories of rights as antithetical to basic American free-doms. It punished mercilessly those who advocated a more expansive definition and a more concrete commitment to those rights. And it demanded uncondi-tional loyalty.[21]

Opportunities and Threats in the Post–Cold War Era

The end of the Cold War de-linked the struggle for human rights from the geopolitical conflict between East and West. This provided an opening for economic and social rights to be promoted without being associated with the policies of an ideological enemy. Despite the U.S. government's ongoing opposition to economic and social rights, human rights and humanitarian organizations were able to reframe these rights as being consistent with a liberal state rather than requiring a form of totalitarian socialism in their implementation. The end of the Cold War also allowed funding organizations to provide support for eco-nomic and social rights without being labeled as communists.[22]

The end of the Cold War facilitated but certainly did not determine the increasing adoption of subsistence rights. A deeper explanation of these trends requires an examination of the actions taken by NGOs themselves and the internal characteristics—their guiding principles, strategic interests, and organizational structures—that led NGOs to support or disregard subsistence rights.

NGO Characteristics and Subsistence Rights

HUMAN RIGHTS NGOS AND THE INITIAL REJECTION OF SUBSISTENCE RIGHTS

The changing political context of the Cold War and its aftermath created structural conditions that led most NGOs to reject subsistence rights in the first period but led some to adopt them in the later period. This raises two key questions. Even in the context of ideological opposition to economic and social rights during the Cold War, why did northern human rights NGOs, which often confronted their own governments on other issues, neglect subsistence rights for so long? And, after the Cold War's end, why did NGOs adopt subsistence rights differentially, with some doing so wholeheartedly, others partially, and others not at all?

In answer to these questions, NGOs' organizational cultures played a key role. Some organizations long opposed subsistence rights based on the Western liberal assertion that these were not rights at all because they were not justiciable. For example, as the founding director of Human Rights Watch, Aryeh Neier, has argued:

I think of rights as only having meaning if it is possible to enforce them. I don't think rights are an abstract concept—I think they are a contract between the citizen and the state or community, and the citizen has to be able to enforce his or her side of that contract. Enforcing that contract means that there must be some mechanism of enforcement, and judicial enforcement seems to be the mechanism that we have hit upon in order to enforce rights. Therefore, from my standpoint, if one is to talk meaningfully of rights, one has to discuss what can be enforced through the judicial process. . . . The concern I have about economic and social rights is when there are broad assertions which broadly speak of the right to shelter, education, social security, jobs, health care . . . then I think we get into territory that is unmanageable through the rights process or the judicial process. . . . So I think it's dangerous to the idea of civil and political rights to allow this idea of economic and social rights to flourish.[23]

As Neier makes clear, philosophical opposition to subsistence rights qua rights was related to the prominent role of law and lawyers in the human rights movement. For most human rights scholars and practitioners, rights arose originally out of moral ideals, but law provided the only legitimate and effective way to implement those ideals on the ground.[24] (As a result, human rights practitioners have tended to be legal professionals, and human rights scholarship has occurred primarily in law schools.) These same scholars and practitioners assigned a uniquely valid status to civil and political rights because these rights were codified in constitutions, bills of rights, and statutes in northern societies in a manner in which economic and social rights were not. Whereas the former were justiciable, the latter, with their ostensibly aspirational character, were not.

These problems also raised strategic, institutional, and material barriers to human rights organizations' work on subsistence rights. Northern human rights organizations believed that their well-developed institutional methodologies were not congruent with the promotion of economic and social rights. The primary advocacy strategy that human rights organizations have developed is the "naming and shaming" of specific violators through the generation of public outrage against them. This methodology involves carefully researching to pinpoint specific violators, publicizing the legal violation through report writing and media outreach, and mobilizing public campaigns in support of specific victims and vulnerable groups. Many human rights practitioners have argued that subsistence rights do not fit well into naming and shaming campaigns because they lack a clear violation or discrete perpetrator. As Kenneth Roth has stated:

I have been to countless conferences and debates in which advice is freely offered about how international human rights organizations must do more to protect [economic and social] rights. Fair enough. Usually, the advice reduces to little more than sloganeering. People lack medical care; therefore, we should say that their right to health has been violated. People lack shelter; therefore, we should say that their right to housing has been violated. People are hungry; therefore, we should say that their right to food has been violated. Such "analysis," of course, wholly ignores such key issues as who is responsible for the impoverished state of a population, whether the government in question is taking steps to progressively realize the relevant rights, and what the remedy should be for any violation that is found. More to the point, for our purposes, it also ignores which issues can *effectively be taken up by international human rights organizations that rely on shaming and public pressure* and which cannot.[25]

Thus the perceived misfit between economic and social rights and the practical and strategic demands of human rights advocacy has long stifled the promotion of these rights.

Although the UDHR proclaims all human rights equal, NGOs must focus their advocacy on the issues, methods, targets, and geographic areas that are most effective in maximizing their impact, promoting rights awareness, and raising their own profiles.[26] Historically, these issues have tended to be civil and political rights violations covered by the mainstream media, within relatively large countries that were subject to the influence of northern aid and where these organizations maintained an ongoing presence.[27] Organizations justifiably recognized the need to be strategic about their institutional survival and the effectiveness of their campaigns. In the context of the Cold War, when the overwhelming majority of attention and resources in the global North were directed toward civil and political rights, the major human rights organizations survived and thrived precisely by defining their mandates narrowly.[28] Amnesty International, for example, grew from a small office in London in the early 1960s to one of the most far-reaching and influential NGOs on the planet by focusing mostly on political prisoners.[29]

As such, one of the biggest concerns that northern NGOs have had about adopting subsistence rights has been overstretching organizational resources, staff capabilities, and methodological expertise, which would ultimately reduce their effectiveness.[30] Organizations such as Human Rights Watch and Amnesty International were concerned that venturing too far into subsistence rights would create dissent among staff and activists who believed the rights too controversial, confusing, or outside of the NGOs' original mandates.[31] Staff members feared that promoting subsistence rights would dilute these organizations' public images as impartial providers of objective information.[32] For example, some Amnesty International staff members have been concerned that the organization has lost much of its moral authority by venturing into subsistence rights and other politically controversial issues at the cost of its traditional mandate on prisoners of conscience. These "guardians" of Amnesty's traditional mandate argued that while it was possible to objectively report on a prisoner's torture, defending economic and social rights requires taking a more political (and thus less moral) stance.[33] One of the most important pragmatic concerns, therefore, has been that the major human rights organizations do not have the internal capacity and appropriate methods to advocate for subsistence rights effectively.

More generally, human rights scholars and practitioners have argued that promoting economic and social rights would dilute the human rights movement's always tenuous hold on public attention and governmental support. For example, in the early 1980s Philip Alston noted the oft-cited concern that "a proliferation of new rights would be much more likely to contribute to a serious devaluation of the human rights currency."[34] Thus a concern over "rights inflation" has been a common way for the human rights movement to defend the political effectiveness of a more limited set of rights.

For all of these reasons, groups such as Human Rights Watch and Amnesty International long focused on civil and political rights, reinforcing the international legal distinction from economic and social rights. Phillip Alston, former chairman of the UN Committee on Economic, Social and Cultural Rights, lamented during the early 1990s that

"Human Rights Watch has had an ideological or philosophical objection to economic and social rights, and does not participate in any way [in the Committee]. Hundreds of NGOs send representatives to the UN Commission on Human Rights to protest violations of civil and political rights. At our sessions, you'll find just one representative, a fellow from the Habitat International Coalition, sitting rather quietly. Lawyerly NGOs, accustomed to traditional legal argument, cannot accommodate economic and social rights within their comfortable framework."[35]

HUMAN RIGHTS NGOs AND THE DIFFERENTIAL ADOPTION OF SUBSISTENCE RIGHTS

The expansion of subsistence rights work began when the human rights community acted as if the end of the Cold War and the spread of economic neoliberalism were opportunities to engage in economic and social rights work rather than barriers to entry. At first this work was carried out by actors other than the main human rights gatekeepers. Antipoverty activists in the north and south, "freed from the ideological and material constraints of the Cold War,"[36] began to advocate for the right to subsistence despite the hesitations of traditional human rights organizations. Groups in the south, especially in Latin America and Eastern Europe, who had pressured their own governments for years on civil and political rights, began to incorporate subsistence rights into their daily work.[37] The end of the Cold War and the rapid process of democratization around the world also allowed new human rights organizations to form in the former Soviet bloc and throughout the south.[38] Many of these local and national groups, such as the Centro de Estudios Legales y Sociales in Argentina, the Programa Venezolana de Educación Derechos Humanos (Provea) in Venezuela, and the Asociación Pro Derechos Humanos in Peru, advocated for economic and social rights and collaborated with the emerging organizations in the north that were devoted exclusively to them.[39] Increasingly these organizations published reports on economic and social rights violations and the right to subsistence, often related to access to land.[40] It is not surprising that these national organizations in the global south were more concerned with subsistence rights early on than groups in the north, given that they were often located within areas of extreme poverty and had personal connections with people suffering from economic deprivation.[41]

At the same time that socialist regimes were being dismantled after the Cold War, states throughout the world accelerated moves to liberalize trade and investment policies, privatize public services, and whittle away at social guarantees against poverty.[42] This created significant new threats to subsistence in many regions of the world, as southern farmers were forced to compete with northern industrialized agriculture and southern governments shrank their safety nets. As new organizations were forming in the south and increasingly taking on subsistence rights, antipoverty activists in the north responded by demonstrating under the banner of human rights as well. Marchers in Seattle, Bangkok, Genoa, and elsewhere carried signs demanding economic and social rights, among other slogans.[43] Human rights became one of several main organizing frames for mobilizations against "neoliberal globalization" and what demonstrators viewed as an unjust global economic system. Antipoverty activists also created organizations in the north, such as FIAN and COHRE, that pursued economic and social rights outside of the human rights gatekeepers' mandate limitations.

Eventually the leading human rights organizations in the north began to hear the growing calls—from partner organizations and their members throughout the world—to expand their work.[44] Amnesty International's recent history is instructive in understanding the shift toward economic and social rights, both because of its prominence within the human rights community and because of its historically narrow mandate in working on torture and political prisoners. Amnesty International is one of the main human rights gatekeepers that maintain the resources, personnel, reputation, and political access to define and certify the international human rights agenda. Indeed, Amnesty International's work "is often equated with the worldwide human rights struggle."[45]

As Curt Goering notes, Amnesty International's history has been marked by a process of "gradual incrementalism, that is, a cautious expansion of the boundaries of AI's work."[46] Around the early 1980s, several debates began within Amnesty International about expanding its mandate beyond the focus on political prisoners. These discussions included whether the organization would denounce torture and the death penalty, violations committed by nonstate actors, or violations against persons because of their sexual orientation or whether it would adopt a position on the use of force to protect human rights.[47] Thousands of members within Amnesty International's global grassroots network were also debating whether the organization should move into the promotion of economic and social rights. Dissatisfied with Amnesty International's progress in this regard, several of its activists broke off and eventually formed FIAN, an organization devoted specifically to the right to food. At the 1991 International Council Meeting, Amnesty International amended its mandate, enabling its activists to denounce human rights abuses by nonstate actors as well as adopt gay prisoners of conscience. This opened the door for further work on economic and social rights as well.[48]

By the mid-1990s Amnesty International began to informally include economic and social rights in its educational and promotional materi-als.[49] Researchers who realized that these rights were intimately tied to violations of civil and political rights "sneaked" economic and social rights into their background reports. Thematic reports on indigenous people (1992), women (1995), and children (1998) made increasing reference to economic and social rights in the context of the organiza-tion's main concerns over civil and political rights violations. However, as recently as its 1997 International Council Meeting, a formal policy of focusing on violations of specific economic and social rights was re-jected based on the notion that these rights fell too far outside of its mandate.

By the early twenty-first century, however, momentum had swung within Amnesty International toward involvement with economic and social rights. Senior staff members came to believe that adopting eco-nomic and social rights was the best way to respond to a number of trends occurring both within and outside the organization—such as the salience of global poverty, young people's involvement in human rights activism, and the critiques of the Western human rights regime in the global south. Numerous discussions took place within the organization over whether to adopt economic and social rights, and a fragile consen-sus emerged that, despite the methodological difficulties, these rights were too important to ignore. Leaders who originally feared that eco-nomic and social rights advocacy would "dilute their core mission" real-ized that their relevance and legitimacy as global human rights organi-zations increasingly depended on expanding that mission to include a focus on extreme poverty.[50] Within Amnesty International, this was led by Secretary General Pierre Sané, who initiated a process in 1993 to reevaluate the organization's role in the world and adapt to current trends.[51] In addition, northern human rights organizations had been seeking to expand their membership (and thus their base of funding and activism) among youth and among new regions of the world such as Asia and Africa. Amnesty International was concerned about its reputa-tion as a "white middle-class organization" and sought to be "relevant in developing countries."[52] When the antiglobalization movement ignited in the late 1990s in the global north, the message was reinforced that the legitimacy of human rights organizations depended in part on advo-cating for economic and social rights.[53]

Amnesty International officially expanded its mandate at its con-tentious 2001 International Council Meeting (ICM) in Dakar, Senegal. Its chapters, particularly from the global south, demanded that the or-ganization adopt a "full spectrum" approach involving equal attention to both civil and political and economic, social, and cultural rights. Oth-ers cautioned against such a leap beyond its traditional core concerns.

Ultimately the ICM adopted a "messy compromise" extending the organization's traditional emphasis on nondiscrimination from the political to the economic sphere.[54] Since the ICM in 2001, Amnesty International has developed a long-term strategy on economic and social rights, engaged in research and reporting on specific violations, created advisory bodies within the organization, and produced promotional materials on economic and social rights.[55] Amnesty International describes their expanded work in these terms: "We are integrating the new emphases on economic[,] social and cultural rights into our work gradually and carefully. We prioritize according to the severity and pervasiveness of the human rights abuse concerned, the potential for Amnesty International to make an impact and the relationship this has with our previous work."[56] This expansion into economic and social rights has responded to the urgent needs of the poor, even if the term "subsistence rights" was not used. At the same time, the focus on arbitrary and discriminatory conduct fits Amnesty International's existing methodology, increasing the new strategy's chance of success both within the organization and on the ground.

Amnesty International also retains a strong promotional aspect to its work, and it is now in the beginning stages of expanding its work on subsistence rights by developing a global campaign specifically related to this theme.[57] The Global Campaign for Human Dignity will comprise a four- to six-year commitment toward specific poverty-focused goals, similar to the global campaign to stop violence against women that Amnesty launched in 2004. This would represent a deeper, long-term, and more programmatic approach to subsistence rights, and Amnesty International members are in the midst of shaping the specific contours of this campaign. The Global Campaign for Human Dignity will have three main demands: accountability, or making economic and social rights legally enforceable; access, or ensuring that the most vulnerable can obtain basic services; and agency, or respecting the right of the poor to control their own livelihoods. The campaign will focus on two strategic areas of subsistence rights work—health and housing—by initiating advocacy projects in key countries, which will enable Amnesty International to "campaign for individual remedies for those abuses while building momentum for broader policy and legal changes at the national and international level."[58]

This increasing interest among the leading human rights organizations in subsistence rights has been bolstered by a growing willingness among institutional donors to fund economic and social rights work.[59] These donors, such as the Ford Foundation and the Mertz Gilmore Foundation, were influenced by the growth in the promotion of these rights in the global south. Donors witnessed a "dramatic increase in requests for funding" in the late 1990s from organizations focusing on economic and social rights, most of whom were local and national groups from the developing world.[60] Ideological and logistical barriers that had hindered northern organizations from promoting them at the international level were less relevant to human rights organizations in the south. As one donor described, when she had conversations with the staff of human rights organizations in the Philippines and Venezuela about their economic and social rights work, "I was blown away because the issues that had stuck conversation at the international level were almost—not completely, but almost—beside the point at the national level. When people come to you as a human rights organization on the ground with issues of food, housing, whatever . . . then you just figure out ways to do this. It was like, they couldn't say, 'No, the standards are too vague,' or 'No, there's this issue of justiciability.' You just have to do it. So they were sort of breaking through some of [these barriers]."[61]

Conversely, while the foregoing factors encouraged Amnesty International to move toward adoption of subsistence rights, the other major human rights gatekeeper, Human Rights Watch (HRW) has been more reluctant. HRW's distinct organizational culture helps explain this outcome. As discussed earlier, both Kenneth Roth, the current director of HRW, and Aryeh Neier, the former director, have expressed doubts about the validity and effectiveness of economic and social rights. They argue that, unlike Amnesty International, HRW does not have a strong base of grassroots activists and therefore relies more heavily on media campaigns and lobbying actions that involve shaming a specific perpetrator for a clear legal violation. They are wary of what Roth calls the "sloganeering" of economic and social rights, or broad moral assertions of rights, which they believe would limit the effectiveness of rights strategies.[62] As a result, HRW's work on economic and social rights was initially limited to situations in which it reinforced or flowed from the organization's already existing work on civil and political rights.[63] After a process of internal debate, in 2003, HRW expanded this policy to include all economic and social rights, but its work on these rights remains methodologically restricted to situations in which a clear legal violation, identifiable violator, and achievable remedy exist—most commonly in the case of arbitrary or discriminatory governmental conduct.[64]

By contrast, Amnesty International has pursued the path of economic and social rights more broadly and deeply than has HRW. As a global network of grassroots groups, Amnesty International was more directly connected with antiglobalization activists and advocates for the poor in the global south, many of whom were urging human rights organizations to begin addressing extreme poverty as early as the 1980s. Amnesty International's strong membership base not only pressured it to adopt subsistence rights but also created incentives for it to adopt a more programmatic, rather than legalistic, notion of these rights. What Roth dismisses as "sloganeering" Amnesty International may view as an opportunity to mobilize its membership into action. Thus it can adopt a Global Campaign for Human Dignity that maintains a broader focus than would single instances of legal violations. In essence, Amnesty International's methodology of social change centers around mobilizing its dynamic membership, while HRW's lack of membership necessitates a focus on a specific method of advocacy, which entails a more legal definition of rights and thus a hesitant approach to subsistence rights.

Yet even within Amnesty International, the expansion of work into subsistence rights has been resisted by some staff members who fear the dilution of its core identity, the loss of its reputation for solid and impartial research, and a diminution in their own authority within the organization. For example, in 2003, dozens of staff members at its International Secretariat signed a protest letter to Secretary General Irene Khan, arguing that the expansion of its work into economic and social rights would require that less attention be directed toward prisoners of conscience and that these prisoners would suffer as a result.[65] Once again, the resistance has resulted from the intermingling of both principled and strategic rationales.

Notably, even the cautious, partial, and belated adoption of subsistence rights by powerful gatekeepers such as Amnesty International and HRW is seen as a mixed blessing by smaller rights NGOs whose central focus has long been subsistence rights.[66] On the one hand, the gatekeeper organizations provide the resources and the sense of legitimacy to certify subsistence rights as valid and worthy of promotion. They are powerful enough to define what constitutes a human rights violation; thus only with their participation is the expansion of economic and social rights widely recognized.[67] On the other hand, as the gatekeeper organizations expand their mandates, it will inevitably spread their resources more thinly. And because they are the most powerful players, they consume a large proportion of the overall funding for subsistence rights work, shaping how these rights are understood and the dominant methodologies used to pursue them. For rights advocates who have long promoted subsistence rights, the gatekeeper NGOs' recent entry into the field has the potential to drown out the capacity-building work and intensive research often done by smaller, local human rights organizations.[68] Therefore many are ambivalent about the participation of the human rights gatekeepers, even as they welcome the advance of subsistence rights advocacy overall.

ANTIPOVERTY NGOS AND SUBSISTENCE RIGHTS

At roughly the same time that human rights NGOs began to adopt subsistence rights, social justice groups and humanitarian organizations were doing the same, through a human rights approach to poverty and development. Paul Nelson and Ellen Dorsey observe that the "use of human rights standards to influence social and economic policy is growing rapidly."[69] For example, the Poor People's Economic Human Rights Campaign, a national coalition of grassroots groups fighting for subsistence rights, grew from a handful of members to more than sixty within a five-year period.[70] When Food First, a national antihunger research and advocacy group, organized congressional hearings on U.S. food policy as part of its 1998 "Economic Human Rights: The Time Has Come" campaign, more than 180 local social justice groups participated nationwide.[71]

Other examples of the connection between human rights and social justice movements in the last ten years are too numerous to mention, but a few cases may serve to illustrate the trend. Local constituency-based groups have begun to frame some of their mobilizing campaigns in rights-based terms, such as the Kensington Welfare Rights Union in Philadelphia, the Women's Economic Agenda Project in Oakland, the Coalition to Protect Public Housing in Chicago, and the Coalition for Immokalee Workers in Florida. National advocacy groups and coalitions based primarily in Washington, D.C., and New York, such as Public Citizen, the Bank Information Center, the Center of Concern, the Center for Economic Justice, the Washington Office on Latin America, the One Campaign, and the National Mobilization against Sweatshops, are similarly using rights language to lobby policymakers or raise public awareness about poverty. All of these groups occasionally receive assistance from legal aid programs such as Legal Momentum, the NAACP Legal Defense Fund, the Urban Justice Center, and the National Law Center on Homelessness and Poverty, who are themselves increasingly willing to apply international human rights law in addition to national law to the issues that affect the poor. Academic institutes, such as the Center for Human Rights and Global Justice at New York University and the Center for Health and Human Rights at Harvard University, are supporting this trend by conducting research and publishing reports on the links between human rights and social justice issues. Finally, networks have emerged in the past decade, such as the U.S.

Human Rights Network and ESCR-Net, whose explicit goals are to facil-itate communication and collaboration between social justice and human rights organizations.

Likewise, the major relief and development NGOs began around the end of the 1990s to officially adopt human rights and incorporate them into their programming. One of the first NGOs to advocate a closer rela-tionship between human rights and development was the Human Rights Council of Australia, which published *The Rights Way to Develop-ment* in 1995 urging a more consistent incorporation of human rights standards, especially economic and social rights, into the planning of development aid.[72] Although *The Rights Way* received a "mixed reaction" from other humanitarian organizations, the idea of adopting rights-based approaches to development eventually caught on.[73] Most of the major international humanitarian NGOs have now adopted them, in-cluding CARE, Oxfam, Save the Children, ActionAid, World Vision, and dozens of others. Oxfam is one of the NGOs that has taken subsistence rights the furthest, as all twelve of its autonomous national offices have signed onto Oxfam International's strategic plan (2001–4) that defined its focus as the "realization of economic and social rights within the wider human rights continuum."[74] Oxfam began using human rights language as early as the mid-1990s but has only recently begun to imple-ment the rights-based approach programmatically.[75] Oxfam Interna-tional named former UN high commissioner for human rights Mary Robinson as honorary president, and as Oxfam America's president Ray Offenheiser states, "The conscious choice to center all programming on a rights-based approach and to focus more particularly on economic and social rights has represented a major organizational shift for all Oxfam affiliates."[76]

Yet there still remains widespread resistance within social justice and humanitarian organizations to adopting a human rights approach to ex-treme poverty. Many social justice groups still find "a deep resistance to framing their work in human rather than single-identity/issue terms."[77] The majority of social justice organizations rely occasionally on human rights language when it fits a particular campaign strategy or frame a par-ticular program consistently in human rights terms while other programs within the same organization are not explicitly rights oriented. For exam-ple, Public Citizen frames its Water for All program fairly consistently in human rights terms but much less so its other programs on food, energy policy, democracy, or global trade.[78] For many of these groups, adopting a rights-based approach to poverty revolves around whether it is an effec-tive method of political advocacy rather than debating whether these rights are valid legal instruments. Thus, although social justice activists adhere to the fundamental philosophical principles underlying subsistence rights, these groups adopt a human rights orientation only when it fits their strategic goals within a particular social context.

Bread for the World, a national Christian antihunger advocacy group, began its work in 1975 with a human rights orientation (through lobbying for the right-to-food resolution in Congress) but has since mostly abandoned an explicit rights-based approach.[79] Even though many of Bread for the World's fifty thousand members are personally motivated by human rights principles, the organization has found that framing hunger primarily around religious themes is much more effective for its constituency. Staff members at Bread for the World tend to associate human rights with legal strategies, such as lobbying for U.S. ratification of the International Covenant on Economic, Social and Cultural Rights, and feel that taking on such an approach would be impractical because it would "totally change Bread's structure and mission." In addition, Bread for the World's organizing strategy is centered on pragmatic, short-term, tangible goals that make an immediate difference in the lives of poor people, and human rights strategies can be perceived as ill-suited to this approach. Finally, Bread for the World's staff members understand the U.S. government's historic antipathy toward economic and social rights and have therefore made the decision to apply their limited resources to other approaches when trying to change U.S. policy.

Similarly, not all humanitarian NGOs or projects have explicitly adopted human rights language, for reasons related to the organizations' identities or histories. Faith-based development organizations such as Catholic Relief Services, Mercy Corps, Lutheran World Relief, and World Vision have been less eager to adopt a human rights approach than have secular organizations.[80] Although these faith-based organizations have adopted policies and principles that are mostly consistent with a rights-based approach, they have tended to frame their approach in terms that resonate with their core constituencies who have a religious worldview. Each organization's guiding principles are "closely tied to the core values and beliefs that drive each one."[81] Thus, for example, Catholic Relief Services uses a "justice lens" to approach its development work, based on the principles of Catholic social justice, that is often called a human rights approach by outsiders. Mercy Corps employs human rights language regularly but subsumes it within a "civil society" approach, in part because of the concern that "rights language might make people uncomfortable."[82] Some faith-based NGOs that have adopted a rights-based approach, such as World Vision, openly acknowledge that human rights language should be used only when it fits into larger religious principles. As a World Vision representative has stated, "Christians may use the language of human rights in a development context but they will use it where it is in agreement with a Christian worldview. There will be times when it is not appropriate. There will be times when something is being claimed as a right which is in direct con-. flict with Christian principles or where the consequences of a human rights approach is not felt to be Christian. It may also be the case that Christian agencies believe that a rights-based approach is not as appropriate as another [approach]."[83]

Other humanitarian NGOs, religious or secular, may be reluctant to adopt a rights-based approach because of strategic concerns—they have no experience with policy advocacy, they are tied to institutional donors that oppose subsistence rights, they can't afford to be confrontational with host governments, or they fear a complete change in mission and organizational structure.[84] For example, because the U.S. Agency for International Development (USAID) does not fund rights-based approaches, organizations such as Catholic Relief Services, which receives a large proportion of its funds from USAID, are not likely to promote their work via rights language. Some NGOs, such as the International Committee of the Red Cross (ICRC), depend on a strict interpretation of neutrality in order to fulfill their missions in extremely sensitive political situations, such as visiting prisoners of war on both sides of a conflict. While the ICRC's mission is not inconsistent with human rights principles, the perception of human rights work as involving more open political advocacy could become a hindrance to its work and is certainly opposed to its identity.[85] Other NGOs have expressed a fear that rights-based approaches require a fundamental shift in an organization's mission toward political and legal advocacy and a shift in staff competencies toward legal expertise and have therefore dismissed a human rights approach.[86]

In sum, adopting a human rights approach to poverty has prompted both support and resistance, depending on the organization and the context in which it works. As organizations restructure their operations, staff members are inevitably displaced, and traditional areas of work (e.g., service delivery or prisoners of conscience) may receive less attention and suffer as a result. And yet, as a senior staff member at Amnesty International acknowledged, for decades northern human rights practitioners "kept the large majority of the world's victims outside" of their collective efforts.[87] As human rights, social justice, and humanitarian organizations increasingly adopt subsistence rights, they are beginning to make the human rights framework more relevant to the fifth of the world's people living in extreme poverty. Emerging NGO practice on subsistence rights has resulted in increasing attention and resources devoted to those rights, and this effort is producing results. At the international level, the UN Committee on Economic, Social and Cultural Rights, in collaboration with human rights NGOs, has done much work to elaborate the content of these rights and monitor them through the state reporting mechanism. More than one hundred national constitutions throughout the world now protect at least some rights to subsistence, and increasingly courts in places as diverse as India, South Africa, and Argentina are expressing their willingness to review the constitutionality of states' economic and social policies.

Conclusion

Analysts who examine NGO motivations often treat strategic considerations with suspicion, envisioning two distinct worlds—the principled and the strategic—which necessarily compete with each other. There seems to be a widespread assumption that, in the realm of civil society, not only should NGOs be motivated by principled ideas, but also they should be able to promote these principles with "purity"—absent any consideration of the strategic limitations in their environment, the need for material resources to carry out their mission effectively, or their own organizational structure and interests. For example, Stephen Hopgood questions Amnesty International's more pragmatic approach and its recent expansion into new rights, implying that its moral integrity has been diluted by strategic attempts to respond to the concerns of its members, raise money professionally, and be politically effective. He envisions a separation between the principled and strategic realms, claiming that "moral authority is the opposite of tactical; it aspires to truth."[88] Other analysts have encouraged Amnesty International to "ensure that strategic considerations do not play too large a role" in its work, as if somehow human rights ought to be promoted in a less strategic manner.[89] Likewise, scholars who highlight the strategic aspects of NGO practice are often described as cynical or critical of civil society motivations.[90]

This chapter posits a different kind of relationship between strategic interests and principled ideas, one that is mutually constitutive rather than inherently conflictual. Both principled and strategic factors played a large part in the rejection and subsequent gradual acceptance of subsistence rights by northern NGOs. Normative entrepreneurs within these organizations expressed their deeply held beliefs and responded to what they perceived as opportunities within their strategic environments—for example, the end of the Cold War, the intractability of global poverty, and the legitimacy of rights language—by promoting subsistence rights as a way to effectively meet these opportunities. Groups that continue to resist subsistence rights have both principled and strategic concerns in mind as well.

The largest source of philosophical opposition to subsistence rights revolves around the argument that they are not really human rights because they are not justiciable in courts, or because they impose a set of positive duties on the state that are impossible to fulfill. However, scholars and practitioners have increasingly adopted a position that subsistence rights are potentially just as enforceable as civil and political rights (indeed, advances in legislation and a few court decisions around the globe are demonstrating that possibility), that all human rights impose both positive and negative duties on states and other actors, and that subsistence rights obligations are not overly burdensome.[91] Therefore there is clearly a principled basis for all of these organizations to adopt subsistence rights—in their beliefs about the UDHR, the centrality of subsistence rights, the importance of political engagement, and the social obligation to address the root causes of extreme poverty.

Yet the timing of the trend, and the inevitable costs and benefits that result, cannot be explained without reference to these organizations' attempts to respond strategically to material and political opportunities. The end of the Cold War created a context in which organizations could pursue subsistence rights without their own survival being threatened. Human rights organizations began to expand their mandate when it became clear that their legitimacy and credibility were at stake. Yet their engagement with subsistence rights remains limited by concerns over organizational capacity, overstretching resources, and the effectiveness of new approaches. Institutional donors adopted subsistence rights for largely principled reasons, but the new streams of funding that they provided created a material incentive for NGOs to frame their work on extreme poverty in human rights terms.

Principled and strategic (or ideational and rational) factors are therefore not mutually exclusive or even in conflict in this case. Principled motives must always be mediated by strategic and organizational concerns. Those who dismiss subsistence rights as invalid are not likely to find rights-based approaches to poverty particularly effective or conducive to organizational survival and growth. Those who believe philosophically in subsistence rights must still find a way to promote them effectively. Otherwise the organization will not survive to carry out its work. Organizational interests are primarily generated from and expressed through ideas, and ideas are built on a foundation of interests and promoted through strategic, often calculated, practice.

The growth of subsistence rights work among northern NGOs has resulted from the way in which these organizations (and new groups entering the field) have defined their interests, interpreted the human rights domain, and calculated the anticipated effectiveness of their methods in accomplishing their self-defined goals. Thus when human rights NGOs such as Amnesty International expand their mandate to promote subsistence rights, they are responding to an idea based on an essential human need (physical survival), in a manner that strategically pursues their organizational interests (organizational survival, membership growth, effectiveness, or geographical balance), interests that are constructed through the exchange of ideas. When social justice groups adopt human rights language to promote antipoverty policies, they are strategically appropriating an idea that they fundamentally believe in (the inherent dignity of people) to appeal to particular constituencies that further the groups' normatively driven mission.

Restrictions in an NGO's strategic environment necessarily dictate that NGOs focus on a geographically and substantively limited range of concerns, compared with the universe of possible needs. Indeed, as NGOs ponder how they can effectively fit within that environment, it is possible that some of their strategic interests may interfere with the pursuit of their principled goals. Yet most of the strategic deliberation that NGOs engage in is directed toward effectively realizing those very goals and is intimately tied into contested interpretations of what those principled goals should be. In that sense, the rise of new rights is not a story of principled ideas versus strategic interests but of how strategy and principles are inextricably intertwined.

Chapter 9
Local Claims, International Standards, and the Human Right to Water

Paul J. Nelson

In recent years, conflicts over water have become increasingly common around the world. In many of these disputes, the "right to water" has been a central claim. In Cochabamba, Bolivia, activists invoked water rights in 2000 to oppose privatization of municipal water services, becoming a global cause célèbre. In India since the late 1990s, farmers and consumers have resisted Coca-Cola's plans to use local water in soft drinks, winning support both at home and abroad. Transnational advocacy networks have also fought proposals by the World Bank and other international financial institutions to fund water privatization schemes. Finally, at the United Nations, NGOs long demanded acceptance of a human right to water. In November 2002, the UN Committee on Economic, Social and Cultural Rights formally recognized this right. According to its General Comment 15, this right "entitles everyone to sufficient, safe, acceptable, physically accessible and affordable water for personal and domestic uses."[1] As such, the right includes individual freedoms, such as continuing access to water supplies and freedom from arbitrary disconnections. It also includes entitlements, many in the form of obligations on states, inter alia, to recognize water rights in law, adopt a national water strategy, and ensure that water is affordable and accessible to all.[2]

Given that clean water is critical to health, quality of life, and productivity, these recent struggles over water rights are significant in themselves. In addition, water conflicts are important case studies for clarifying the role of economic, social, and cultural (ESC) rights in trade and other policy issues. From a theoretical standpoint, they also help broaden our understanding of transnational advocacy strategies, methods, and movements. This chapter's account of the period from the late 1990s through 2005 demonstrates the diverse political origins of "new rights" and reveals the power—but also the limitations—of human rights claims in affecting economic and social policy. I make four arguments. First, activists have asserted water rights primarily in reaction to privatization of local water systems and liberalization of international trade and investment rules related to water. At the same time, such claims are part of a broader trend toward rights-based advocacy in many social justice movements worldwide. This twin context of threat and opportunity explains the rapid rise of water movements at the local and international levels during the late 1990s.

Second, in these campaigns, water rights claims have been prominent but have rarely stood alone. In many countries, they are bound together with other themes, including nationalism and opposition to foreign investment. In the international arena, the mix of arguments is more complex. It includes both hostility to transnational corporations and international financial institutions and promotion of water as a global public good or global commons.

Third, the national and international advocacy efforts have been mutually supportive but loosely linked. There is dynamic interaction between domestic water campaigns and a broad set of transnational NGOs motivated variously by human rights, environmental quality, consumer protection, corporate accountability, trade regulation, and World Bank reform.

Finally, the groundswell of domestic and international activism since the mid-1990s helped impel the UN Committee on Economic, Social and Cultural Rights to recognize the right to water in its 2002 General Comment 15. In turn, General Comment 15 strengthened the legitimacy of water rights claims, unleashing more intensive advocacy, particularly at the international level. The general comment's influence on domestic water activists, while important, has been smaller. Many domestic movements continue to rely primarily on moral arguments concerning water rights or on national legal guarantees rather than appealing explicitly to international human rights law.

The remainder of this chapter first introduces the human right to water in the international system. The second section examines the national and international tracks on which water rights have been debated, providing brief accounts from Ghana, South Africa, and India. The concluding section offers an interpretation of the experience and its relevance for the "gatekeeper model" developed in this volume.

The Right to Water and Its Context

Local social movements and international activists advance water rights in two ways: as a legal standard backed by a growing body of national and international law and as a political claim articulating their interests. This section first probes the claim's legal basis. It then discusses the political context for its rise: opportunities presented by a broader movement toward rights-based social justice advocacy and threats posed by increasing water privatization.

HUMAN RIGHTS STANDARDS

Water is not mentioned in either the Universal Declaration of Human Rights (UDHR) or the International Covenant on Economic, Social and Cultural Rights (ICESCR).[3] But the absence of an explicit standard did not prevent advocates such as Peter Gleick and nongovernmental organizations (NGOs) such as the Center for Economic and Social Rights from claiming that access to water is a human right. Their argument had a legal basis: a right to water was arguably assumed in some human rights agreements, and water could be shown to be a foundation for the broader right to life and right to health. Article 24(c) of the Convention on the Rights of the Child (CRC), for example, describes steps that states parties should take to implement the right to the highest attainable standard of health, including steps to reduce infant and child mortality and to provide adequate food and "supplies of clean drinking water."[4] The Convention on the Elimination of All Forms of Discrimination against Women (CEDAW) places access to water on the list of services that must be provided to women without discrimination (along with housing, electricity, sanitation, transport, and communication).[5] Outside of the major human rights treaties, water issues are included in other international statements and declarations, including the constitution of the World Health Organization (WHO; 1946), the declaration of the UN Conference on the Environment and Development (UNCED; 1992), and the Millennium Declaration (2000).[6]

The absence of water from core human rights instruments encouraged development of a further argument, articulated in General Comment 15: that access to water is so tightly linked to explicit guarantees that it too must be considered a right. As General Comment 15 concisely argues, water is "inextricably related to the right to the highest attainable standard of health" pursuant to ICESCR Article 12.[7] It also "clearly falls within the category of guarantees essential for securing an adequate standard of living" under ICESCR Article 11, as the list of goods needed for such a living standard is not exhaustive.[8] In this view, water rights' omission from rights treaties resulted not from the framers' affirmative decision to exclude it but from their inability to imagine a world in which water access would be contested.[9]

THE NEW RIGHTS ADVOCACY

Using these arguments, advocates have promoted the human right to water since the mid-1990s. Two factors encouraged them to make these claims: a receptive international environment among like-minded organizations and a set of external threats. With regard to the former, in the mid-1990s progressive NGOs and social movements explored new approaches to long-standing global social problems such as poverty, disease, and homelessness. Together, these diverse and largely uncoordinated efforts constituted what I have called elsewhere "new rights advocacy."[10] This approach has three facets: recognition of new ESC rights such as the right to water; usage of conventional human rights principles, analyses, and methodologies to advance the new rights; and establishment of innovative campaigns focusing global attention on previously neglected problems. Primary proponents of the new rights advocacy include development agencies that have adopted rights-based approaches, traditional human rights NGOs that have expanded their mandates beyond civil and political rights to ESC rights, and newly formed NGOs that have focused specifically on ESC rights.[11] Many such NGOs are now linked in an International Network for ESC Rights, founded with support from the Ford Foundation in 2003.[12]

PRIVATIZATION AND LIBERALIZATION

New threats to water access, primarily in the form of large-scale water privatization schemes, also spurred advocates to make rights claims. Although corporate water provision is long-standing in a few countries such as the United Kingdom, water privatization expanded rapidly beginning in the late 1980s as part of a larger trend toward selling off state-run industries and utilities. On the whole, public water systems in developing countries are inefficient and deliver water of uncertain quality. They also serve the wealthy far better than the poor: slums, shantytowns, and temporary urban settlements are rarely served well, with residents in those areas often paying a premium for water delivered by truck.[13] In this context, reforms were (and are) clearly needed. Many countries turned to privatization, hoping to increase efficiency, reduce waste, broaden service, and create incentives for infrastructure improvements. For their part, multinational water corporations quickly invested in water trade and services in the developing world. Thus, by 2001, ninety-three countries had partially privatized water and wastewater services.[14]

While citizens of some developing countries have accepted water privatization, two elements in private contracts, rate increases and pre-payment, have sparked resistance in many other places.[15] Because corporations seek profits, privatization usually entails higher water fees, although price concessions are sometimes made to low-income consumers.[16] To help guarantee their investment, companies also often require prepayment, particularly in impoverished areas. Consumer reaction to these policies is often negative. Rate hikes and higher connection fees have galvanized citizen movements in Bolivia, Argentina, Ghana, New Zealand, India, and elsewhere, while prepaid meters have had the same effect in countries including South Africa, Brazil, the Philippines, Nigeria, and the United States.[17]

Multinational corporations' dominance of water service contracts heightens local suspicions that providers will raise rates and ignore consumer needs. In addition, water services corporations have benefited from substantial World Bank support, including financing, insurance against investment risks, and adjudication of disputes through the International Center for Settlement of Investment Disputes (ICSID). The World Bank's facilitating role has galvanized opposition among international critics and domestic antiglobalization movements.[18] The World Bank, in the eyes of many water activists, has a "shared agenda [with] the global water giants" that results in "corporate interests overriding basic human needs and livelihoods" in the World Bank's financing of water system reforms.[19]

Water Rights on the Rise

The combination of civil society's receptivity to water rights and privatization's threat to public access has precipitated rights claims in both national and international spheres. In this section, I first examine a number of domestic water movements that have raised such claims, then turn to water rights activism directed primarily at international institutions.

Within countries, the most frequent advocates are consumers protesting actual or impending changes in municipal water management. Organizing at the neighborhood level, they often create citywide movements and sometimes form national NGOs and NGO coalitions. While these movements sometimes engage in mass mobilizations, they also use administrative and judicial institutions. Whatever their strategy, many domestic water movements invoke water rights, sometimes referencing national constitutional, statutory, or policy commitments, other times citing broader human rights norms. In some cases, local advocates have promoted their causes overseas or otherwise gained support from transnational NGOs interested in water rights. As examples of these dynamics, consider the following brief accounts of recent water politics in Ghana, South Africa, and India.[20]

GHANA

In 2001, the Ghanaian government, backed by World Bank financing and expertise, proposed privatization of the country's municipal water systems. This plan quickly sparked domestic opposition that came to be embodied in the Ghana National Coalition against the Privatisation of Water. The coalition objected to the government's fast-track implementation of privatization, opacity in contracting, and perceived favoritism toward multinational corporations.[21]

To bolster its cause, the coalition sought support from overseas NGOs. It was successful in this strategy for two reasons. First, the World Bank's prominent role meant that international critics of its policy were receptive to the coalition's appeals. Second, Ghanaian advocates effectively marketed their cause overseas. For one thing, in 2001 the coalition organized a national NGO forum on water, aimed both at educating the world about the privatization scheme and at raising the coalition's international profile. More important, coalition leaders embarked on foreign speaking tours and sponsored an international fact-finding mission to Ghana.[22] Washington-based NGOs such as the Citizens' Network for Essential Services and the International Water Working Group (IWWG) responded with support for the National Coalition and public opposition to the World Bank's role.[23] In the United Kingdom, the World Development Movement pressured British water company Biwater to withdraw from competition for the contract in Ghana and mobilized opposition to European Union trade and aid policies promoting water privatization in Ghana and elsewhere.

SOUTH AFRICA

South Africa's 1996 constitution provides the "right to have access to . . . sufficient food and water," in addition to a variety of civil, political, and other social and economic rights.[24] This provision has neither deterred the government from water privatization nor moved it to halt South Africa's production of prepaid water meters for domestic and foreign use. But the constitutional right to water access has also created a strong basis for domestic opposition to the privatization schemes. Such resistance has been widespread, aggravated in particular by corporations' use of the meters, which sharpen the perception that privatized water will violate poor citizens' rights.[25] Invoking the constitution's water rights provision, privatization opponents have gone to South Africa's courts to fight privatization. South Africa's water conflicts, like Ghana's, have also become internationally prominent. The IWWG, for instance, showcases the South African conflicts in its global campaign for water rights and against prepaid meters.[26]

INDIA

India is also experimenting with privatization, and human rights arguments are prominent in citizen challenges to the 2002 National Water Policy providing for private ownership and management of water systems.[27] The case profiled here, however, involves conflict over Coca-Cola's use of local water supplies. In the 1990s, the company built some sixty-eight bottling plants in India. In the states of Kerala and Uttar Pradesh, local farmers and consumer groups argued that the plants drained fresh water from underground aquifers, polluted other water sources, and deprived families of water for personal and agricultural use. The company disputed these claims. Four of its sixty-eight bottling plants in India draw on municipal water supplies, while most use water from the plants' own wells.[28]

In their advocacy against Coca-Cola, the Indian movements weave together human rights arguments, environmental concerns, and antiglobalization sentiments.[29] Several cases have been heard in Indian courts, testing water rights against property rights and contractual claims.[30] In one case, local panchayat authorities in Kerala ruled that the company's operations must cease because they deprived residents of water resources. This was later overruled by state-level courts. But on June 15, 2006, Kerala's newly elected chief minister, V. S. Achuthanandan, denounced water "being taken from poor communities to produce drinking water for the rich" and agreed to "proactive measures" to prevent further soil and groundwater pollution. These measures included a temporary ban on the production and sale of Coca-Cola (and Pepsi) in the state.[31] In a similar local conflict in Mehdiganj, Uttar Pradesh, leaders of a community movement maintained a protest vigil at a Coca-Cola bottling plant in March 2006 and announced a hunger strike on June 23, 2006, demanding that the plant be closed.[32] Although controversy over the Mehdiganj plant continues, Coke's announcement of a $20 million water conservation initiative in 2007 was seen by its Indian critics as largely in response to their efforts.[33] These Indian conflicts have attracted transnational NGO support, most importantly from the India Resource Center, a small California-based NGO fighting "corporate globalization" in India.[34]

INTERNATIONAL MOBILIZATION

As suggested by the foregoing accounts, transnational support for local water movements came not from major human rights NGOs but from three other sources: solidarity networks with links to a particular country or city, water rights activists such as the Canadian-based Blue Planet Project, and antiprivatization advocates opposed to the World Bank and International Monetary Fund (IMF). Since the mid-1990s, these three sets of groups have asserted water rights claims in numerous international venues as well. For example, the 1998 Water Manifesto, supported by individuals and organizations from five continents, stated that "water is a fundamental, inalienable individual and collective right" and that "it is up to society as a whole to guarantee the right of access . . . without discrimination."[35] In 2001, the Blue Planet Project called on governments to pledge that water would not be "privatized, commodified, traded or exported for commercial purpose" and that it would be "exempted from all existing and future international and bilateral trade and investment agreements."[36]

Such advocacy, along with the many internationally reported conflicts over water privatization in developing countries, formed the backdrop against which the UN Committee on Economic, Social and Cultural Rights issued General Comment 15. For international water rights advocates, issuance of the general comment was a pivotal moment. It stamped the United Nations' approval on activists' long-standing arguments, increasing their legitimacy and sparking intensified mobilization. While they are not tightly coordinated, the many transnational NGOs engaged in such activities place water rights at the core of their campaigns.[37] For instance, the New York–based Center for Economic and Social Rights (CESR) has advocated a rights-based approach to water since 2003, citing international agreements and national laws. CESR also urges that the WHO's daily water standard, 20–40 liters per household and within a reasonable distance, become a benchmark for national policy and litigation. As another example, the IWWG, a coalition headquartered at Washington, D.C.-based Public Citizen, focuses its advocacy on the IMF, the World Bank, and the World Trade Organization's (WTO) General Agreement on Trade in Services (GATS). In the wake of General Comment 15, IWWG began referring to water access as a human right and on that basis criticized prepaid water meters.[38] South African and international advocacy organizations take similar positions against the meters, based on General Comment 15.[39] Finally, the UK-based WaterAid, a specialized charity focused on water, sanitation, and hygiene, adopted a "human rights approach" to all of its work in 2003, with obvious implications for its water-related project assistance. Wat-erAid has also expanded its advocacy work by initiating a critique of "private sector participation" in water system reforms.[40]

In 2003–5, other NGOs issued a flood of new reports, position papers, and advocacy initiatives promoting water rights. Among these NGOs were Brot für die Welt; World Economy, Ecology and Development (WEED); Jubilee South; Amnesty International; COHRE; and the inter-American network La Red VIDA.[41] Major reports by the WHO, COHRE, and the American Association for the Advancement of Science systematically frame water as a human rights issue.[42] A 2004 report by the International Union for the Conservation of Nature (IUCN) argues for wider recognition of the human right to water as a tool to improve decisions about the allocation and management of water supplies.[43] Finally, a joint NGO demand that donor countries cease funding the World Bank's water privatization facility (the Public-Private Infrastructure Advisory Facility) references the human right to water.[44]

Notably absent from these many new initiatives were the mainstream human rights NGOs, Amnesty International, and Human Rights Watch. Amnesty International responded to the release of General Comment 15 with a statement of support, followed by efforts to encourage the inclusion of human rights perspectives in the 2003 meeting of the influential, corporate-sponsored World Water Forum.[45] But neither NGO has entered the water debates more actively nor have two other large human rights NGOs, Human Rights First and Physicians for Human Rights. This likely reflects these organizations' historical focus on civil and political, rather than economic and social, rights. In this context, water rights have not fit well with the core mission of these human rights NGOs, although Amnesty International has recently changed its stance on these issues.[46] But for the most part, the major rights organizations neither pushed for the changes embodied in General Comment 15 nor used the general comment as the basis for water rights activism.

Conclusion

Water rights advocacy has increased at both domestic and international levels since the mid-1990s. Within countries, as the brief case studies in this chapter illustrate, the water rights frame serves as a powerful mobilizing tool. While activists have had limited success in using water rights affirmatively to encourage much-needed improvements in public utility operations, they have had greater success in deploying them to block privatization schemes, especially where national laws or constitutions guarantee water rights. Thus far, South African and Argentinean activists have achieved the most in this regard. Elsewhere, governments and corporations have abandoned or modified a growing number of privatization schemes due to public protest or litigation.[47] As a result, the World Bank is now questioning the financial and political viability of such schemes in developing countries.[48] At the international level, years of activism helped encourage the UN Commission to issue General Comment 15, solidifying the previously uncertain international legal status of water rights and contributing to new NGO activism.

Nonetheless, the meaning and implications of water rights remain contested. Water rights typically butt against property rights claims and therefore remain relatively weak as enforceable legal claims. In many cases, too, international institutions formulating water policy have ignored water rights. Within international institutions, official policy clearly favors market mechanisms and public-private partnership arrangements to mobilize capital and provide water services. Months after the release of General Comment 15, for instance, a major international report on water issues related to the Millennium Development Goals made no mention of water rights and instead touted foreign investment as the preferred means of meeting water needs.[49] A follow-up report published in 2006 softens the focus on private financing but again overlooks water rights.[50]

What does the water rights case suggest about the theoretical concepts developed in this volume? While this chapter has surveyed too few cases to offer definitive conclusions, a number of hypotheses may be suggested. First, many water conflicts remain primarily domestic issues. Where national laws are strong, domestic activists may see no advantage in internationalizing their causes. Second, despite the strength of some domestic advocacy, other local activists seek transnational NGO support. And as the cases surveyed in this chapter indicate, NGOs sometimes become active. Gatekeeper human rights NGOs have not played a major role, however, probably because the cases do not fit with their decades-long focus on civil and political rights. Rather smaller NGOs, particularly those specializing in water or ESC rights, have been the critical players. Beyond fit between local and transnational concerns, the reasons that the various NGOs do or do not become involved relate closely to factors discussed in this volume. Such NGOs, with their limited resources, cannot become involved in all water conflicts, but they do in some cases respond to appeals from local water rights groups. The Ghanaian Coalition undertook the most concerted effort to attract overseas NGOs, probably because national law provided little help in the fight against privatization. In addition, whatever the level of local outreach, transnational NGOs are drawn to national water disputes having important international implications. In some cases, this is because the disputes involve entities with which the NGOs are engaged in ongoing conflicts. These include international financial institutions such as the World Bank and multinational corporations such as Coca-Cola, as the Ghanaian and Indian cases indicate. Similarly, in South Africa, the international importance of a fight over water in a country that both protects water rights and acts as a major exporter of prepaid meters drew strong NGO interest.

Third, in addition to their role in certain local water conflicts, transnational NGOs specializing in water issues sought support and legitimation for their water rights claims. As indicated earlier, until recently, major human rights NGOs have steered clear of this issue. But the United Nations proved a more receptive institution for these demands. After years of water rights activism in the 1990s, a major breakthrough occurred when the UN Committee on Economic, Social and Cultural Rights issued General Comment 15. While local activists in developing countries have not used this international standard extensively, transnational water NGOs have sought to use the ruling to implement in practice the abstract promise of General Comment 15. Even Amnesty International, as part of its broader embrace of economic and social rights, has now been moved to promote water rights internationally.

Finally, national- and international-level water campaigns may be best characterized as mutually supportive, parallel campaigns with significant interaction but without a mutual agenda or strategy. Jordan and van Tuijl have pointed out that transnational campaigns vary in the degree of articulation of national and transnational participants.[51] While some are collaborative efforts to block a national change, others involve international actors whose primary concern is in another political arena and who cooperate and communicate but do not follow coordinated strategies. It is possible that the formal recognition of a human right to water will lead to more coordinated advocacy, but this would require a substantial shift from the present loosely linked relationships.

Notes

Chapter 1. Introduction

1. Vienna Declaration, World Conference on Human Rights, Vienna, June 14–25, 1993, UN Doc. A/CONF.157/24 (pt. 1), 20 (1993).

2. Thomas Risse, Stephen C. Ropp, and Kathryn Sikkink, eds., *The Power of Human Rights: International Norms and Domestic Change* (Cambridge: Cambridge University Press, 1999). See also Sanjeev Khagram, James V. Riker, and Kathryn Sikkink, eds., *Restructuring World Politics: Transnational Social Movements, Networks, and Norms* (Minneapolis: University of Minnesota Press, 2002); Ann Florini, ed., *The Third Force: The Rise of Transnational Civil Society* (Tokyo: Japan Center for International Change and Carnegie Endowment for International Peace, 1999).

3. Margaret Keck and Kathryn Sikkink, *Activists beyond Borders: Advocacy Networks in International Politics* (Ithaca, N.Y.: Cornell University Press, 1998), 27.

4. Universal Declaration of Human Rights, adopted December 10 1948, G.A. Res. 217A (III), UN GAOR, 3rd sess. (Resolutions, pt. 1), 71, UN Doc. A/810 (1948); International Covenant on Civil and Political Rights, adopted December 16, 1966, G.A. Res. 2200 (XXI), UN GAOR, 21st sess., supp. no. 16, UN Doc. A/6316 (1966), 999 UNTS 171 (entered into force March 23 1976).

5. International Covenant on Economic, Social, and Cultural Rights, adopted December 16, 1966, G.A. Res. 2200 (XXI), UN GAOR, 21st sess., supp. no. 16, art. 15, UN Doc. A/6316 (1966), 993 UNTS 3 (entered into force January 3, 1976); International Convention on the Elimination of All Forms of Racial Discrimination, adopted December 21, 1965, 660 UNTS 195 (entered into force January 4, 1969).

6. For the importance of such organizations, see Zehra F. Arat and Peter H. Juviler, eds., *Non-State Actors in the Human Rights Universe* (Bloomfield, Conn.: Kumarian, 2006).

7. Andrew Cortell and James W. Davis, "Understanding the Domestic Impact of International Norms: A Research Agenda," *International Studies Review* 2, no. 1 (2000): 65–87.

8. Curt Goering, "Amnesty International and Economic, Social and Cultural Rights," in *Ethics in Action: The Ethical Challenges of International Human Rights Nongovernmental Organizations*, ed. Daniel A. Bell and Jean-Marc Coicaud (Cambridge: Cambridge University Press, 2007), 204–17.

9. See, e.g., Keck and Sikkink, *Activists beyond Borders*; Thomas Risse and Kathryn Sikkink, "The Socialization of International Human Rights Norms into

Domestic Practices: Introduction," in *The Power of Human Rights*, ed. Risse, Ropp, and Sikkink, 1–38. Both these works assume that local groups initiate network formation and note but do not highlight tensions within networks. For examination of intranetwork conflicts, see Shareen Hertel, *Unexpected Power: Conflict and Change among Transnational Activists* (Ithaca, N.Y.: Cornell University Press, 2006).

10. For elaboration of this process, see Clifford Bob, *The Marketing of Rebellion: Insurgents, Media, and International Activism* (Cambridge: Cambridge University Press, 2005).

11. The sociological literature on countermovements is extensive but focuses on domestic, rather than transnational, opponents. See, e.g., David S. Meyer and Suzanne Staggenborg, "Movements, Countermovements, and the Structure of Political Opportunity," *American Journal of Sociology* 101, no. 6 (1996): 1628–60; Mayer N. Zald and Bert Useem, "Movement and Countermovement Interaction: Mobilization, Tactics, and State Involvement," in *Social Movements in an Organizational Society*, ed. Mayer N. Zald and John D. McCarthy (New Brunswick, N.J.: Transaction Books, 1987), 247–73; Clarence Y. H. Lo, "Countermovements and Conservative Movements in the Contemporary U.S.," *Annual Review of Sociology* 8 (1982): 107–34.

12. Michael Ignatieff, *Human Rights as Politics and Idolatry* (Princeton, N.J.: Princeton University Press, 2001).

13. John Kingdon, *Agendas, Alternatives, and Public Policies*, 2nd ed. (New York: HarperCollins, 1995).

14. See Clifford Bob, "Gunning for the Globe: Movement and Countermovement in the Small Arms Control Process," paper presented at the annual meeting of the International Studies Association, March 2, 2007. Analogously, in American politics, lobbyists vigorously promote certain policies, often by searching out problems to which the policy may be offered as a "solution." Deborah Stone, *Policy Paradox: The Art of Political Decision Making*, rev. ed. (New York: W. W. Norton, 2001).

15. See Mary Ann Glendon, *Rights Talk: The Impoverishment of Political Discourse* (New York: Free Press, 1991).

16. For an example of rights claims concealing hard-edged political goals, see Aryeh Neier, "Not All Human Rights Groups Are Equal," *New York Times*, May 27, 1989, 22.

17. For the distinction between negative and positive liberty, see Isaiah Berlin, "Two Concepts of Liberty," in *The Proper Study of Mankind: An Anthology of Essays*, ed. Henry Hardy (New York: Farrar, Straus, and Giroux, 2000).

18. Ronald Dworkin, *Taking Rights Seriously* (Cambridge, Mass.: Harvard University Press, 1978); Michael Ignatieff, "The Attack on Human Rights," *Foreign Affairs* (November–December 2001: 102–17.

19. For detailed discussion of the factors that go into NGO decisions about adopting local social movements, see Bob, *The Marketing of Rebellion*. For analogous ideas in a different context, see Joanne Bauer, ed., *Forging Environmentalism: Justice, Livelihood, and Contested Environments* (Armonk, N.Y.: M. E. Sharpe, 2006).

20. Philip Alston, "Conjuring Up New Human Rights: A Proposal for Quality Control," *American Journal of International Law* 78: 3 (1984): 607.

21. Ignatieff, *Human Rights as Politics*, 90; see also Amy Gutman, Introduction, in ibid., x; William Schulz, *In Our Own Best Interest: How Defending Human Rights Benefits Us All* (Boston: Beacon Press, 2001), 15.

22. Alston, "Conjuring Up New Human Rights," 616.

23. Ignatieff, *Human Rights as Politics.*

24. Joshua William Busby, "Bono Made Jesse Helms Cry: Jubilee 2000, Debt Relief, and Moral Action in International Politics," *International Studies Quarterly* 51, no. 2 (2007): 247–75.

25. Aspects of this little-studied issue are discussed in Doris Buss and Didi Herman, *Globalizing Family Values: The Christian Right in International Politics* (Minneapolis: University of Minnesota Press, 2003).

26. David M. Smolin, "Overcoming Religious Objections to the Convention on the Rights of the Child," *Emory International Law Review* 20 (Spring 2006): 81–110.

Chapter 2. Orphaned Again?

1. Charli Carpenter, Kai Greig, Donna Sharkey, and Robyn Wheeler, *Protecting Children Born of Sexual Violence and Exploitation in Conflict Zones: Findings from Consultations with Humanitarian Practitioners* (Pittsburgh, Pa.: University of Pittsburgh, GSPIA/Ford Institute of Human Security, 2005).

2. Elisabeth Rehn and Ellen Johnson Sirleaf, *Women, War and Peace* (New York: UNIFEM, 2002), 13.

3. This list has grown since UN secretary general Kofi Annan first announced "children and armed conflict" as a specific issue area within the UN system. It now includes an array of concerns such as displaced children, girls, child soldiers, orphans, and children affected by HIV/AIDS. See Charli Carpenter, "Setting the Advocacy Agenda: Issue Emergence and Non-Emergence around Children and Armed Conflict," *International Studies Quarterly* 51, no. 1 (2007): 1–35; Carmen Sorger and Eric Hoskins, "Protecting the Most Vulnerable: War-Affected Children," in *Human Security and the New Diplomacy,* ed. Rob McRae and Don Hubert (Montreal: McGill University Press, 2001), 134–52.

4. UNICEF, "Children Born of Sexual Violence in Conflict Zones: Considerations for UNICEF Response," outcome document of meeting held November 23, 2005, on file with author (2006), 1.

5. Ibid., 3.

6. Ann Mische, "Cross-Talk in Movements: Reconceiving the Culture-Network Link," in *Social Movements and Networks: Relational Approaches to Collective Action,* ed. Mario Diani and Doug McAdam (Oxford: Oxford University Press, 2004), 258–81; Sidney Tarrow, *The New Transnational Activism* (Cambridge: Cambridge University Press, 2005); Florence Passy, "Social Networks Matter: But How?" in *Social Movements and Networks,* ed. Diani and McAdam, 21–49.

7. The results of these focus groups were also published as an interim report through the Ford Institute of Human Security at the University of Pittsburgh. See Carpenter et al., *Protecting Children Born of Sexual Violence.*

8. In any conversational setting where I discussed my research topic, I was also contributing to the process of social construction. Therefore I kept detailed field notes of my experiences at international conferences, at UN meetings where I was invited to present briefings of my research, at consultancies with the humanitarian sector, in the classroom, over the phone with members of the press, and among my colleagues. The records of these interactions provided a supplementary source of data on how this topic does or does not fit into international rights discourse.

9. On children of rape in contemporary hotspots, see Kathy Evans, "Legacy of War: Kuwait's Littlest Victims," *Calgary Herald*, July 29, 1993, B4; Stacy Sullivan, "Born under a Bad Sign," *Newsweek*, September 23, 1996, 49; Helena Smith, "Rape Victims Babies Pay the Price of War," *Observer*, April 16, 2000, 1–5; Siam Powell, "East Timor's Children of the Enemy," *Weekend Australian*, March 10, 2001, 1; Emily Wax, "Rwandans Struggle to Love Children of Hate," *Washington Post*, March 29, 2004, 24; Sudarsan Raghavan, "Rape Victims, Babies Face Future Labeled as Outcasts," *Miami Herald*, December 7, 2004, http://www.peace-women.org/news/Sudan/Dec04/outcasts.html/ (accessed September 5, 2007). On children of foreign soldiers in historical conflicts, see Robert McKelvey, *The Dust of Life: America's Children Abandoned in Vietnam* (Seattle: University of Washington Press, 1999); Olga Rains, Lloyd Rains, and Melynda Jarratt, *Voices of the Left-Behind* (Montreal: Dundurn Press, 2006).

10. Bina D'Costa, "War Babies: The Question of National Honor," http://www.drishtipat.org/1971/docs/warbabies_bina.pdf, excerpted from "The Gendered Construction of Nationalism: From Partition to Creation" (Ph.D. thesis, Australian National University, 2003) (accessed April 15, 2008).

11. Bianifer Nowrojee, *Shattered Lives: Sexual Violence during the Rwandan Genocide and Its Aftermath* (New York: Human Rights Watch, 1996); Marie Mukangendo, "Caring for Children Born of Rape," in *"Born of War": Protecting Children of Sexual Violence Survivors in Conflict Zones*, ed. Charli Carpenter (Bloomfield, Conn.: Kumarian Press, 2007), 40–52.

12. Kai Grieg, *The War Children of the World* (Bergen, Norway: War and Children Identity Project, 2001), http://www.warandchildren.org (accessed September 8, 2007). This report includes, however, children born of exploitative relations between local women and occupation soldiers who are then abandoned by their birth fathers, as well as those born to rape victims. It includes war children who are now adults as well as those under age eighteen.

13. Cynthia Price Cohen, "The United Nations Convention on the Rights of the Child: A Feminist Landmark," *William and Mary Journal of Women and Law* 3 (1997): 29–78.

14. Joana Daniel, "No Man's Child: The War-Rape Orphans" (M.A. thesis, Boltzmann Institute of Human Rights, University of Vienna, 2003); Siobhan McEvoy, "Human Rights Culture and Children Born of Rape," in *"Born of War,"* ed. Carpenter. pp. 49–179.

15. World Health Organization, *Reproductive Health during Conflict and Displacement: A Guide for Program Managers* (Geneva: WHO, 2000); Graca Machel, "The Impact of Armed Conflict on Children: A Critical Review of Progress Made and Obstacles Encountered in Increasing Protection for War-Affected Children" (Winnipeg, Manitoba: International Conference on War-Affected Children, 2000); Rehn and Sirleaf, *Women, War and Peace*; Charlotte Lindsey, *Women Facing War* (Geneva: ICRC, 2001); United Nations Secretary General, *Women, Peace and Security: Study for the Secretary General pursuant to Security Council Resolution 1325 (2000)* (New York: United Nations, 2002).

16. Robyn Carpenter, "Surfacing Children: Limitations of Genocidal Rape Discourse," *Human Rights Quarterly* 22, no. 2 (2000): 428–77; Daniel, "No Man's Child"; Patricia Weitsman, "The Discourse of Rape in Wartime: Sexual Violence, War Babies and Identity," paper presented at the annual meeting of the International Studies Association, February 26–March 1, 2003.

17. Becirbasic Belma and Dzenana Secic, "Invisible Casualties of War" (London: Institute for War and Peace Reporting, 2002), http://www.bosnia.org.uk/

news/news_body.cfm?newsid=1666 (accessed September 9, 2007); Lydia Polgreen, "Darfur's Babies of Rape Are on Trial from Birth," *New York Times*, February 11, 2005, A1.

18. Gatekeepers are powerful and well-recognized organizations "whose decisions to back a [cause] activate other organizations and individuals across the world." Clifford Bob, *The Marketing of Rebellion: Insurgents, Media and International Activism* (New York: Cambridge University Press, 2005), 18.

19. Based on the density of in-links on the Internet as well as a number of verbal references to organizations in interviews and focus groups, the most influential hubs in this issue network include UNICEF, the UN Office of the Special Representative to the Secretary-General for Children and Armed Conflict (OSRSG), Save the Children Federation, the Watchlist for Children and Armed Conflict, and the Child Rights Information Network.

20. By contrast, 76 percent of websites mentioned child soldiers, 70 percent mentioned children separated from their families or orphans, 60 percent mentioned displaced children, and 36 percent mentioned girls as particular categories of concern. The thirty-three organizations were identified using a manual hyperlink analysis, beginning with the Watchlist on Children and Armed Conflict website and including every linked organization within three degrees of separation whose site contained a web page specifically focused on children and armed conflict as a multi-issue policy area. For the complete results of this study, see Carpenter, "Setting the Advocacy Agenda."

21. Almost all practitioners with whom I have spoken report that programming earmarked for war babies is nonexistent. Conversely, many practitioners claim that although war babies are not singled out for attention, this does not necessarily mean that they are underserved. Without local assessment, however, it is impossible to tell whether this is the case.

22. Personal interview, Sarajevo, Bosnia and Herzegovina, April 2004.

23. Personal correspondence, June 2004.

24. The agenda-setting influence of academics can be illustrated by the following example. A UNICEF program officer in Sarajevo told me that he first began thinking about this category of child when he did an interview with a researcher, Joana Daniel, for her M.A. thesis on children of rape. "It surprised me to realize that UNICEF of all places would have paid so little attention to this issue," he said. Later he spearheaded the first UN fact-finding study on Bosnia's children of rape. However, efforts in New York seemed driven by other dynamics.

25. Isabel Matheson, "Darfur War Breeds 'Dirty Babies,'" *BBC Online*, December 15, 2004, http://news.bbc.co.uk/2/hi/africa/4099601.stm (accessed September 8, 2007); Raghavan, 2004.

26. Personal correspondence, June 2004.

27. Zeid Al-Hussein, *A Comprehensive Strategy to Eliminate Sexual Exploitation and Abuse in U.N. Peacekeeping Operations*, UN Doc A/59/710, 2005.

28. To some extent the perception that one can adequately protect the babies by meeting the mothers' needs may stem from the particular configuration of gender discourse prevalent at UNICEF as an organization. In Maggie Black's words, "From the moment of its birth, UNICEF accepted as a matter of course that the well-being of children was inseparable from the well-being of those in whose wombs they were conceived." Maggie Black, *Children First: The Story of UNICEF, Past and Present* (Oxford: Oxford University Press, 1996), 183.

29. This decision was extremely significant insofar as "U.N. policy is driven by

the issuance of certain reports and studies that are, in turn, adopted as Security Council resolutions." Angela Raven-Roberts, "Gender Mainstreaming in United Nations Peacekeeping Operations: Talking the Talk, Tripping over the Walk," in *Gender, Conflict and Peacekeeping*, ed. Dyan Mazurana, Angela Raven-Roberts, and Jane Parpart (New York: Rowman and Littlefield), 43–64. The decision not to circulate a given report (as well as the decision not to fund a study in the first place) constitutes a decision not to adopt or advocate for an issue within UN institutions.

30. UNICEF, "Children Born of Sexual Violence."

31. Focus groups at the University of Pittsburgh with humanitarian practitioners in 2004–5 found that far more participants drew linkages between these babies' needs and the umbrella issue of sexual violence than with the umbrella issue of child protection. See Charli Carpenter, "Studying Issue (Non)-Adoption in Transnational Advocacy Networks," *International Organization* 61, no. 2 (2007): 643–67.

32. Ibid.

33. Focus group transcript, New York, December 2004, on file with author.

34. UNICEF, "Children Born of Sexual Violence."

35. Carpenter et al., *Protecting Children Born of Sexual Violence.*

36. This is particularly obvious when it comes to women's advocates' understanding of infanticide as a human rights problem. "It is absolutely vital," said one women's rights activist, "that we not treat [rape survivors who kill their infants] as cold-blooded murderers." A participant in a focus group argued that "in cases where the woman has no other options, I have to say that I don't think infanticide is an impermissible alternative." And one renowned author on forced pregnancy argued that infanticide against such babies by their mothers "might be considered healthy." Beverly Allen, *Rape Warfare: The Hidden Genocide in Bosnia-Herzegovina and Croatia* (Minneapolis: University of Minnesota Press, 1996), 99. Such arguments are made through the lens of women's human rights rather than child rights and demonstrate that the two are not always unproblematically interchangeable, as is sometimes assumed in human rights discourse. See Charli Carpenter, "'Women, Children and Other Vulnerable Groups': Gender, Strategic Frames and the Protection of Civilians as a Transnational Issue," *International Studies Quarterly* 49, no. 2 (2005): 295–334. One Ugandan study found that demobilized girl soldiers who conceived as a result of sexual slavery gave the babies names such as "A bad thing happened to me." See Eunice Apio, "Challenges of Integrating Children Born in Armed Conflict: A Study of Children Born of the Lord's Resistance Army, Gulu Municipality, 1990–2003" (M.A. thesis, Makerere University, 2002).

37. Carpenter, "Setting the Advocacy Agenda."

38. Margaret Keck and Kathryn Sikkink, *Activists beyond Borders: Advocacy Networks in International Politics* (Ithaca, N.Y.: Cornell University Press, 1998), distinguish between problems, issues, and campaigns. In the human rights area, problems are preexisting grievances that may not yet have been defined as issues. Issues are created when advocates name a problem as a human rights violation and put it on the agenda. For example, the capture and covert execution of dissidents has been a problem throughout history but only emerged as an issue when Amnesty International defined the concept of "disappearances." Campaigns involve concerted efforts by multiple organizations lobbying for specific outcomes around a certain issue. Campaigns and coalitions sometimes form around, but are distinct from, specific issues. See Sanjeev Khagram, James Riker,

and Kathryn Sikkink, "From Santiago to Seattle: Transnational Advocacy Groups Restructuring World Politics," in *Restructuring World Politics: Transnational Social Movements, Networks and Norms*, ed. Sanjeev Khagram, James Riker, and Kathryn Sikkink (Minneapolis: University of Minnesota Press, 2002), 3–24. Thus the Campaign to Stop the Use of Child Soldiers was a campaign around the issue of child soldiers, aimed specifically at codifying a prohibition on child recruitment in international law (and now, at encouraging ratification). The child soldiers issue, however, is much broader, as is the issue pool within the "children and armed conflict" network. Most of these issues do not result in specific campaigns. Here we are interested in how problems become identified as issues.

39. Keck and Sikkink, *Activists beyond Borders*, 26–28.

40. Martha Finnemore and Kathryn Sikkink, "Taking Stock: The Constructivist Research Program in International Relations and Comparative Politics," *Annual Review of Political Science* 4, no. 1 (2001): 391–416; Ethan Nadelmann, "Global Prohibition Regimes: The Evolution of Norms in International Society," *International Organization* 44, no. 4 (1990): 479–526; David H. Lumsdaine, *Moral Vision in International Politics: The Foreign Aid Regime, 1949–1989* (Princeton, N.J.: Princeton University Press, 1993); Richard Price, "Reversing the Gun Sights: Transnational Civil Society Targets Land Mines," *International Organization* 52, no. 3 (1998): 613–44.

41. This perspective, associated in particular with Richard Price's work on weapons taboos, suggests that the promotion of new moral standards is most likely to succeed if these can be grafted onto preexisting taboos. For example, the chemical weapons taboo was popularized partly because it built on an earlier prohibition on the use of poisons in warfare. See Richard Price and Nina Tannenwald, "Norms and Deterrence: The Nuclear and Chemical Weapons Taboos," in *The Culture of National Security: Norms and Identity in World Politics*, ed. Peter J. Katzenstein (New York: Columbia University Press, 1996), 114–53. Advocates of the Ottawa Convention banning antipersonnel landmines sought to move debate over landmines away from arms control discourse and graft it onto the relatively robust norm of civilian immunity by emphasizing landmines' indiscriminate effects. Price, "Reversing the Gun Sights."

42. This might be viewed as one example of a broader rhetorical strategy deployed by policy gatekeepers to block policy changes. Joshua Busby describes a similar type of norm-based strategy deployed by conservatives early in the Jubilee 2000 debt relief campaign to resist the idea of debt forgiveness. The idea was resisted not merely for material reasons but by the argument that it would do more harm than good, enabling corrupt regimes. See Joshua Busby, "Bono Made Jesse Helms Cry: Jubilee 2000, Debt Relief, and Moral Action in International Politics," *International Studies Quarterly* 51, no. 2 (2007): 247–75.

43. Personal interview, New York, June 2005.

44. Focus group, Geneva, Switzerland, February 2005.

45. For more in-depth discussion of this issue, see the essays in Carpenter, *Born of War*.

46. For example, while "women and children" is often treated as a single constituency in advocacy discourse, hyperlink analysis of the organizations "doing" women and armed conflict overlap with those organizations "doing" children and armed conflict by only 60 percent, suggesting that these are distinct, though highly interdependent, advocacy communities. Carpenter, "Women, Children and Other Vulnerable Groups."

47. Mische, "Cross-Talk in Movements," 261.
48. Tarrow, *New Transnational Activism*, 165.
49. Personal interview, June 2003.
50. Personal interview, August 2003.
51. Tarrow, *New Transnational Activism*, 165.
52. Heated disagreements broke out within several focus groups about whether to conceptualize infanticide as a crime against an infant or against the mother, insofar as the situation 'forced her' to kill her baby. Others held that infanticide should not be considered criminal at all because in some ways it constituted the mother's last best avenue to exercise self-determination. As important as the clear-cut causal chain described by Keck and Sikkink may be, the question of where the chain leads is also critical. Politically acceptable perpetrators may be as or more important than politically acceptable victims. According to one interviewee, "With trafficking questions you can follow them, blame the evil traffickers; here, you're delving into a much more intimate and personal realm and there are those fine lines and no one knows what to do with them." Personal interview, New York, June 2005.
53. Mische, "Cross-Talk in Movements."
54. Telephone interview, UNICEF consultant, December 2005.
55. Personal interview, UN OSRSG staff person, August 2003.
56. Some other cases in which activists have unsuccessfully attempted to pitch issues as human rights abuses to gatekeepers include the campaigns to treat infant male circumcision as genital mutilation and to outlaw conscription in national armies. If the referent point is "categories of concern" rather than rights specifically, current examples of vulnerable populations lacking advocacy attention would include the needs of the able-bodied disfigured in war-torn societies or, until quite recently, girl soldiers. A methodology for identifying a population of non-issues for comparison within specific advocacy arenas is presented in Charli Carpenter, "Governing the Global Agenda: 'Gatekeepers' and 'Issue Adoption' in Transnational Advocacy Networks," working paper, presented at the Global Governors Working Group, George Washington University, 2007.
57. Jutta Joachim, "Framing Issues and Seizing Opportunities: The U.N., NGOs and Women's Rights," *International Studies Quarterly* 47, no. 2 (2003): 247–74.
58. Keck and Sikkink *Activists beyond Borders*.
59. David S. Meyer and Nancy Whittier, "Social Movement Spillover," *Social Problems* 41, no. 2 (1994): 277–98.

Chapter 3. "Dalit Rights Are Human Rights"

Originally published in a slightly different form as Clifford Bob, "'Dalit Rights Are Human Rights': Caste Discrimination, International Activism, and the Construction of a New Human Rights Issue," *Human Rights Quarterly* 29, no. 1 (February 2007): 167–93. Reprinted by permission of the publisher.
1. A word in the Marathi language of western India, "Dalit" means "broken up," "ground to pieces," or "oppressed." Popularized by Dalit leader Dr. B. R. Ambedkar during India's colonial period, the term is the self-identification preferred by those seeking to internationalize issues of caste discrimination. In domestic Indian politics, the term is also commonly, although not uniformly, utilized. In this chapter, I use the term "Dalit" to discuss contemporary attempts to

internationalize issues of caste discrimination, whereas I use "Untouchable" to discuss historical or nonpolitical issues. Gandhi's term for the group, *"Harijan"* (People of God), achieved some popularity during the late colonial and early independence eras. However, as part of broader Untouchable conflict with Gandhi and the Congress Party, *"Harijan"* was long attacked as patronizing; it is little used in contemporary Dalit politics. In 1936, the British developed a "schedule" of Untouchable castes who would receive various compensatory benefits from the colonial state, and these schedules have been maintained since Independence. The terms "scheduled castes" and "SCs" remain common in Indian legal discourse today but do not have the political resonance of "Dalit." For discussion of the politics of group naming, see Oliver Mendelsohn and Marika Viiczany, *The Untouchables: Subordination, Poverty and the State in Modern India* (New York: Cambridge University Press, 1998), 2–5 .

2. Ibid., 1; Human Rights Watch, *Broken People: Caste Violence against India's "Untouchables"* (New York: Human Rights Watch, 1999).

3. Human Rights Watch, *Caste Discrimination: A Global Concern* (New York: Human Rights Watch, 2001), 1.

4. Ibid.

5. See, e.g., Rajakrishnan Ramasamy, *Caste Consciousness among Indian Tamils in Malaysia* (Petaling Jaya, Malaysia: Pelanduk, 1984); Expanded Working Paper on Discrimination Based on Work and Descent Submitted by Mr. Asbjørn Eide and Mr. Yozo Yokota, UN ESCOR, Comm'n Hum. Rts., Sub-Comm'n Promot. Protect. Hum. Rts., 56th sess., Prov'l Agenda Item 5, UN Doc. E/CN.4/Sub.2/2004/31 (2004). Countries covered by the report included Burkina Faso, India, Japan, Kenya, Mali, Federated States of Micronesia, Nepal, Pakistan, Senegal, Sri Lanka, and Yemen.

6. See Mendelsohn and Vicziany, *Untouchables*, 2–5.

7. Keck and Sikkink define TANs as loosely formed groupings of NGOs, activists, foundations, journalists, bureaucrats, and others all bound by "shared values, a common discourse, and dense exchanges of information and services." Margaret E. Keck and Kathryn Sikkink, *Activists beyond Borders: Advocacy Networks in International Politics* (Ithaca, N.Y.: Cornell University Press, 1998). See also Ann M. Florini, ed., *The Third Force: The Rise of Transnational Civil Society* (Washington, D.C.: Brookings Institution, 2000); Thomas Risse, Stephen C. Ropp, and Kathryn Sikkink, eds., *The Power of Human Rights: International Norms and Domestic Change* (Cambridge: Cambridge University Press, 1999).

8. Universal Declaration of Human Rights (UDHR), adopted December 10, 1948, G.A. Res. 217A (III), UN GAOR, 3d sess. (Resolutions, pt. 1), 71, UN Doc. A/810 (1948); International Covenant on Civil and Political Rights (ICCPR), adopted December 16, 1966, G.A. Res. 2200 (XXI), UN GAOR, 21st sess., supp. no. 16, UN Doc. A/6316 (1966), 999 UNTS 171 (entered into force March 23, 1976); International Covenant on Economic, Social and Cultural Rights (ICESCR), adopted December 16, 1966, G.A. Res. 2200 (XXI), UN GAOR, 21st sess., supp. no. 16, art. 15, UN Doc. A/6316 (1966), 993 UNT.S. 3 (entered into force January 3, 1976); International Convention on the Elimination of All Forms of Racial Discrimination (ICERD), adopted December 21, 1965, 660 UNT.S. 195 (entered into force January 4, 1969).

9. Clifford Bob, *The Marketing of Rebellion: Insurgents, Media, and International Activism* (New York: Cambridge University Press, 2005).

10. Mendelsohn and Vicziany, *Untouchables*.

11. Ibid.

12. Ibid.

13. Christophe Jaffrelot, "Sanskritization vs. Ethnicization in India: Changing Identities and Caste Politics before Mandal," *Asian Survey* 40, no. 5 (2000): 756–66.

14. Mendelsohn and Vicziany, *Untouchables.*

15. Christophe Jaffrelot, *Dr. Ambedkar and Untouchability: Fighting the Indian Caste System* (New York: Columbia University Press, 2004).

16. Even after conversion, however, many Untouchables still suffer discrimination not only from Hindus but also from members of their new communities.

17. For discussion of Gandhi's views, see Christophe Jaffrelot, *India's Silent Revolution: The Rise of the Lower Castes in North India* (New York: Columbia University Press, 2003), 11–32; Mendelsohn and Vicziany, *Untouchables.*

18. Jaffrelot, *India's Silent Revolution.*

19. Ibid.

20. For further discussion of Ambedkar's views, his conflicts with Gandhi, and the important compromises he made in the Poona Pact, see Jaffrelot, *India's Silent Revolution*, 19–25; Eleanor Zelliot, *From Untouchable to Dalit: Essays on the Ambedkar Movement* (New Delhi: Manohar, 1992).

21. For political and legal aspects of the reservation system, see Marc Galanter, *Competing Equalities: Law and the Backward Classes in India* (Berkeley: University of California Press, 1984). Reservations also cover the "scheduled tribes," indigenous groups found in India.

22. Myron Weiner, *The Child and the State in India: Child Labor and Education Policy in Comparative Perspective* (Princeton, N.J.: Princeton University Press, 1991), 3–5.

23. National Human Rights Commission, "Central and State Authorities Urged to Prevent Atrocities against SCs: NHRC Releases Report on Atrocities against SCs," October 19, 2004, http://www.nhrc.nic.in/disparchive.asp?fno=837 (accessed January 25, 2008); Human Rights Watch, *Broken People.*

24. For detailed discussion of the rise of Untouchable and lower caste parties in north India, see Jaffrelot, *India's Silent Revolution;* Ghanshyam Shah, ed., *Dalit Identity and Politics: Cultural Subordination and the Dalit Challenge* (New Delhi: Sage Publications, 2001).

25. Sudha Pai, *Dalit Assertion and the Unfinished Democratic Revolution: The Bahujan Samaj Party in Uttar Pradesh* (New Delhi: Sage Publications, 2002).

26. Mendelsohn and Vicziany, *Untouchables.*

27. Francine R. Frankel, "Caste, Land and Dominance in Bihar: Breakdown of the Brahmanical Social Order," in *Dominance and State Power in Modern India: Decline of a Social Order,* ed. Francine R. Frankel and M. S. A. Rao (Oxford: Oxford University Press, 1989).

28. Eva-Maria Hardtmann, *"Our Fury Is Burning": Local Practice and Global Connections in the Dalit Movement* (Stockholm: Almquist and Wiksell International, 2003), 150–82; John C. B. Webster, *Religion and Dalit Liberation: An Examination of Perspectives* (New Delhi: Manohar, 2002); Christopher S. Queen, *Engaged Buddhism in the West* (Boston: Wisdom, 2000).

29. Fourteenth Periodic Reports of States Parties Due in 1996: India, 4/29/96, Committee on the Elimination of Racial Discrimination (CERD), 49th sess., UN Doc. CERD/C/299/Add.3 (State Party Report, 1996).

30. For examples of these arguments, see ibid.

31. Barbara Joshi, ed., *Untouchable! Voices of the Dalit Liberation Movement* (London: Zed Books, 1986).

32. Ibid.; telephone interview with ACJP leader, April 26, 2001; telephone interviews with Human Rights Watch staff person, April 10, 20, 2001; personal interview with Human Rights Watch manager, March 14, 2001; personal interview with Dalit Liberation Education Trust leader, in Buffalo, New York, October 15, 2004. Consistent with Duquesne University's Institutional Review Board approval for my research, I audiotaped my interviews and granted my informants confidentiality. Audiotapes are on file in Special Collections, Gumberg Library, Duquesne University.

33. Joshi, *Untouchable!*

34. Held in New York City, the conference had among its sponsors Columbia University, the City University of New York, the New York Council for the Humanities, the Ford Foundation, the Smithsonian Institution, and the National Science Foundation. See ibid.

35. See, e.g., Bob, *Marketing of Rebellion.*

36. Telephone interview with ACJP leader.

37. See Joshi, *Untouchable!* (testimony of Laxmi Berwa to UN Sub-commission on Human Rights, August 31, 1982).

38. Ibid., 137.

39. ACJP, "Accomplishments of Ambedkar Center for Justice and Peace in Internationalizing the Dalit Issue in the Last 15 Years," http:/www.web.net/~acjp/accomplish.html (accessed January 25, 2008).

40. ICERD, Art. 1 (emphasis added). India ratified ICERD in 1969.

41. See, e.g., Fourteenth Periodic Reports, para. 7. Notably, in its periodic reports under ICERD, India did provide limited information on the situation of the scheduled castes as a "courtesy" to the treaty committee.

42. Ibid.

43. Concluding Observations of the Committee on the Elimination of Racial Discrimination: India, 9/17/96, CERD, 49th sess., UN Doc. CERD/C/304/Add.13 (Concluding Observations/Comments), para. 14 (1996).

44. Ibid.

45. Human Rights Watch, *India: Politics by Other Means: Attacks against Christians in India* (New York: Human Rights Watch, 1999).

46. Interview with ACJP leader; interviews with Human Rights Watch staff person; interview with Human Rights Watch manager.

47. Telephone interview with Ford Foundation program officer, May 16, 2001.

48. Ibid.

49. Ibid. With its long experience in India, the Ford Foundation identified some of the Dalit civil society organizations invited to attend the planning meeting.

50. NCDHR, Signature campaign sheet, folder 3: Memorandum to PM 1999, in NCDHR, *Dalit Rights: Advocacy Materials & Documents* (Compact disk, 2002).

51. Ibid.

52. Ibid. (emphasis in original).

53. NCDHR, Signature campaign back cover, folder 3: Memorandum to PM 1999, in NCDHR, *Dalit Rights.*

54. First World Dalit Convention, "Declaration," http:/www.ambedkar.org/Worldwide_Dalits/first_world_dalit_convention.htm (accessed January 25, 2008).

55. International Dalit Solidarity Network (IDSN), http://www.idsn.org/ (accessed January 25, 2008.

56. Ibid. IDSN's international associates are Human Rights Watch, International Movement against All Forms of Discrimination and Racism, Lutheran

World Federation, Asian Human Rights Commission, Minority Rights Group International, Anti-Slavery International, Robert F. Kennedy Memorial Foundation, ICMICA/Pax Romana, World Council of Churches, FORUM-ASIA, Commonwealth Human Rights Initiative, and Franciscans International. Dalit solidarity networks have been established in the United Kingdom, France, Germany, the Netherlands, Denmark, Sweden, and the United States. Ibid.

57. See NCDHR, black paper, in NCDHR, *Dalit Rights.*

58. See NCDHR, Signature campaign front cover, folder 3, in NCDHR, *Dalit Rights.*

59. Telephone interview with Unitarian Universalist Holdeen India program manager, May 1, 2001; telephone interview with Robert F. Kennedy Memorial manager, May 2, 2001.

60. Barbara Crossette, "An 'Untouchable' Says Caste Is Truly a Human Rights Issue," *New York Times*, November 16, 2000, A6.

61. Discrimination Based on Work and Descent: Sub-Commission on Human Rights Resolution 2000/4, UN ESCOR, Comm'n Hum. Rts., Sub-Comm'n Promot. Protect. Hum. Rts., 52nd sess., 17th mtg., para. 1, UN Doc. E/CN.4/Sub.2/Res/2000/4 (2000).

62. Ibid.

63. Ibid.

64. Working paper by Rajendra Kalidas Wimala Goonesekere on the Topic of Discrimination Based on Work and Descent, Submitted Pursuant to the Sub-Commission Resolution 2000/4, UN ESCOR, Comm'n Hum. Rts., Sub-Comm'n Promot. Protect. Hum. Rts., 53rd sess., Prov'l agenda item 5, UN Doc. E/CN.4/Sub.2/2001/16 (2001).

65. Ibid., para. 1.

66. Ibid., para. 7.

67. Ibid.

68. Ibid.

69. Ibid., para. 9.

70. Ibid., para. 49.

71. Expanded Working Paper Submitted by Asbjørn Eide and Yozo Yokota Pursuant to Sub-Commission Decision 2002/108, UN ESCOR, Comm'n Hum. Rts., Sub-Comm'n Promot. Protect. Hum. Rts., 55th sess., Prov'l agenda item 5, para. 58, UN Doc. E/CN.4/Sub.2/2003/24 (2003).

72. Ibid., para. 7.

73. Ibid.

74. Ibid.

75. Discrimination Based on Work and Descent: Sub-Commission on Human Rights Resolution 2004/17, UN ESCOR, Comm'n Hum. Rts., Sub-Comm'n Promot. Protect. Hum. Rts., 56th sess., Prov'l agenda item 5, UN Doc.E/CN.4/Sub.2/Res/2004/17 (2004).

76. See IDSN, "Dalits Break through UN Wall of Silence on Caste," http://www.idsn.org/documents/un/pdf/chrmedia.pdf (accessed January 10, 2005).

77. NCDHR, "World Conference against Racism," http://www.dalits.org/WCAR.htm (accessed December 5, 2001).

78. Yogesh Varhade, "UN Prepcom for WCAR, Geneva May 1–5, 2000 and Dalit 'Traitors,'" (undated), http://www.ambedkar.org/UN/UN%20Prepcom.htm (accessed January 25, 2008).

79. See, e.g., "India: Govt. Flayed for Denying Visas," *Hindu*, February 28,

2001, http://www.hinduonnet.com/2001/02/28/stories/0228000f.htm (accessed January 25, 2008); Human Rights Watch, "Indian Government Tries to Block Caste Discussion," February 22, 2001, hrw.org/english/docs/2001/02/22/india270.htm (accessed January 25, 2008).

80. World Conference against Racism, Racial Discrimination, Xenophobia and Related Intolerance (WCAR), "Draft Programme of Action (Item 9 of the Provisional Agenda)," para. 73 (2001), http://www.racism.gov.za/substance/confdoc/themespoa.htm (accessed January 25, 2008).

81. WCAR, "India: Statement by H. E. Mr. Omar Abdullah," September 2, 2001, http://www.un.org/WCAR/statements/indiaE.htm (accessed January 25, 2008).

82. General Recommendation 29, article 1, para. 1 (Descent), CERD, 61st sess., UN Doc. CERD/C/61/Misc.29/rev.1 (2002).

83. Ibid. In addition, General Recommendation 29 urged that in implementing these measures states take cognizance of multiple discrimination faced by women members of "descent-based communities."

84. Ibid.

85. Ambassador Piet de Klerk, human rights ambassador of the Netherlands, speech before the "Stop Caste Discrimination—Support the Dalits" campaign, Utrecht, the Netherlands (October 9, 2004), http://www.idsn.org/tekst/developments.htm (accessed January 25, 2008).

86. European Parliament, "Annual Report on Human Rights in the World in 2002 and European Union's Human Rights Policy," 2002/2011(INI), para. 55 (2003).

87. Amy Gutmann, Introduction, in *Human Rights as Politics and Idolatry*, ed. Michael Ignatieff (Princeton, N.J.: Princeton University Press, 2001), vii–x.

88. Sidney Tarrow, *Power in Movement: Social Movements and Contentious Politics* (New York: Cambridge University Press, 1998), 176–95.

89. Susan Burgerman, *Moral Victories: How Activists Provoke Multilateral Action* (Ithaca, N.Y.: Cornell University Press, 2001).

90. NCDHR, Memorandum, folder 1: Inaugural Folder: Campaign Initial Memorandum, in NCDHR, *Dalit Rights*.

91. Ibid.

92. See Keck and Sikkink, *Activists beyond Borders*, 27.

93. See National Human Rights Commission, "Central and State Authorities Urged to Prevent Atrocities against SCs." Others have argued as well that state incapacity or lack of resources provides only a partial explanation for continuing discrimination and violence against Untouchables—and that caste-based discrimination, pervading both society and state, is the critical factor. See, e.g., Weiner, *Child and the State.*

94. See Hardtmann, *"Our Fury Is Burning."*

95. Ibid., 216–20.

96. IDSN, "Explaining Caste Systems," http://www.idsn.org/ (accessed January 25, 2008).

97. IDSN, "Dalits Break through the UN Wall of Silence," www.idsn.org/documents/un/pdf/chrmedia.pdf (including a link to the UN Sub-commission resolution) (accessed June 5, 2006). For further discussion of this dynamic during the period preceding the WCAR, see Hardtmann, *"Our Fury Is Burning."*

98. See, e.g., Human Rights Watch, *India: Politics by Other Means.*

99. NCDHR, Signature campaign sheet, folder 3: Memorandum to PM 1999, in NCDHR, *Dalit Rights*.

100. Peter N. Prove, "Working Paper on Discrimination on the Basis of Work and Descent: Call for Submissions," http://www.ambedkar.org/UN/WorkingPaper.htm (accessed January 25, 2008).

101. IDSN website, http://www.idsn.org/index.htm (accessed January 25, 2008).

102. Despite its democracy, however, India's human rights record is mixed. See Caroline Beer and Neil Mitchell, "Comparing Nations and States: Human Rights and Democracy in India," *Comparative Political Studies* 39, no. 8 (2006): 996–1018.

Chapter 4. Applying the Gatekeeper Model of Human Rights Activism

1. Wendy Wong, "Narrowing the Options: The Formation of Human Rights Norms in Amnesty International's Network, 1961–1980," paper presented to the 2007 annual meeting of the American Political Science Association annual meeting, August 30–September 1, 2007.

2. Amnesty International, "The Campaign to Eradicate Female Genital Mutilation: A Role for Amnesty International," October 1, 1997, http://www.amnesty.org/ailib/intcam/femgen/fgm3.htm (accessed April 25, 2006).

3. Stephen Hopgood, *Keepers of the Flame: Understanding Amnesty International* (Ithaca, N.Y.: Cornell University Press, 2006), 4.

4. Ibid., 7.

5. Ibid. See also Tom Buchanan, "'The Truth Will Set You Free': The Making of Amnesty International," *Journal of Contemporary History* 37, no. 4 (2002): 575–97.

6. See Peter R. Baehr, "Amnesty International and Its Self-Imposed Limited Mandate," *Netherlands Quarterly of Human Rights* 12, no. 2 (1994): 5–21.

7. Amnesty International, "About Amnesty International," http://www.amnesty.org/en/who-we-are/about-amnesty-international (accessed May 1 2007).

8. Amnesty International, "Amnesty International's Statute," http://www.amnesty.org/en/who-we-are/accountability/statute (accessed December 4, 2007).

9. Ibid.

10. "AI and Homosexuality," November 1986, from the head of the Research Department, POL, 03/IEC 12/86, quoted in Hopgood, *Keepers of the Flame*, 117.

11. Author interview with AI activist Nancy Flowers, Baltimore, Maryland, July 7, 2007.

12. Hopgood, *Keepers of the Flame*, 117.

13. Ibid.

14. Author interview with AI activist Cynthia Rothschild, August 18, 2007.

15. Decision 7 of AI's 1979 International Council Meeting.

16. Author interview with Flowers.

17. Author interview with Rothschild.

18. See Hopgood, *Keepers of the Flame*, 95–100.

19. Ibid., 117.

20. Laurence Helfer and Alice Miller, "Sexual Orientation and Human Rights: Toward a United States and Transnational Jurisprudence," *Harvard Human Rights Journal* 9 (1996): 61–103.

21. See, e.g., Amnesty International, "Cameroon: Twelve Female Students Expelled from School on Suspicion of Being Lesbians," http://www.amnestyusa.org/Country_Information/Cameroon/page.do?id=1106557&n1=3&n2=36&n

3=1040 (accessed January 25, 2008); Amnesty International, "Uganda: Lesbian, Gay, Bisexual and Transgender People Targeted," August 29, 2006, http://web.amnesty.org/library/Index/ENGAFR590062006?open&of=ENG-UGA (accessed January 25, 2008); Amnesty International, "Stonewalled—Still Demanding Respect: Police Abuses against Lesbian, Gay, Bisexual and Transgender People in the USA," March 23, 2006, http://web.amnesty.org/library/index/engamr510012006 (accessed January 25, 2008); Amnesty International, "PR China: Possible Disappearance of Dr. Wan Yanhai," September 3, 2002, http://action.web.ca/home/lgbt/alerts.shtml?x=18407 (accessed January 25, 2008).

22. Gary Pool, "Filling the Gaps in Amnesty International's Freedom College," *Humanist*, November–December 1997, http://findarticles.com/p/articles/mi_m1374/is_n6_v57/ai_19989937/pg_3 (accessed January 25, 2008).

23. Amnesty International, *Breaking the Silence* (New York: Amnesty International, 1994). AI-UK followed up with a significantly rewritten second edition in 1997.

24. Amnesty International, "Crimes of Hate, Conspiracy of Silence: Torture and Ill-Treatment Based on Sexual Identity," June 22, 2001, http://web.amnesty.org/library/index/engact400162001 (accessed January 25, 2008).

25. Ibid.

26. See Behind the Mask, "Amnesty International Calls for Adoption of Resolution on Sexual Orientation at UN Commission on Human Rights," April 23, 2003, http://www.mask.org.za/article.php?cat=&id=29 (accessed January 25, 2008).

27. See Amnesty International Lesbian, Gay, Bisexual and Transgender Network (AILGBTN), http://www.ai-lgbt.org (accessed January 25, 2008).

28. See Amnesty International USA, "OUTfront: Lesbian, Gay, Bisexual and Transgender Human Rights," http://www.amnestyusa.org/outfront (accessed January 25, 2008).

29. AILGBTN, "General Info: Gay and Bisexual Issues," http://www.ai-lgbt.org/general_info.htm (accessed January 25, 2008).

30. Amnesty International OUTfront, "Human Rights Concerns: Breaking the Silence," http://www.amnestyusa.org/outfront/dangerousliving/About OUTfront.doc (accessed January 25, 2008).

31. Author interview with Rothschild.

32. As the AI-Canada web page states: "Amnesty has widened its focus beyond freedom of opinion. Today we oppose human rights abuses based on discrimination: 'identity-based' abuses. Amnesty members now work for people who are targeted because of how they are seen—in discriminatory ways—by others. Examples include lesbian and gay people, Indigenous people and women." Amnesty International Canada, "History—Changing World: New Directions for Amnesty," http://www.amnesty.ca/about/history/history_of_amnesty_international/changing_world.php (accessed January 25, 2008).

33. See Jeri Laber, *The Courage of Strangers: Coming of Age with the Human Rights Movement* (New York: Public Affairs, 2002).

34. The author, who absorbed this comment, was the only openly gay researcher. At the time, one secretary and one program assistant could also be counted as out-of-the-closet employees, making the count three out of about one hundred employees. (Note: The quotations in this paragraph are reconstructions, not verbatim accounts.)

35. These statements refer to the author's experiences at HRW in 1993–94.

36. This observation is drawn from the author's participation in human rights activism at the time, including service on the board of directors of the IGLHRC.

37. However, the public statements of the Women's Rights Division carefully avoided reference to "lesbians," "LGBT," or "sexual orientation" as issues it "work[s] on." The division's website states: "We work on issues relating to a vast array of women's concerns, including women workers, domestic violence, sexual violence, women and HIV/AIDS, women and armed conflict, international justice, trafficking, refugees and internally displaced persons, gender-based asylum claims, women's status in the family, women's legal status, women in state custody, sexual autonomy, and reproductive rights." Human Rights Watch, "Frequently Asked Questions about the Women's Rights Division of Human Rights Watch," http://www.hrw.org/women/faq.html (accessed January 25, 2008; web page states that it was last updated in 2006).

38. Ibid.

39. IGLHRC website, http://www.iglhrc.org (accessed January 16, 2008).

40. See Human Rights Watch and IGLHRC, "Public Scandals: Sexual Orientation and Criminal Law in Romania," January 1998, http://www.hrw.org/ reports97/Romania (accessed January 16, 2008).

41. Author interviews with Scott Long, June 12, 2006; Jessica Stern, June 12, 2007; Cynthia Rothschild, September 2, 2007; and Julie Dorf, October 24, 2007. See also HRW Lesbian, Gay, Bisexual and Transgender Rights Program, http://www.hrw.org/doc/?t=lgbt (accessed January 18, 2008).

42. Human Rights Watch, "Netherlands: Threat to Return Gay and Lesbian Iranians: HRW Letter to Minister Verdonk," March 8, 2006, http://www.hrw .org/english/docs/2006/03/08/nether12776.htm (accessed January 16, 2008).

43. Human Rights Watch, "Guatemala: Transgender People Face Deadly Attacks," February 21, 2006, http://hrw.org/english/docs/2006/02/21/ guatem12696.htm (accessed January 16, 2008).

44. Human Rights Watch, "South Africa Murder Highlights Violence against Lesbians," March 3, 2006, http://hrw.org/english/docs/2006/03/02/safric12753 .htm (accessed January 16, 2008).

45. Human Rights Watch, "Russia: Gay Pride Parade Should Not Be Banned," February 27, 2006, http://hrw.org/english/docs/2006/02/27/russia12728.htm (accessed January 16, 2008).

46. See Human Rights Watch, "In a Time of Torture: The Assault on Justice in Egypt's Crackdown on Homosexual Conduct," March 2004, http://hrw.org/reports/2004/egypt0304/ (accessed January 16, 2008); "Hated to Death: Homophobia, Violence and Jamaica's HIV/AIDS Epidemic," November 2004, http://hrw.org/reports/2004/jamaica1104/ (accessed January 16, 2008).

47. Michael McClintock, *Everyday Fears: A Survey of Violent Hate Crimes in Europe and North America*, August 8, 2005, http://www.humanrightsfirst.org/discrimination/pdf/everyday-fears-intro-080805.pdf (accessed January 16, 2008).

48. International Human Rights Law Group, "Report on the Regional Preparatory Conferences for the Conference on the Americas," 2001, http://www .globalrights.org/site/DocServer/chileprepcomeng.pdf?docID=198 (accessed January 16, 2008). International Human Rights Law Group was later renamed Global Rights.

49. Amnesty International USA, Gender Public Advocacy Coalition, Global Rights, Human Rights Campaign Fund, Immigration Equality, International Gay and Lesbian Human Rights Commission, Lambda Legal Defense & Educa-

tion Fund, Inc., Law and Policy Program of the Columbia School of Public Health, National Center for Lesbian Rights, National Gay and Lesbian Task Force, Sylvia Rivera Law Project, *Lesbian, Gay, Bisexual, Transgender and Intersex Human Rights in the United States: A Shadow Report* (Washington, D.C.: Global Rights, 2006) (on file with author).

50. Yogyakarta Principles, March 2007 (on file with author).

51. Successful candidates are granted either "general category" status, if they are "concerned with most of the activities of the ECOSOC and its subsidiary bodies," or "special category" status, if they "have a special competence in, and are concerned specifically with, only a few of the fields of activity covered by the ECOSOC." Only general category NGOs may propose items for the ECOSOC agenda and circulate statements at ECOSOC meetings. UN Department of Economic and Soocial Affairs, "Consultative Status with ECOSOC," http://www .un.org/esa/coordination/ngo/.

52. See generally ILGA, http://www.ilga.org (accessed January 18, 2008).

53. See Wayne Morgan and Kristen Walker, "Rejecting (In)tolerance: Tolerance and Homosexuality," *Melbourne University Law Review* (1995): 202–24, 213–14.

54. ILGA, "ILGA's Public Stance against Paedophilia and Commitment to the Protection of Children," July 13, 2006, http://www.ilga.org/news_results.asp ?LanguageID=1&FileCategory=10&FileID=861 (accessed January 25, 2008).

55. Douglas Sanders, Kurt Krickler, and Rodney Croome, "Finding a Place in International Law," July 20, 1997, http://www.geocities.com/mhc_human rights/SANDERS.html (January 25, 2008).

56. ILGA, "Unfair Treatment of ILGA's Application at the UN: Ongoing Struggle for LGBT NGOs to Get the Right to Speak at the United Nations in Their Own Name," January 23, 2006, http://ilga.org/news_results.asp?Language ID=1&FileCategory=1&FileID=738 (accessed January 25, 2008).

57. Human Rights Watch, "Letter to US Secretary of State Condoleezza Rice," January 25, 2006, http://hrw.org/english/docs/2006/01/25/iran12536.htm (accessed January 25, 2008).

58. Ibid.

59. ILGA, "Final Petition for LGBT Groups' ECOSOC Status," July 22, 2006, http://www.ilga.org/news_results.asp?LanguageID=1&FileCategoryID=1&FileI D=855&ZoneID=7 (accessed January 25, 2008).

60. ILGA, "UN Credibility at Stake as ECOSOC Addresses Applications of NGOs Working on Sexual Orientation Issues," July 24, 2006, http://www.ilga .org/news_results.asp?LanguageID=1&FileCategoryID=1&FileID=868&ZoneID =7 (accessed January 25, 2008).

61. Ibid.

62. ILGA, "Gaining the Right to Speak in Our Own Name at the United Nations," April 10, 2006, http://www.ilga.org/news_results.asp?LanguageID=1&File ID=936&FileCategory=44&ZoneID=7 (January 25, 2008).

63. ILGA, "ILGA Officially Asks the Latin American and Caribbean Group at the United Nations to Co-Sponsor Brazilian Resolution," April 17, 2004, http://www.ilga.org/news_results_b.asp?FileID=42 (accessed January 25, 2008).

64. Economic and Social Council, "Economic and Social Council Adopts Decisions on Recommendations Contained in Report of Committee on Non-Governmental Organizations," July 20, 2007, http://www.un.org/News/Press/docs/ 2007/ecosoc6301.doc.htm (accessed January 25, 2008).

65. ILGA, "Gaining the Right to Speak at the UN: United Nations Grant Consultative Status to Groups Working to Address Sexual Orientation and Gender

Identity Issues," July 24, 2007, http://www.ilga.org/news_results.asp? LanguageID= 1&FileCategoryID=44&FileID=1090&ZoneID=7 (accessed January 25, 2008).

66. Sonja Licht, "Women as Agents of Change in Conflict and Post-Conflict Situations," September 15, 2002, http://www.lse.ac.uk/Depts/global/Publications/HumanSecurityReport/LichtWomen.pdf (accessed January 25, 2008), 3.

67. See Charlotte Bunch and Niamh Reilly, *Demanding Accountability: The Global Campaign and Vienna Tribunal for Women's Human Rights* (New York: Center for Women's Global Leadership, 1994).

68. See Julie Mertus and Pamela Goldberg, "A Perspective on Women and International Human Rights after the Vienna Declaration: The Inside/Outside Construct," *New York University Review of International Law & Policy* 26 (1994): 201.

69. IGLHRC and Center for Women's Global Leadership, "Written Out: How Sexuality Is Used to Attack Women's Organizing," 2000, http://www.iglhrc.org/files/iglhrc/reports/Written%20Out.pdf (accessed January 25, 2008), 53–70.

70. Sonia Katyal, "Exporting Identity," *Yale Journal of Law and Feminism* 14 (2002): 97–166.

71. See Rosalind P. Petchesky, "Sexual Rights: Inventing a Concept, Mapping an International Concept," in *Framing the Sexual Subject: The Politics of Gender, Sexuality and Power*, ed. Richard Parker, Regina Maria Barbosa, and Peter Aggleton (Berkeley: University of California Press, 1999), 81–101. See also Yasmin Tambiah, "Sexuality and Human Rights," in *From Basic Needs to Basic Rights: Women's Claim to Human Rights*, ed. Marge Schuler (Washington, D.C.: Women, Law, and Development International, 1995).

72. Mark Blaisus, ed., *Sexual Identities, Queer Politics* (Princeton, N.J.: Princeton University Press, 2001), 120.

73. United Nations Population Information Network, "Report of the International Conference on Population and Development," para. 7.2, http://www.un.org/popin/icpd/conference/offeng/poa.html (accessed January 25, 2008).

74. United Nations Fourth World Conference on Women, "Platform for Action," September 1995, para. 96, http://www.un.org/womenwatch/daw/beijing/platform/health.htm#diagnosis (accessed January 25, 2008).

Chapter 5. From Resistance to Receptivity

1. UNAIDS, *2007 AIDS Epidemic Update* (Geneva: UNAIDS, 2007).

2. Tony Barnett and Alan Whiteside, *AIDS in the Twenty-First Century: Disease and Globalization* (Houndsmill, UK: Palgrave Macmillan, 2001); Andrew T. Price-Smith, *The Health of Nations: Infectious Disease, Environmental Change, and Their Effects on National Security and Development* (Cambridge, Mass.: MIT Press, 2001).

3. UNAIDS, "Human Rights and HIV," http://www.unaids.org/en/PolicyAndPractice/HumanRights/default.asp (accessed December 19, 2007).

4. International Federation of Red Cross and Red Crescent Societies, "HIV/AIDS," http://www.ifrc.org/what/health/hivaids/index.asp (accessed July 23, 2007).

5. Human Rights Watch, "HIV/AIDS and Human Rights," http://www.hrw.org/doc/?t=hivaids&document_limit=0,5 (accessed July 23, 2007).

6. Physicians for Human Rights, "Health Action AIDS: About the Health Ac-

tion AIDS Campaign," http://physiciansforhumanrights.org/hiv-aids/about/ (accessed July 23, 2007).

7. Katarina Tomasevski, Sofia Gruskin, Zita Lazzarini, and Aart Hendriks, "AIDS and Human Rights," in *AIDS in the World*, ed. Jonathan M. Mann, Daniel J. M. Tarantola, and Thomas W. Netter (Cambridge, Mass.: Harvard University Press, 1992), 539.

8. Ibid., 560.

9. Paul Farmer, *Pathologies of Power: Health, Human Rights, and the New War on the Poor* (Berkeley: University of California Press, 2003), 230.

10. David P. Fidler, *International Law and Infectious Diseases* (Oxford: Clarendon Press, 1999), 170.

11. David P. Fidler, "Public Health and International Law: The Impact of Infectious Diseases on the Formation of International Legal Regimes, 1800–2000," in *Plagues and Politics: Infectious Disease and International Policy*, ed. Andrew T. Price-Smith (Houndsmill, UK: Palgrave Macmillan, 2001), 267.

12. See Benedict Carton, "The Forgotten Compass of Death: Apocalypse Then and Now in the Social History of South Africa," *Journal of Social History* 37, no. 1 (2003): 199–218; William H. McNeill, *Plagues and Peoples* (Garden City, N.Y.: Anchor Books, 1976); Maynard W. Swanson, "The Sanitation Syndrome: Bubonic Plague and Urban Native Policy in the Cape Colony, 1900–1909," *Journal of African History* 18, no. 3 (1977): 387–410.

13. Swanson, "Sanitation Syndrome."

14. Anthony Boadle, "Cuba Fights AIDS with Free Drugs, not Quarantine," *Reuters*, November 30, 2005, http://www.globalexchange.org/countries/americas/cuba/3613.html (accessed January 11, 2006).

15. Peter Baldwin, *Disease and Democracy: The Industrialized World Faces AIDS* (Berkeley: University of California Press, 2005), 53–59.

16. David L. Kirp and Ronald Beyrer, *AIDS in the Industrialized Democracies* (New Brunswick, N.J.: Rutgers University Press, 1992), 14; Wendy E. Parmet and Daniel J. Jackson, "No Longer Disabled: The Legal Impact of the New Social Construction of HIV," *American Journal of Law and Medicine* 23, no. 1 (1997): 10–11.

17. Brett C. Stockdill, "ACT-UP (AIDS Coalition to Unleash Power)," in *Protest, Power, and Change: An Encyclopedia of Nonviolent Action from ACT-UP to Women's Suffrage*, ed. Roger S. Powers and William B. Vogele (New York: Garland, 1997), 9–10.

18. Michael Bronski, "The Truth about Reagan and AIDS," *Z Magazine* 17, no. 1 (2004). http://zmagsite.zmag.org/Jan2004/bronski0104.html (accessed July 23, 2007).

19. Steven Epstein, *Impure Science: AIDS, Activism, and the Politics of Knowledge* (Berkeley: University of California Press, 1996), 221–22.

20. Michael Kirby, "Human Rights and the HIV Paradox," *Lancet* 348 (1996): 1217–18.

21. Tomasevski et al., "AIDS and Human Rights," 567.

22. Ibid.

23. Jonathan M. Mann, Daniel J. M. Tarantola, and Thomas Netter, "The Global Response," in *AIDS in the World*, ed. Mann, Tarantola, and Netter, 228.

24. Tomasevski et al., "AIDS and Human Rights," 568.

25. David F. McFadden, *International Cooperation and Pandemic Disease: Regimes and the Role of Epistemic Communities in Combating Cholera, Smallpox, and AIDS* (Ph.D. diss., Claremont Graduate University, 1995), 171.

26. Yves Beigbeider, "Challenges to the World Health Organization," in *The Politics of Emerging and Resurgent Infectious Diseases*, ed. Jim Whitman (Houndsmill, UK: Palgrave, 2000), 184.

27. Amir Attaran and Jeffrey Sachs, "Defining and Refining International Donor Support for Combating the AIDS Pandemic," *Lancet* 357 (2001): 60.

28. Thomson Prentice, "World AIDS Specialists Fall Out on Key Initiatives," *The Times* (London) March 21, 1990, http://www.lexisnexis.com (accessed December 19, 2007).

29. PBS Frontline, "The Age of AIDS," May 30, 2006 (Boston: WGBH, 2006).

30. Leon Gordenker, Roger A. Coate, Christer Jönsson, and Peter Söderholm, *International Cooperation in Response to AIDS* (London: Pinter, 1995), 74.

31. Ann Gibbons, "New Head for the WHO Global Program on AIDS," *Science* 248 (1990): 1306.

32. World Health Organization, *1991 Progress Report, Global Program on AIDS* (Geneva: World Health Organization, 1992), 6.

33. After Nakajima left the position in 1998, many criticized him for unimaginative leadership and failing to keep WHO relevant as new health challenges emerged. See Richard Horton, "WHO: The Casualties and Compromises of Renewal," *Lancet* 359 (2002): 1605–11.

34. David Chandler, "Leader of Global Fight against AIDS Resigns," *Boston Globe*, March 17, 1990, 21.

35. Prentice, "World AIDS Specialists."

36. Gibbons, "New Head," 1306.

37. Chandler, "Leader of Global Fight," 21.

38. Prentice, "World AIDS Specialists."

39. Michael Balter, "Global Program Struggles to Stem the Flood of New Cases," *Science* 280 (1998): 1863.

40. Sharon Kingman, "Dr. Jonathan Mann? Now Just WHO Was He...?" *Independent* (London), October 28, 1990, 8.

41. "AIDS Meeting Faces Conflicting Views," *St. Louis Post-Dispatch*, July 20, 1992, 1A.

42. Lawrence K. Altman, "A Focus on Caring as Well as Curing," *New York Times*, August 15, 1993, 9.

43. Harvard School of Public Health, "In Memoriam: Jonathan Mann," September 11, 1998, http://www.hsph.harvard.edu/ats/Sep11/ (accessed July 23, 2007).

44. Michael Balter, "UN Readies New Global AIDS Plan," *Science* 266 (1994): 1312–13; Lisa Garbus, "The UN Response," in *AIDS in the World II*, ed. Jonathan M. Mann and Daniel J. M. Tarantola (Oxford: Oxford University Press, 1996), 369.

45. Sofia Gruskin, Aart Hendriks, and Katarina Tomasevski, "Human Rights and Responses to HIV/AIDS" in *AIDS in the World II*, ed. Mann and Tarantola, 328–29.

46. Mann made a similar appeal in response to a lack of government action on AIDS. In 1992, he called for creation of new "blue" political parties to call attention to health concerns, similar to "green" parties emphasizing environmental protection. See Marlene Cimons, "A Call for Global Health Action: AIDS Expert Urges New Political Party," *Chicago Sun-Times*, July 20, 1992, 8.

47. Amnesty International, "Health and Human Rights: Fighting AIDS by Fighting for Human Rights and Human Dignity," April 2003, http://www.amnestyusa.org/hiv_aids/fightingaids.html (accessed February 6, 2006).

48. Human Rights Watch, "HIV/AIDS and Human Rights," 2002, http://www.hrw.org/wr2k2/hivaids.html (accessed February 2, 2006).

49. Joseph Amon, "Preventing the Further Spread of HIV/AIDS: The Essential Role of Human Rights," in *Human Rights Watch World Report 2006*, http://www.hrw.org/wr2k6/wr2006.pdf (accessed February 2, 2006), 54.

50. Ibid., 67.

51. Farmer, *Pathologies of Power*, 217–25.

52. Laura Jamison, "A Commitment to Change," *Amnesty International Magazine*, Fall 2006, http://www.amnestyusa.org/Fall_/A_Committment_to_Change/page.do?id=1105195&n1=2&n2=19&n3=358 (accessed November 29, 2007).

53. Paul Farmer, "Challenging Orthodoxies in Health and Human Rights," address presented at the American Public Health Association annual meeting, November 5, 2006, http://www.pih.org/inforesources/essays/APHA_2006_keynote-Paul_Farmer.pdf (accessed November 29, 2007).

54. National Economic and Social Rights Initiative, "Board of Directors," http://www.nesri.org/about_us/board.html (accessed November 29, 2007).

55. Farmer, "Challenging Orthodoxies," 9.

56. Alan Berkman, Jonathan Garcia, Miguel Munoz-Laboy, Vera Paiva, and Richard Parker, "A Critical Analysis of the Brazilian Response to HIV/AIDS: Lessons Learned for Controlling and Mitigating the Epidemic in Developing Countries," *American Journal of Public Health* 95, no. 7 (2005): 1163–64.

57. Paulo R. Teixiera, Marco Antonio Vitoria, and Jhoney Barcarolo, "Antiretroviral Treatment in Resource-Poor Settings: The Brazilian Experience," *AIDS* 18, supp. 3 (2004): S5–S7.

58. Sonia Correa, Peter McIntyre, Carla Rodrigues, Anabela Paiva, and Cecilia Marks, "The Population and Reproductive Health Program in Brazil, 1990–2002: Lessons Learned—A Report to the John D. and Catherine T. MacArthur Foundation," *Reproductive Health Matters* 13, no. 25 (2005): 77.

59. Correa et al., "Population and Reproductive Health Program," 75.

60. Jane Galvao, "Brazil and Access to HIV/AIDS Drugs: A Question of Human Rights and Public Health," *American Journal of Public Health* 95, no. 7 (2005): 1111–12.

61. Correa et al., "Population and Reproductive Health Program," 73.

62. Ibid.

63. Steven Friedman and Shauna Mottiar, "A Rewarding Engagement? The Treatment Action Campaign and the Politics of HIV/AIDS," *Politics and Society* 33, no. 4 (2005): 513–14.

64. Pam Das, "Interview with Zackie Achmat—Head of the Treatment Action Campaign," *Lancet Infectious Diseases* 4, no. 7 (2004): 468.

65. Ibid., 467.

66. Peter Dwyer, "Dying to Fight," *Transformation* 53 (2003): 77–79.

67. Peris S. Jones, "'A Test of Governance': Rights-Based Struggles and the Politics of HIV/AIDS Policy in South Africa," *Political Geography* 24, no. 4 (2004): 436.

68. Steven Robins, "'Long Live, Zackie, Long Live': AIDS Activism, Science, and Citizenship after Apartheid," *Journal of Southern African Studies* 30, no. 3 (2004): 665.

69. Joan Fitzpatrick and Ron C. Skye, "Republic of South Africa v. Grootboom, Case No. CCT 11/00.2000(11) BCLR 1169 and Minister of Health v. Treatment Action Campaign, Case No. CCT 8/02," *American Journal of International Law* 97 (2003): 675–77; Friedman and Mottiar, "A Rewarding Engagement?" 532–33.

70. Treatment Action Campaign, "The HIV Campaign: A Discussion of the Response of the South African Government," submission to African peer review mechanism, February 2006, http://www.tac.org.za (accessed February 17, 2006), 6.

71. Friedman and Mottiar, "A Rewarding Engagement?" 547.

72. Zackie Achmat, "The Treatment Action Campaign, HIV/AIDS, and the Government," *Transformation* 54, no. 1 (2004): 77–80.

Chapter 6. Disability Rights and the Human Rights Mainstream

The author gratefully acknowledges the comments provided on earlier drafts of this chapter by Clifford Bob, Katherine Guernsey, and Julie Mertus. Shortcomings in the chapter belong to the author alone.

1. See, e.g., Human Rights Watch, "Uzbekistan: Dissident Forced into Psychiatric Detention," press release, September 3, 2005, http://hrw.org/english/docs/2005/09/03/uzbeki11684.htm (accessed January 2, 2008); Human Rights Watch, "Uzbekistan: Psychiatric Punishment Used to Quash Dissent: Government Deploys Stalinist-Era Tactic against Leading Human Rights Defender," October 20, 2005, http://hrw.org/english/docs/2005/10/20/uzbeki11905.htm (accessed January 2, 2008).

2. Convention on the Rights of Persons with Disabilities, http://www.un.org/disabilities/defult.asp?id-150. For documents relating to the development of the international convention, including the draft working group convention text, see http://www.worldenable.net.

3. Much of this section is based on National Council on Disability, *Understanding the Role of an International Convention on the Human Rights of People with Disabilities* (Washington, D.C.: National Council on Disability, 2002; Janet E. Lord, principal author). For more on traditional models of disability, see Gareth Williams, "Theorizing Disability," in *Handbook of Disability Studies*, ed. Gary L. Albrecht, Katherine D. Seelman, and Michael Bury (Thousand Oaks, Calif.: Sage Publications, 2003), 123.

4. Simi Linton, *Claiming Disability: Knowledge and Identity* (New York: New York University Press, 1998), 11.

5. "Disabled people's organizations" are membership organizations directed by persons with disabilities themselves, whereas "service organizations" have traditionally been led by nondisabled persons.

6. Antidiscrimination legislation has been passed in some forty-five countries. Gerard Quinn and Theresia Degener, *Human Rights Are for All: The Current Use and Future Potential of United Nations Human Rights Instruments in the Context of Disability* (Geneva: United Nations Office of the High Commissioner for Human Rights, 2002), sec. 4.6.

7. Doris Zames Fleischer and Freida Zames, *The Disability Rights Movement: From Charity to Confrontation* (Philadelphia: Temple University Press, 2000); Richard K. Scotch, *From Good Will to Civil Rights: Transforming Federal Disability Policy*, 2nd ed. (Philadelphia: Temple University Press, 2001).

8. RI later changed its name when its mandate expanded to include adults.

9. Diane Drieder, *The Last Civil Rights Movement* (New York: St. Martin's Press, 1989), 28.

10. See http://www.rehab-international.org/about/history.html. This move caused consternation among some disability rights leaders who saw the move as

a disingenuous legitimation strategy for an organization still dominated by medical and rehabilitation professionals, as opposed to disabled activists.

11. G.A. Res. 217A (III), UN Doc. A/810, 71 (1948).

12. G.A. Res. 2200A, 21 UN GAOR, supp. no. 16, 52, UN Doc. A/6316 (1966).

13. G.A. Res. 2200A, 21 UN GAOR, supp. no. 16, 49, UN Doc. A/6316 (1966).

14. The UDHR makes only one narrow reference to disability. Art. 25 provides, "Everyone has the right to a standard of living adequate for the health and well-being of himself and his family, ... and the right to security in the event of unemployment, sickness, disability, widowhood, old age or other lack of livelihood in circumstances beyond his control." Regional human rights conventions make similarly limited mention of disability. See African [Banjul] Charter on Human and Peoples' Rights, adopted June 27, 1981, OAU Doc. CAB/LEG/ 67/3 rev. 5, 21 I.L.M. 58 (1982), (October 21, 1986), Art. 18(4); Additional Protocol to the American Convention on Human Rights in the Area of Economic, Social and Cultural Rights, O.A.S. Treaty Series No. 69 (1988), signed November 17, 1988, Art. 18. Specific mention of disability appears in some international human rights treaties, such as the Convention on the Rights of the Child, G.A. Res. 44/25, annex, 44 UN GAOR Supp. (no. 49), 167, UN Doc. A/44/49 (1989) (entered into force September 2, 1990), Arts. 2(1) and 23.

15. For a major UN study tracking the failure of the existing human rights treaty system to integrate disability rights, see Quinn and Degener, *Human Rights Are for All.*

16. Declaration on the Rights of Mentally Retarded Persons, G.A. Res. 2856 (XXVI), 26 UN GAOR Supp. (no. 29), 93, UN Doc. A/8429 (1971). Declaration on the Rights of Disabled Persons, G.A. Res. 3447 (XXX), 30 UN GAOR Supp. (no. 34), 88, UN Doc. A/10034 (1975).

17. Declaration on the Rights of Mentally Retarded Persons, G.A. Res. 2856 (XXVI), 26 UN GAOR Supp. (no. 29), 93, UN Doc. A/8429 (1971; emphasis added).

18. Ibid. (emphasis added).

19. G.A. Res. 37/52 (1982).

20. For more on these efforts, see generally Bengt Lindqvist, "Standard Rules in the Disability Field," in *Human Rights and Disabled Persons: Essays and Relevant Human Rights Instruments,* ed. Theresia Degener and Yolan Koster-Dreese (Boston: Martinus Nijhoff, 1995), 64–65.

21. UN Standard Rules on the Equalization of Opportunities for Persons with Disabilities, G.A. Res. 48/96, December 20, 1993, UN Doc. A/RES/48/96; G.A. Res. 119, UN GAOR, 46th sess., supp. no. 49, annex at 188–92, UN Doc. A/46/49 (1991). For more on the MI Principles, see Eric Rosenthal and Leonard S. Rubenstein, "International Human Rights Advocacy under the 'Principles for the Protection of Persons with Mental Illness,'" *International Journal of Law and Psychiatry* 16 (1993): 257–300.

22. See Statement of the World Network of Users and Survivors of Psychiatry, for the Meeting of Experts on the International Convention to Promote and Protect the Rights and Dignity of Persons with Disabilities, Mexico City, June 11–14, 2002, http://www.wnusp.net/wnusp%20evas/Dokumenter/WNUSP%20 Mexico%20statement.html (accessed January 2, 2008). For documentation of abuses against people with mental disabilities, see the publications of Mental Disability Rights International, http://www.mdri.org/publications/index.htm.

23. Holly Burkhalter, quoted in Michael Winerip, "The Global Willowbrook," *New York Times Magazine,* January 16, 2000, http://query.nytimes.com/gst/full

page.html?res=9B00E2D71F3BF935A25752C0A9669C8B63 (accessed January 2, 2008).

24. Disabled people's organizations with Economic and Social Council consultative status and forming the IDA include DPI, RI, World Blind Union, World Federation of the Deaf, World Federation of the Deafblind, Inclusion International, and the World Network of Users and Survivors of Psychiatry. Recently, an eighth group has joined the IDA, the International Federation of Hard of Hearing People.

25. Report of the United Nations Consultative Expert Group Meeting on International Norms and Standards Relating to Disability, Berkeley, California, December 1998, http://www.un.org/esa/socdev/enable/disberk0.htm (accessed January 2, 2008).

26. Report of the Interregional Seminar and Symposium on International Norms and Standards Relating to Disability, Hong Kong, December 1999, http://www.worldenable.net/hongkong99/default.htm (accessed January 2, 2008). See also Theresia Degener, "International Disability Law—A New Legal Subject on the Rise: The Interregional Experts Meeting in Hong Kong, Dec. 13–17, 1999," *Berkeley Journal of International Law* 18, no. 1 (2000): 180–95.

27. Participants included DPI, II, RI, the World Blind Union, and the World Federation of the Deaf, as well as various national NGOs. ˙

28. Beijing Declaration on the Rights of People with Disabilities in the New Century, March 12, 2000, http://icrpd.net/ratification/documents/en/Extras/Beijing%20Declaration%20on%20the%20Rights%20of%20People%20with%20Disabilities%20in%20the%20New%20Century.pdf, para. 7 (accessed January 2, 2008).

29. The network consisted of the Landmine Survivors Network, the Center for International Rehabilitation, the Inter-American Institute on Disability, the United States International Council on Disabilities, the American Association of People with Disabilities, the American Council of the Blind, Mental Disability Rights International, Not Dead Yet, Support Coalition International, and the World Institute on Disability.

30. Groups such as DPI worked hard to engage AI and HRW in the disability convention process. They arranged meetings between the chairman of DPI and leaders of AI and HRW and had the DPI delegation at the ad hoc committee share information with AI and HRW participants.

31. This argument was made by the chair of the World Network of Users and Survivors of Psychiatry during the course of ad hoc committee negotiations.

32. Summit on Human Rights and Disability, National Council on Disability, Washington, D.C., April 8, 2002 (transcript on file at National Council on Disability). Later that year, Kenneth Roth introduced an MDRI report by stating that the human rights movement's "embrace of this broad sector of humanity [the disabled] has barely begun. Remedying this failure is a major challenge facing the movement." Kenneth Roth, foreword to MDRI, "Not on the Agenda: Human Rights of People with Disabilities in Kosovo," 2002, http://www.mdri.org/pdf/KosovoReport.pdf (accessed January 2, 2008).

33. See National Council on Disability, *Understanding the Role of an International Convention*, 41–43, 58.

34. Notably, however, a number of other important human rights NGOs, including Global Rights (formerly International Human Rights Law Group) and Human Rights First (formerly Lawyers Committee for Human Rights), did not become involved.

35. One exception was the London-based group Interrights, which embraced

disability as an issue for its strategic litigation strategy. See Interrights, *Annual Report 2003* (London: Interrights, 2003).

36. See generally Michael Ashley Stein and Janet E. Lord, "Future Prospects for the United Nations Convention on the Rights of Persons with Disabilities," in *The UN Convention on the Rights of Persons with Disabilities: European and Scandinavian Perspectives,* ed. Oddný Mjöll Arnardóttir and Gerard Quinn (forthcoming).

37. For a comprehensive analysis of the monitoring system established by the convention, see Janet E. Lord and Michael Ashley Stein, "The Committee on the Rights of Persons with Disabilities," in *The United Nations and Human Rights: A Critical Appraisal,* ed. Frédéric Mégret and Philip Alston, 2nd ed. (Oxford: Oxford University Press, 2008).

38. See http://www.ideanet.org/content.cfm?id=5F5A&memberMenuid=0.

39. For the Disability Rights Promotion International website, see http://www.yorku.ca/drpi/index.html (accessed January 2, 2008).

40. See Mental Disability Advocacy Center, http://www.mdac.info/ (accessed January 2, 2008).

41. The University of Minnesota Human Rights Resource Center, by contrast, has recently included a title on the rights of people with disabilties in its leading human rights education series. Janet E. Lord, Katherine N. Guernsey, Joelle M. Balfe and Valerie L. Karr, *Human Rights. YES! Action and Advocacy on the Rights of Persons with Disabilities* (Minneapolis: University of Minnesota Human Rights Resource Center, 2007).

Chapter 7. New Rights for Private Wrongs

1. Annika Rahman and Nahid Toubia, eds., *Female Genital Mutilation: A Guide to Laws and Policies Worldwide* (New York: St. Martin's Press, 2000); Rosemarie Skaine, *Female Genital Mutilation: Legal Cultural and Medical Issues* (Jefferson, N.C.: McFarland & Co., 2005). See Rahman and Toubia, *Female Genital Mutilation,* 15–39, for a list of conventions and charters that include FGM.

2. Alison Brysk, *Human Rights and Private Wrongs: Constructing Global Civil Society* (New York: Routledge, 2005).

3. There are three types of FGM: type 1, clitoridectomy, where part or all of the clitoris is removed; type 2, excision, which involves complete clitoridectomy and removal of part or all of the labia minora; and type 3, infibulation, the most severe form of FGM, where the clitoris and labia minora are removed, and the labia majora are cut and sewn together.

4. World Health Organization, "Female Genital Mutilation," http://www.who.int/mediacentre/factsheets/fs241/en/ (accessed April 19, 2006).

5. Rahman and Toubia, *Female Genital Mutilation,* 26.

6. Ibid.

7. Margaret Keck and Kathryn Sikkink, *Activists Beyond Borders: Advocacy Networks in International Politics* (Ithaca, N.Y.: Cornell University Press, 1998), 67–69.

8. Ibid.

9. Jomo Kenyatta, *Facing Mount Kenya: The Tribal Life of the Gikuyu* (New York: Vintage, 1962), 128.

10. Efua Dorkenoo, *Cutting the Rose: Female Genital Mutilation, the Practice and Its Prevention* (London: Minority Rights, 1995).

11. Kay Boulware-Miller, "Female Circumcision: Challenges to the Practice as a Human Rights Violation," *Harvard Women's Law Journal* 8 (1985): 159.

12. Elizabeth Heger Boyle, *Female Genital Cutting: Cultural Conflict in the Global Community* (Baltimore: Johns Hopkins University Press, 2002), 65.

13. Inter-African Committee on Traditional Practices Affecting the Health of Women and Children, http://www.iac-ciaf.org/ (accessed April 19, 2006). Currently, the IAC has branches in twenty-two of the twenty-eight countries that practice FGM and continues to work at the local, regional, and international levels.

14. Nawal El Saadawi, *The Hidden Face of Eve: Women in the Arab World* (London: Zed Books, 1980).

15. Rainbo, http://www.rainbo.org/

16. Boyle, *Female Genital Cutting*, 41.

17. Ibid., 45.

18. Ibid., 48.

19. Rahman and Toubia, *Female Genital Mutilation*.

20. Ibid.; Alison Slack, "Female Circumcision: A Critical Appraisal," *Human Rights Quarterly* 10, no. 4 (1988): 437–86.

21. Skaine, *Female Genital Mutilation*, 46.

22. Christine J. Walley, "Searching for 'Voices': Feminism, Anthropology, and the Global Debate over Female Genital Operations," *Cultural Anthropology* 12, no. 3 (1997): 405–38.

23. Keck and Sikkink, *Activists beyond Borders*, 20.

24. Fran Hosken, *The Hosken Report: Genital and Sexual Mutilation of Females* (Lexington, Mass.: Women's International Network News, 1982).

25. Alice Walker and Pratibha Parmar, *Warrior Marks* (New York: Women Make Movies, 1993).

26. Alice Walker, *Possessing the Secret of Joy* (New York: Harcourt Brace Jovanovich, 1992).

27. Charlotte Bunch, "Transforming Human Rights from a Feminist Perspective," in *Women's Rights, Human Rights: International Feminist Perspectives*, ed. Julie Peters and Andrea Wolper (New York: Routledge, 1994), 11–17; Hilary Charlesworth, "What Are Women's International Human Rights?" in *Human Rights of Women: National and International Perspectives*, ed. Rebecca J. Cook (Philadelphia: University of Pennsylvania Press, 1994), 58–84; Bonnie Smith, ed., *Global Feminisms since 1945* (New York: Routledge, 2000); Keck and Sikkink, *Activists beyond Borders*.

28. Convention on the Elimination of All Forms of Discrimination against Women (CEDAW), adopted by G.A. Res. 34/180 (December 18, 1979).

29. Boulware-Miller, "Female Circumcision," 162–63.

30. Ibid., 163.

31. Ibid.

32. Boyle, *Female Genital Cutting*, 42.

33. Boulware-Miller, "Female Circumcision."

34. General Recommendation No. 14, Female Circumcision (9th sess., 1990), http://www.un.org/womenwatch/daw/cedaw/recommendations/recomm.htm (accessed June 8, 2006).

35. Declaration on the Elimination of Violence against Women, G.A. Res. 48/104, Art. 2 (December 20, 1993), http://www.ohchr.org/english/law/eliminationvaw.htm (accessed June 8, 2006).

36. Vienna Declaration and Programme of Action, World Conference on Human Rights, June 25, 1993, http://www.ohchr.org/english/law/vienna.htm (accessed April 25, 2006).

37. See http://www.unfpa.org/icpd/icpd.htm.

38. World Health Organization, *Female Genital Mutilation: An Overview* (Geneva: World Health Organization, 1998), 53.

39. *Female Genital Mutilation: A Joint WHO/UNICEF/UNFPA Statement* (Geneva: World Health Organization, 1997).

40. Amnesty International, "Why and How Amnesty International Took Up the Issue of Female Genital Mutilation," October 1, 1997, http://www.amnesty .org/ailib/intcam/femgen/fgm2.htm (accessed April 25, 2006).

41. Saba Bahar, "Human Rights Are Women's Right: Amnesty International and the Family," in *Global Feminisms since 1945: Rewriting Histories*, ed. Bonnie G. Smith (New York: Routledge, 2000), 268–69.

42. Amnesty International, *It's in Our Hands: Stop Violence against Women* (New York: Amnesty International, 2004), 15.

43. Amnesty International, *Women in the Front Line* (New York: Amnesty International, 1991).

44. Amnesty International, "Why and How."

45. Ibid.

46. Amnesty International, *Human Rights Are Women's Right* (London: Amnesty International, 1995).

47. Bahar, "Human Rights Are Women's Right," 272.

48. Amnesty International, "Why and How."

49. Amnesty International, *It's in Our Hands*, 15.

50. Amnesty International, "Why and How."

51. See Amnesty International, "The Campaign to Eradicate Female Genital Mutilation: A Role for Amnesty International," October 1, 1997, http://www .amnesty.org/ailib/intcam/femgen/fgm3.htm (accessed April 25, 2006).

52. In addition, Doctors without Borders attempts to ensure that the practice is not performed in facilities where the agency works and that instruments provided by Doctors without Borders are not used for the procedure. Medecins Sans Frontieres, "Female Genital Cutting," September 13, 1999, http://www.msf .org/msfinternational/invoke.cfm?component=article&objectid=7128255C-EC70-11D4–B2010060084A6370&method=full_html (accessed April 19, 2006).

53. World Medical Association, "Policy: The World Medical Association Statement on Female Genital Mutilation," 45th World Medical Assembly, Budapest, Hungary, October 1993, http://www.wma.net/e/policy/c10.htm (accessed April 19, 2006).

54. Skaine, *Female Genital Mutilation*.

55. Boyle, *Female Genital Cutting*, 46.

56. Hosken, *Hosken Report*, 315.

57. Claude E. Welch, *Protecting Human Rights in Africa: Roles and Strategies of Non-Governmental Organizations* (Philadelphia: University of Pennsylvania Press, 1995), 92.

58. See Nadia Wassef, "Ending Female Genital Mutilation without Human Rights: Two Approaches—Egypt," Carnegie Council on Ethics and International Affairs, August 6, 2000, http://www.cceia.org/viewMedia.php/prmTemplateID/8/prmID/631 (accessed April 19, 2006).

59. Boyle, *Female Genital Cutting*.

60. Rahman and Toubia, *Female Genital Mutilation*, 10.

61. Georgia Dullea, "Female Circumcision a Topic at UN Parley," *New York Times,* July 18, 1980, B4.

62. Ibid.

63. Elizabeth Heger Boyle and Kristin Carbone-Lopez, "Movement Frames and African Women's Explanations for Opposing Female Genital Cutting," *International Journal of Comparative Sociology* 47, no. 6 (2006): 435–65.

64. Shareen Hertel, *Unexpected Power: Conflict and Change among Transnational Activists* (Ithaca, N.Y.: Cornell University Press, 2006).

65. Slack, "Female Circumcision."

66. UNICEF, "UNICEF Hails Progress toward Ending Female Genital Cutting," February 6, 2006, http://www.unicef.org/media/media_30925.html (accessed April 26, 2006).

67. Ibid.

68. Barbara Crossette, "Sabiny Elders of Uganda Lead Women from Circumcision," *Chicago Tribune,* August 9, 1998, 6.

69. Tina Rosenberg, "Mutilating Africa's Daughters: Laws Unenforced, Practices Unchanged," *New York Times,* July 5, 2004, http://www.nytimes.com/2004/07/05/opinion/05MON3.html?ex=1201669200&en=afbf39f756e2b194&ei=507 0 (accessed April 25, 2006).

70. Scheherezade Faramarzi, "'It Won't Be Obeyed': Egypt Has an Uphill Battle to End Female Circumcision," *Chicago Tribune,* March 7, 1999, 10.

71. Melron Nicol-Wilson, "Ending Female Genital Mutilation without Human Rights: Two Approaches—Sierra Leone," Carnegie Council on Ethics and International Affairs, August 6, 2006, http://www.cceia.org/viewMedia.php/prm TemplateID/8/prmID/630 (accessed April 19, 2006).

72. Susan Igras, Jacinta Muteshi, Asmelash Wolde Mariam, and Saida Ali, "Integrating Rights-based Approaches into Community-based Health Projects: Experiences from the Prevention of Female Genital Cutting Project in East Africa," August 2002, http://www.crin.org/docs/resources/publications/hrbap/int egrating_rba_CARE_Ethiopia.pdf (accessed April 25, 2006).

73. Skaine, *Female Genital Mutilation,* 211.

74. Nirit Ben-Ari, "Changing Tradition to Safeguard Women," *Africa Recovery* 17, no. 1 (2003): 4.

75. Daniel Maharaj, "Kenya to Ban Female Genital Excision," *Los Angeles Times,* December 15, 2001, A18.

76. "Ending a Dangerous Ritual," *Los Angeles Times,* October 24, 2002, B16.

77. Boyle, *Female Genital Cutting.*

78. Center for Reproductive Rights, "Female Genital Mutilation (FGM): Legal Prohibitions Worldwide," http://www.reproductiverights.org/pub_fac_fgmicpd .html (accessed May 10, 2006). Countries that have banned FGM include Benin, Burkina Faso, Central African Republic, Chad, Côte d'Ivoire, Djibouti, Egypt, Ethiopia, Ghana, Guinea, Kenya, Niger, Senegal, South Africa, Tanzania, and Togo.

79. Magdi Abdelhadi, "Egypt Forbids Female Circumcision," *BBC News,* June 28, 2007, http://news.bbc.co.uk/2/hi/middle_east/6251426.stm (accessed July 11, 2007).

80. NotJustSkin.Org, "Female Genital Cutting," http://www.notjustskin.org/en/fgc.html (accessed May 10, 2006); Slack, "Female Circumcision."

81. Skaine, *Female Genital Mutilation.*

82. U.S. Department of State, "Female Genital Mutilation (FGM) or Female Genital Cutting (FGC): Individual Country Reports," June 1, 2001, http://www .state.gov/g/wi/rls/rep/crfgm/ (accessed September 9, 2007); Boyle and Carbone-Lopez, "Movement Frames and African Women's Explanations."

83. Skaine, *Female Genital Mutilation*; Rahman and Toubia, *Female Genital Mutilation.*

84. Skaine, *Female Genital Mutilation.*

85. Slack, "Female Circumcision," 478; Maharaj, "Kenya to Ban Female Genital Excision."

Chapter 8. Economic Rights and Extreme Poverty

1. Universal Declaration of Human Rights, adopted December 10, 1948, G.A. Res. 217A (III), UN GAOR, 3rd sess. (Resolutions, pt. 1), 71, UN Doc. A/810 (1948).

2. International Covenant on Civil and Political Rights, adopted December 16, 1966, G.A. Res. 2200 (XXI), UN GAOR, 21st sess., Supp. no. 16, UN Doc. A/6316 (1966), 999 UNT.S. 171 (entered into force March 23 1976).

3. International Covenant on Economic, Social and Cultural Rights, adopted December 16, 1966, G.A. Res. 2200 (XXI), UN GAOR, 21st sess., Supp. no. 16, UN Doc. A/6316 (1966), 993 UNT.S. 3 (entered into force January 3, 1976).

4. International Commission of Jurists, "History," http://www.icj.org/article.php3?id_article=2957&id_rubrique=11&lang=en (accessed August 1, 2007).

5. World Organization against Torture, "Economic, Social and Cultural Rights," http://www.omct.org/index.php?id=SCR&lang=eng&PHPSESSID=7cb3c655f1f705ba3908f0e00f4c3414 (accessed August 1, 2007).

6. International Federation for Human Rights, "Globalization and ESC Rights," http://www.fidh.org/rubrique.php3?id_rubrique=182 (accessed August 1, 2007).

7. For general information on FIAN International, see http://www.fian.org. For COHRE, see http://www.cohre.org. For the Center on Economic and Social Rights, see http://www.cesr.org. (All accessed December 1, 2005.)

8. This definition is extrapolated from Henry Shue, *Basic Rights: Subsistence, Affluence and U.S. Foreign Policy* (Princeton, N.J.: Princeton University Press, 1996), 13.

9. ICESCR, Art. 11(1).

10. Shue, *Basic Rights,* 5, 19.

11. UNDP, *Human Development Report 2000: Human Rights and Human Development* (New York: Oxford University Press, 2000), 73.

12. United Nations High Commissioner for Human Rights, "Human Rights Dimension of Poverty," http://www.ohchr.org/english/issues/poverty/index.htm (accessed December 1, 2005).

13. Nanak Kakwani and Hyun H. Son, "New Global Poverty Counts," working paper no. 29, UNDP International Poverty Centre, Brazil, September 2006. This study sets the international poverty threshold based on a minimum caloric intake equivalent to $1.22 per day in 1993 purchasing power point parity (PPP) exchange rates.

14. Ibid.

15. World Bank, *World Development Indicators 2004* (Washington, D.C.: World Bank, 2004).

16. Shue, *Basic Rights,* 221, n. 5 (emphasis added). For a detailed history of U.S. rejection of economic and social rights, see Philip Alston, "U.S. Ratification of the Covenant on Economic, Social and Cultural Rights: The Need for an Entirely New Strategy," *American Journal of International Law* 84 (1990): 372–78.

17. See, e.g., Alston, "U.S. Ratification."

18. Anthony Woodiwiss, "The Law Cannot Be Enough: Human Rights and the Limits of Legalism," in *The Legalization of Human Rights: Multidisciplinary Perspectives on Human Rights and Human Rights Law*, ed. Saladin Meckled-Garcia and Basak Çali (London: Routledge, 2006), 33.

19. This has been the case in India, Sri Lanka, Nepal, and elsewhere. See Philip Alston, *Promoting Human Rights through Bills of Rights: Comparative Principles* (Oxford: Oxford University Press, 2000), 507.

20. Telephone interview with Larry Cox, Executive Director, Amnesty International USA, and former senior human rights program officer, Ford Foundation, September 23, 2005.

21. Carol Anderson, *Eyes Off the Prize: The United Nations and the African American Struggle for Human Rights, 1944–1955* (Cambridge: Cambridge University Press, 2003), 5, 276.

22. Interviews with Ann Blyberg, Director, International Human Rights Internship Program, Washington, D.C., August 1, 10, 2005.

23. Aryeh Neier, "Perspectives on Economic, Social and Cultural Rights," lecture at the American University Washington College of Law, March 1, 2006.

24. Saladin Meckled-Garcia and Basak Çali, "Lost in Translation: The Human Rights Ideal and International Human Rights Law," in *The Legalization of Human Rights: Multidisciplinary Perspectives on Human Rights and Human Rights Law*, ed. Meckled-Garcia and Çali, 11–31.

25. Kenneth Roth, "Defending Economic, Social and Cultural Rights: Practical Issues Faced by an International Human Rights Organization," *Human Rights Quarterly* 26, no. 1 (2004), 64 (emphasis added).

26. James Ron, Howard Ramos, and Kathleen Rodgers, "Transnational Information Politics: NGO Human Rights Reporting, 1986–2000," *International Studies Quarterly* 49 (2005): 557–87.

27. Ibid.

28. Katarina Tomasevski, "Unasked Questions about Economic, Social, and Cultural Rights from the Experience of the Special Rapporteur on the Right to Education (1998–2004): A Response to Kenneth Roth, Leonard S. Rubenstein, and Mary Robinson," *Human Rights Quarterly* 27, no. 2 (2005): 714.

29. Jonathan Power, *Like Water on Stone: The Story of Amnesty International* (Boston: Northeastern University Press, 2001), 119.

30. Ibid., xv.

31. Interview with former Amnesty International senior policy staff member, Chiang Mai, Thailand, June 11, 2003 (conducted in confidentiality). See also Stephen Hopgood, *Keepers of the Flame: Understanding Amnesty International* (Ithaca, N.Y.: Cornell University Press, 2006).

32. Power, *Like Water on Stone*, xv, 148.

33. Hopgood, *Keepers of the Flame*.

34. Philip Alston, "Conjuring Up New Human Rights: A Proposal for Quality Control," *American Journal of International Law* 78, no. 3 (1984): 614.

35. See Alston's discussion in "Economic and Social Rights and the Right to Health," Harvard Law School Human Rights Program, 1995.

36. Roger Normand, "Facing the Human Rights Abyss," *Nation,* December 10, 2003, http://www.thenation.com/doc.mhtml?i=20031222&s=normand. (accessed August 1, 2005).

37. Interviews with former Amnesty International senior policy staff member and several human rights practitioners from the global south, Chiang Mai, Thailand, June 11, 2003 (conducted in confidentiality). See Leilani Farha, "Bringing

Economic, Social and Cultural Rights Home: Palestinians in Occupied East Jerusalem and Israel," in *Giving Meaning to Economic, Social and Cultural Rights*, ed. Ishafan Merali and Valerie Oosterveld (Philadelphia: University of Pennsylvania Press, 2001), 160; Jim Shultz, "Promises to Keep: Using Public Budgets as a Tool to Advance Economic, Social and Cultural Rights" (Cuernavaca, Mexico: Ford Foundation and FUNDAR, 2002), 22.

38. Power, *Like Water on Stone*, xiv.

39. Chris Jochnick and Paulina Garzon, "Rights-Based Approaches to Development: An Overview of the Field: A Paper Prepared for CARE and Oxfam-America, Funded by the Ford Foundation," October 22, 2002, http://www.crin.org/docs/resources/publications/hrbap/RBA_Oxfam_CARE.pdf (accessed May 1, 2006), 2.

40. Katarina Tomasevski, *Development Aid and Human Rights* (New York: St. Martin's Press, 1989), 146.

41. Katarina Tomasevski, "Indicators," in *Economic, Social and Cultural Rights: A Textbook*, ed. Asbjorn Eide, Catarina Krause, and Allan Rosas (London: Martinus Nijhoff, 1995), 398.

42. See, for example, David Harvey, *A Brief History of Neoliberalism* (Oxford: Oxford University Press, 2007).

43. Interview with former Amnesty International senior policy staff member, June 11, 2003; interview with former Amnesty International USA board member, Washington, D.C., April 14, 2004 (conducted in confidentiality).

44. Lisa VeneKlasen, Valerie Miller, Cindy Clark, and Molly Reilly, "Rights-based Approaches and Beyond: Challenges of Linking Rights and Participation," IDS working paper 235, December 2004, 28; and Amnesty International USA, "Reframing Globalization: The Challenge for Human Rights," annual general meeting, April 19–21, 2002, http://www.amnestyusa.org/events/agm/agm2002/panels.html (accessed January 25, 2008).

45. Anuradha Mittal and Peter Rosset, eds., *America Needs Human Rights* (Oakland, Calif.: Food First Books, 1999), 172.

46. Curt Goering, "Amnesty International and Economic, Social and Cultural Rights," in *Ethics in Action: The Ethical Challenges of International Human Rights Nongovernmental Organizations*, ed. Daniel A. Bell and Jean-Marc Coicaud (Cambridge: Cambridge University Press, 2007), 205.

47. Power, *Like Water on Stone*, xiv.

48. Hopgood, *Keepers of the Flame*, 120.

49. Amnesty International USA, "Reframing Globalization."

50. Raymond C. Offenheiser and Susan Holcombe, "Challenges and Opportunities of Implementing a Rights-based Approach to Development: An Oxfam America Perspective" (Boston: Oxfam America, 2001), 7. See also Ann Blyberg and Dana Buhl, *Ripple in Still Water: Reflections by Activists on Local- and National-Level Work on Economic, Social and Cultural Rights* (Washington, D.C.: Institute for International Education, International Human Rights Internship Program, 1997); Roth, "Defending Economic," 72.

51. Power, *Like Water on Stone*, xv.

52. Dochas, "Application of Rights Based Approaches—Experiences and Challenges," Dublin, Ireland, remarks of Jim Loughran (Amnesty International), February 12, 2003, http://www.dochas.ie/documents/rba_seminar.pdf (accessed January 25, 2008).

53. Interview with former Amnesty International senior policy staff member, June 11, 2003; interview with former Amnesty USA board member, April 14, 2004.

54. Interview with former Amnesty International senior policy staff member, June 11, 2003.

55. Goering, "Amnesty International," 215.

56. Amnesty International, "Q&A: 'Economic, Social and Cultural Rights are Human Rights,'" http://web.amnesty.org/pages/economist-response-faq-eng (accessed September 24, 2007).

57. Amnesty International, "Amnesty International's Global Campaign for Human Dignity," March 2007, http://www.amnesty.org/en/alfresco_asset/57461c4c-a2a8-11dc-8d74-6f45f39984e5/act350032007en.html (accessed January 25, 2008).

58. Ibid.

59. VeneKlasen et al., "Rights-Based Approaches," 17.

60. Interview with program officer of a U.S. human rights grant-making foundation, New York, July 25, 2005 (conducted in confidentiality).

61. Interview with Blyberg.

62. Roth, "Defending Economic," 65.

63. Neera Chandhoke, "How Global Is Global Civil Society?" *Journal of World-Systems Research* 11, no. 2 (2005): 365.

64. Kenneth Roth, "Response to the Critique of Neera Chandhoke," in *Ethics in Action*, ed. Bell and Coicaud, 198.

65. Hopgood, *Keepers of the Flame*, 1.

66. Telephone interview with the director of a small U.S.-based human rights NGO, July 31, 2005 (conducted in confidentiality).

67. Chandhoke, "How Global," 363.

68. Interview with Blyberg; interview with director of a small U.S.-based human rights NGO, July 31, 2005 (conducted in confidentiality).

69. Paul Nelson and Ellen Dorsey, "New Rights Advocacy: Origins and Significance of a Partial Human Rights–Development Convergence," paper presented at the annual meeting of the International Studies Association, March 17–20, 2004, 37.

70. Ibid., 12.

71. See Mittal and Rosset, *America Needs Human Rights*, viii.

72. For details, see HRCA's website, http://www.hrca.org.au/activities.htm #Development (accessed November 1, 2005).

73. Hans-Otto Sano, "Development and Human Rights: The Necessary, but Partial Integration of Human Rights and Development," *Human Rights Quarterly* 22, no. 3 (2000): 734–52.

74. Oxfam International, "Towards Global Equity: Strategic Plan 2001–04," January 2001, http://www.oxfam.org/es/files/strat_plan.pdf (accessed January 25, 2008), 7.

75. Interview with former senior staff member of Oxfam International, Chiang Mai, Thailand, June 11, 2003 (conducted in confidentiality).

76. Offenheiser and Holcombe, "Challenges and Opportunities," 3.

77. Ford Foundation, "Close to Home: Case Studies of Human Rights Work in the United States," June 2004, http://www.fordfound.org/pdfs/impact/close_to_home.pdf (accessed January 25, 2008), 18.

78. See http://www.citizen.org/ for more information (accessed May 1, 2006).

79. Interviews with Bread for the World senior staff members, Washington, D.C., June 10, 2004 (conducted in confidentiality). This conclusion is also based on the author's attendance at two annual Bread for the World conferences (2003 and 2005) and review of documents in the organization's files.

80. Kimberly Mancino, Anita Malley, and Santiago Cornejo, "Developmental

Relief: NGO Efforts to Promote Sustainable Peace and Development in Complex Humanitarian Emergencies," June 2001, http://www.interaction.org/files.cgi/867_Developmental_Relief_Report_I.pdf (accessed May 1, 2006), 5.

81. Ibid.

82. InterAction, "Discussion on the Rights-based Approach to Development," remarks by Mara Galaty, December 17, 2003, http://www.interaction.org/files.cgi/2581_Notes_RBA_Meeting_December_17_2003.doc (accessed October 1, 2005).

83. Roy McCloughry, "Rights or Wrong? Christian Reflections on a Human Rights Approach to Development," October 2003, http://www.worldvision.org.uk/upload/pdf/orange_paper_4.pdf (accessed January 25, 2008), 16.

84. Jochnick and Garzon, "Rights-Based Approaches to Development," 5; Michael Barnett, "Humanitarianism Transformed," *Perspectives on Politics* 3, no. 4 (2005): 728.

85. Barnett, "Humanitarianism Transformed," 728.

86. Ibid. See also InterAction, "Discussion on the Rights-Based Approach," remarks by Bill O'Neill.

87. Hopgood, *Keepers of the Flame*, 182.

88. Ibid., 159.

89. Ron, Ramos, and Rodgers, "Transnational Information Politics," 576.

90. See, e.g., Stephen M. Saideman, "The Marketing of Rebellion: Insurgents, Media and International Activism," book review in *Perspectives on Politics* 4, no. 2 (2006): 419.

91. See, e.g., Charles Jones, *Global Justice: Defending Cosmopolitanism* (Oxford: Oxford University Press, 1999), 64; Shue, *Basic Rights*, 37.

Chapter 9. Local Claims, International Standards

1. UN Committee on Economic, Social and Cultural Rights, "General Comment 15: The Right to Water," UN Doc. E/C.12/2002/11 (2002), para. 2. General comments are authoritative interpretive statements establishing or clarifying the meaning of human rights covenants and treaties in light of experience.

2. Ibid., paras. 10, 26.

3. Universal Declaration of Human Rights, adopted December 10, 1948, G.A. Res. 217A (III), UN GAOR, 3rd sess. (Resolutions, pt. 1), 71, UN Doc. A/810 (1948); International Covenant on Economic, Social and Cultural Rights, adopted December 16, 1966, G.A. Res. 2200 (XXI), UN GAOR, 21st sess., Supp. no. 16, Art. 15, UN Doc. A/6316 (1966), 993 UNTS 3 (entered into force January 3, 1976).

4. Convention on the Rights of the Child, adopted November 20, 1989, G.A. Res. 44/25 (entered into force September 2, 1990).

5. CEDAW, adopted December 18, 1979, G.A. Res. 34/180 (entered into force September 3, 1981), Art. 14(2)(h). For information on CEDAW, see Philip Alston, "Ships Passing in the Night: The Current State of the Human Rights and Development Debate Seen through the Lens of the Millennium Development Goals," *Human Rights Quarterly* 27, no. 3 (2005): 755–829.

6. Peter Gleick, "The Human Right to Water: Two Steps Forward, One Step Back," in *The World's Water, 2004–2005*, ed. Peter Gleick (Washington, D.C.: Island Press, 2000), 204–12.

7. UN Committee on Economic, Social and Cultural Rights, "General Comment 15," para. 3.

8. Ibid.

9. Gleick, "Human Right to Water."

10. Paul J. Nelson and Ellen Dorsey, "At the Nexus of Human Rights and Development: New Methods and Strategies of Global NGOs," *World Development* 31, no. 12 (2003): 2013–26; Paul J. Nelson and Ellen Dorsey, *New Rights Advocacy: Changing Strategies of Development and Human Rights NGOs* (Washington, D.C.: Georgetown University Press, 2008).

11. Examples of the latter include the Center for Economic and Social Rights, Centre on Housing Rights and Evictions (COHRE), Food Information and Action Network (FIAN), and International Women's Health Coalition. In the developing world, NGOs advancing ESC rights include the Nigerian Social and Economic Rights Action Centre (SERAC); the Indian Tamil Nadu Network for Economic, Social, and Cultural Rights; and IBASE of Brazil.

12. See ESCR-Net, http://www.escr-net.org; Priti Darooka and Carol Pollack, "Human Rights: A Watershed Moment," *FFR: Ford Foundation Report*, Nov. 2003, http://www.fordfound.org/pdfs/impact/ford_reports_fall_2003.pdf (accessed November 24, 2007), 4.

13. David A. McDonald and Greg Ruiters, "Theorizing Water Privatization in Southern Africa," in *The Age of Commodity: Water Privatization in Southern Africa,* ed. David A. McDonald and Greg Ruiters (London: Earthscan, 2005), 13–42; United Nations Development Programme, *Human Development Report 2006* (New York: Oxford University Press, 2006), chap. 2.

14. Alan Snitow and Deborah Kaufman, "The New Economy of Water," Public Broadcasting System, *P.O.V.*, July 13, 2004, http://www.pbs.org/pov/pov2004/thirst/special_neweconomy.html (accessed February 20, 2006). These countries include Argentina, Chile, China, Colombia, the Philippines, South Africa, Australia, and a number of central European countries. Worldwide, however, less than 10 percent of all water is privately provided.

15. Notably, water privatization has inspired human rights claims in a way that state divestiture in other areas has not. This is probably because, unlike other privatized goods, water appears freely in nature, is essential for human survival, and fundamentally affects quality of life.

16. See Ken Conca, *Governing Water: Contentious Transnational Politics and Global Institution Building* (Cambridge, Mass.: MIT Press, 2005), esp. chap. 7, for a discussion of pricing.

17. Ibid., 237–40; Public Citizen, "Is This What Efficiency Looks Like? Prepaid Water Meters," http://www.citizen.org/cmep/Water/humanright/meter/ (accessed August 30, 2007). Notably, the United Kingdom banned the meters in 1998 because of public health risks resulting from use of unsafe water by those who cannot prepay.

18. See, for example, Sara Grusky and Maj Fiil-Flynn, "Will the World Bank Back Down? Water Privatization in a Climate of Global Protest," Public Citizen, April 2004, http://www.citizen.org/documents/worldbank2004.pdf (accessed January 25, 2008).

19. Public Citizen, "World Bank Water Privatization Policies Benefit Corporations, Not Developing Countries," press release, September 25, 2002, http://www.autodealerscam.org/pressroom/release.cfm?ID=1223 (accessed August 31, 2007).

20. I examine these cases not because they are representative of others but because they illustrate key dimensions of domestic water disputes.

21. Ghana National Coalition against the Privatisation of Water, "Accra Declaration on the Right to Water," 2001, http://www.tradeobservatory.org/library .cfm?refid=97679 (accessed November 26, 2007).

22. Rudolf Amenga-Etego and Sara Grusky, "The New Face of Conditionalities: The World Bank and Water Privatization in Ghana," in *The Age of Commodity*, ed. McDonald and Ruiters, 275–90.

23. Sara Grusky, "IMF Forces Water Privatization on Poor Countries," February 2001, http://www.nadir.org/nadir/initiativ/agp/free/imf/water.htm (accessed May 11, 2004); International Water Working Group, "Letter to World Bank President from the Ghana National Coalition against Privatization of Water," February 19, 2002, http://www.citizen.org/cmep/Water/cmep_Water/ articles.cfm?ID=7279 (accessed May 14, 2004).

24. Constitution of South Africa, Art. 27.

25. Anti-Privatisation Forum, "The Struggle against Pre-Paid Water Meters in Soweto," September 10, 2003, http://www.labournet.net/world/0309/ sawater1.html (accessed July 14, 2007); Simon Marvin, Nina Laurie, and Mark Napier, "Pre-Payment: Emerging Pathways to Water Services," 2001, http:// www.aguabolivia.org/newcastle/documentos/Nina-Marvin-southAfrica.htm (accessed June 22, 2005); "Joint Rural Development Services Network and South African Municipal Workers Union (SAMWU) Statement," Johannesburg, August 21, 2000, on file with author.

26. International Water Working Group, "Water for All: International," http://www.citizen.org/cmep/Water/cmep_Water/ (accessed June 16, 2005).

27. Ruchi Pant, "From Communities' Hands to MNCs' BOOTs: A Case Study from India on Right to Water," submitted to Right to Water Project, Rights and Humanity, UK, October 2003, http://www.righttowater.org.uk/pdfs/india_cs .pdf (accessed July 23, 2007).

28. Moni Basu and Scott Leith, "Coca-Cola Using Up Water, Foes in India Contend," *Atlanta Journal-Constitution*, May 29, 2005, http://www.killercoke .org/ajc0529.htm (accessed November 26, 2007).

29. John Vidal, "Coke on Trial as Indian Villagers Accuse Plant of Sucking Them Dry," *Guardian*, November 19, 2003; India Resource Center, "Coca-Cola Challenged on Human Rights Abuses," press release, April 20, 2005, http://www.indiaresource.org/campaigns/coke/2005/cokechallenged.html (accessed July 23, 2007).

30. On this litigation, see Overseas Development Institute, "Right to Water: Legal Forms, Political Channels," briefing paper, July 2004, http://www.odi.org .uk/publications/briefing/bp_july04_waterrights.pdf (accessed June 29, 2006).

31. Plachimada Solidarity Committee and India Resource Center, "Kerala Government Assures Proactive Action against Coca-Cola," press release, June 19, 2006, http://www.indiaresource.org/news/2006/1069.html (accessed July 23, 2007).

32. India Resource Center, "Villagers Begin Hunger Strike to Close Coca-Cola Plant in India," press release, June 23, 2006, http://www.indiaresource.org/ news/2006/1071.html (accessed July 23, 2007).

33. Amit Srivastava, "Indian Campaign Forces Coca-Cola to Announce Ambitious Water Conservation Project," June 30, 2007, http://www.indiaresource .org/campaigns/coke/2007/cokewwf.html (accessed September 30, 2007).

34. Steve Stecklow, "How a Global Web of Activists Gives Coke Problems in India," *Wall Street Journal*, June 7, 2005, 1.

35. Global Committee for the World Water Contract, "The Water Manifesto: The Right to Life," 1998, http://www.f1boat.com/99/watermanifesto.html (accessed July 23, 2007).

36. Blue Planet Project, "The Treaty Initiative to Share and Protect the Global Commons," July 8, 2001, http://www.blueplanetproject.net/documents/A_Plan_of_Action_01.pdf (accessed November 26, 2007).

37. Ken Conca observes that unlike the antidam movement during the same period, the antiprivatization movement lacks "a focal point akin to the role played by the International Rivers Network." Conca, *Governing Water*, 244.

38. IWWG, "Water Is a Human Right," 2004, http://www.citizen.org/cmep/Water/humanright/ (accessed June 29, 2006).

39. Tim Concannon and Hannah Griffiths, "Stealing Our Water: Implications of GATS for Global Water Resources," Food First Institute for Food and Development Policy, November 8, 2001, http://www.foodfirst.org/progs/global/trade/wto2001/stealingwater.html (accessed July 15, 2007); Dale T. McKinley, "The Struggle against Water Privatisation in South Africa," Anti-Privatisation Forum and Coalition against Water Privatisation, September 18, 2004, http://www.waterjustice.org/pv.php?res=77 (accessed July 14, 2007).

40. WaterAid, "New Roles, New Rules: Does Private Sector Participation Benefit the Poor?" briefing paper, London, February 2003, http://www.wateraid.org.uk (accessed July 23, 2007); Water Aid, "Human Rights Approach to Development," http://www.righttowater.org.uk/code/HR_approach.asp (accessed July 23, 2007).

41. Uwe Hoering and Ann Kathrin Schneider, "King Customer? The World Bank's 'New' Water and Its Implementation in India and Sri Lanka," Brot für die Welt and World Economy, Ecology and Development, October 2004, http://www2.weed-online.org/uploads/KingCustomer_engl.fullversion (accessed July 26, 2007); D. Roy Laifungbam, "The Human Right to Water: Necessity for Action and Discourse," Jubilee South, December 12, 2003, http://www.jubileesouth.org/news/EpZyVVlyFygMevRBey.shtml (accessed June 22, 2005); Amnesty International, "World Water Forum," statement, March 23, 2003, http://web.amnesty.org/pages/ec-water-eng (accessed July 26, 2007); Centre on Housing Rights and Evictions, "Legal Resources for the Right to Water: National and International Standards," October 2003, http://www.cohre.org/store/attachments/COHRE%20Sources%208.pdf (accessed July 23, 2007).

42. World Health Organization, *The Right to Water*, 2003, http://www.who.int/water_sanitation_health/rightowater/en/ (accessed June 16, 2005); American Association for Advancement of Science, COHRE, and World Health Organization, *Manual on the Right to Water*, 2004, http://www.righttowater.org.uk/pdfs/manual-flyer.pdf (accessed July 23, 2007).

43. John Scranton, Angela Caesar, and Noémi Nemes, "Water as a Human Right?" IUCN Environmental Policy and Law Paper No. 51, 2004, http://www.iucn.org/themes/law/pdfdocuments/EPLP51EN.pdf (accessed July 26, 2007).

44. World Development Movement, "138 Groups Urge Rich Countries to Pull the Plug on World Bank's Push for Water Privatization," May 15, 2007, http://www.wdm.org/uk/news/pulltheplugonprivatisation15052007.htm (accessed July 14, 2007).

45. Amnesty International, "World Water Forum."

46. See Chapter 8, this volume, discussing reasons that the major human rights NGOs have long neglected economic and social rights—as well as recent changes in this stance.

47. David Hall, Kate Bayliss, and Emanuele Lobina, "Water Privatisation in Africa," Public Services International Research Unit Reports, June 2002, http://www.psiru.org/reports/2002–06–W-Africa.doc (accessed December 3, 2007); Bronwen Morgan, "Building Bridges between Regulatory and Citizen Space: Civil Society Contributions to Water Service Delivery Frameworks in Cross-National Perspective," working paper no. 20, Cultures of Consumption, April 2005, http://www.consume.bbk.ac.uk (accessed June 29, 2006).

48. Michael M. Phillips, "The World Bank Wonders about Utility Privatizations," *Wall Street Journal,* July 21, 2003.

49. James Winpenny, "Financing Water for All: Report of the World Panel on Financing Water Infrastructure," March 2003, http://www.gwpforum.org/servlet/PSP (accessed June 28, 2006). Michael Camdessus, former managing director of the IMF, chaired the commission.

50. Working Group on Financing Water for Agriculture, "Progress Report No 1: Contribution to the Task Force on Financing Water," March 2006, http://www.financingwaterforall.org/fileadmin/Financing_water_for_all/Reports/FW AWG-Agr_Rep_Final.pdf (accessed July 23, 2007).

51. Lisa Jordan and Peter van Tuijl, "Political Responsibility in NGO Advocacy," *World Development* 28, no. 12 (2000): 2051–65.

Contributors

Madeline Baer is a Ph.D. candidate in the Department of Political Science at the University of California, Irvine. She received her B.A. in anthropology from American University and her M.A. in political science from the University of California, Irvine. Her research interests include human rights, social movements, and global water issues.

Clifford Bob is Associate Professor of Political Science at Duquesne University in Pittsburgh. He is the author of *The Marketing of Rebellion: Insurgents, Media, and International Activism* (Cambridge University Press, 2005), which won the 2007 International Studies Association Best Book Award and was named a "Top Book of 2006" by *The Globalist*. He has published widely in academic and policy journals, magazines, and newspapers, including the *American Journal of International Law, Foreign Policy, Social Problems, International Politics*, and the *International Herald Tribune*. He holds a Ph.D. from the Massachusetts Institute of Technology, a J.D. from New York University, and a B.A. from Harvard. His research interests include human rights, globalization, nongovernmental organizations, and transnational advocacy networks.

Alison Brysk is Professor of Political Science and International Studies at the University of California, Irvine. She is the author of *The Politics of Human Rights in Argentina* (Stanford University Press, 1994), *From Tribal Village to Global Village: Indian Rights and International Relations in Latin America* (Stanford University Press, 2000), and *Human Rights and Private Wrongs* (Routledge, 2005). She has edited *Globalization and Human Rights* (University of California Press, 2002), *People Out of Place* (with Gershon Shafir; Routledge, 2004), and *National Insecurity and Human Rights: Democracies Debate Counter-Terrorism* (with Gershon Shafir; University of California Press, 2007).

R. Charli Carpenter is Assistant Professor at the University of Massachusetts-Amherst's Department of Political Science and the author of *Innocent Women and Children: Gender, Norms and the Protection of Civilians* (Ashgate, 2006). She has published extensively on war crimes, humanitarian action, and transnational human rights advocacy and is the editor of *Born of War: Protecting Children of Sexual Violence Survivors in Conflict Zones* (Kumarian, 2007). She is the recipient of a National Science Foundation grant to study issue emergence in transnational networks and is currently writing a book about children's human rights in the former Yugoslavia.

Daniel Chong is Assistant Professor at Rollins College in Orlando, Florida, teaching courses in international relations, human rights, and global social justice. He holds a Ph.D. from the School of International Service at American University. He is working on a book entitled *Reconstructing Rights*, which explains how the application of the human rights framework to global poverty is changing our understanding of how human rights are useful. He has published in *Development and Change* and has an article forthcoming in *Human Rights Review*. In addition to his academic pursuits, he has worked for over a decade in nonprofit organizations engaged in international humanitarian assistance, democracy promotion, peace advocacy, and economic justice.

Janet E. Lord is a human rights law practitioner and scholar specializing in human rights institution building, international disability rights, and inclusive development. She is Adjunct Professor of Law at the University of Maryland School of Law, where she teaches international human rights law, and is a cofounder of BlueLaw International LLP, an international law and international development firm based in Washington, D.C. She is coauthor of *Human Rights. YES! Action and Advocacy on the Rights of Persons with Disabilities* (University of Minnesota Human Rights Center, 2007) and a forthcoming treaty commentary, *The UN Convention on the Rights of Persons with Disabilities* (Cambridge University Press).

Julie Mertus is Professor and Co-Director of the M.A. Program in Ethics, Peace, and Global Affairs at American University. An authority on the Balkans, she has worked on gender and human rights issues for governmental, intergovernmental, and nongovernmental organizations, including UNHCR, USAID, the Norwegian government, the Open Society Institute, Women for Inclusive Security, and the Women's Commission for Refugee Women and Children. Her book *Bait and Switch: Human Rights and U.S. Foreign Policy*, 2nd ed. (Routledge, 2008) was named "human rights book of the year" by the American Political Science Association

Human Rights Section. Her other books include *Human Rights and Conflict* (United States Institute of Peace Press, 2007), *The United Nations and Human Rights* (Routledge, 2005), *Kosovo: How Myths and Truths Started a War* (University of California Press, 1999), and *Local Action/ Global Change*, a training manual on the human rights of women and girls (translated into a dozen languages; a new edition appearing in 2008). A graduate of Yale Law School, her prior appointments include Senior Fellow, U.S. Institute of Peace; Human Rights Fellow, Harvard Law School; Writing Fellow, MacArthur Foundation; Fulbright Fellow (Romania, 1995; Denmark, 2006); and Counsel, Human Rights Watch.

Paul J. Nelson is Associate Professor in the Graduate School of Public and International Affairs, University of Pittsburgh, where he directs the International Development program. He teaches and conducts research on NGOs, human rights, development policy, and international organizations. He worked for fifteen years for several U.S.-based NGOs and is the author, with Ellen Dorsey, of *Human Rights and Development: The New Rights Advocacy* (Georgetown University Press, 2008).

Jeremy Youde is Assistant Professor of Political Science at the University of Minnesota, Duluth. He previously taught at San Diego State University and Grinnell College. His research focuses on the intersection of public health and international politics. He has published in *International Relations; Whitehead Journal of International Relations and Diplomacy; Africa Today;* and *Global Health Governance.* Ashgate published his book, *AIDS, South Africa, and the Politics of Knowledge,* in 2007 as part of its Global Health Series.

Index

Acknowledgments

This volume originates in my interest in testing the frontiers of human rights law, practice, and theory. Before beginning the project, many of the contributors had worked separately on "new" human rights issues— in law firms, nongovernmental organizations, or universities. A series of meetings, some fortuitous, others planned, brought us together to explore the disparate issues covered in this book. While we disagreed on some points, all of us saw value in examining how activists seek to persuade key organizations in the human rights mainstream to encompass new and sometimes controversial issues.

Most of the contributors presented earlier versions of the chapters at the 2006 annual meeting of the International Studies Association and the 2005 annual meeting of the American Political Science Association. In addition, I presented ideas in the introductory chapter as the keynote speaker at the University of Pittsburgh's 2006 Transcending Boundaries Student Conference on Human Rights and the Security Continuum. At all of these venues, I received many useful questions and suggestions. Also helpful were the lengthy and detailed anonymous comments solicited by the University of Pennsylvania Press. This volume originated in ideas I developed but could not pursue in my book, *The Marketing of Rebellion: Insurgents, Media, and International Activism*, and I again thank those who assisted me in that work.

For support that helped make this project possible, I thank the Russo Family Foundation, which awarded me a 2005 course-reduction grant. In addition, institutional support from Duquesne University, particularly its Department of Political Science and Center for Social and Public Policy, was critical to this book's completion. Finally, I thank my wife, Joan Miles, and children, Alex and Natalie, who provided much-needed love and distraction. I dedicate this book to my mother, Renate G. Bob, and my late father, Murray L. Bob.